科技英语丛书

普通生物学专业英语
English for General Biology

主编 周延清 陈晓春

中国科学技术大学出版社

内 容 简 介

本书是作者根据生物学双语教学实践与科研中查阅、撰写生物学专业英语文章的经验体会写成的一部简明生物学专业英语教材,包括生物学专业知识与技术、科技英语翻译技巧和科技论文写作技巧三章内容。第一章分为13个单元,涵盖生物学介绍、生物化学、细胞生物学、分子生物学、细胞工程、动物学、植物学、微生物学、遗传学、生态学、基因工程、水产养殖学、生物信息学和基因组学方面的内容。各单元后都附有英汉对照词汇表和练习题,每隔两个单元有一次口语表达活动。第二章包括科技英语行文规范、习惯表达法、翻译原则和实例方面的内容。第三章包括科技论文的定义、类型、特点、基本格式和写作步骤与技巧方面的内容。书后附有习题答案、各单元选段的英译汉范例及主要参考文献。本书体现了生物学基础知识和新技术的统一性、可读性、实用性和指导性,突出科技英语写作特点,注重中英文翻译技巧与应用,图文并茂。

本书可作为高等院校本科生的生物学专业英语教材和非生物学专业学生的生物选修课教材,也可供生物学相关专业教师、研究生以及科研与管理人员参考使用。

图书在版编目(CIP)数据

普通生物学专业英语 = English for General Biology/周延清,陈晓春主编.—合肥:中国科学技术大学出版社,2012.7(2016.8重印)
ISBN 978-7-312-03014-7

Ⅰ. 普… Ⅱ. ①周… ②陈… Ⅲ. 生物学—英语 Ⅳ. H31

中国版本图书馆 CIP 数据核字(2012)第 091357 号

出版 中国科学技术大学出版社
　　　安徽省合肥市金寨路 96 号,230026
　　　网址:http://press.ustc.edu.cn
印刷 合肥华星印务有限责任公司
发行 中国科学技术大学出版社
经销 全国新华书店
开本 710 mm×960 mm　1/16
印张 16.75
字数 328 千
版次 2012 年 7 月第 1 版
印次 2016 年 8 月第 2 次印刷
定价 27.00 元

Preface
前　言

随着生命科学日新月异的发展以及不同民族、文化和语言之间交流的日益加深,我国高等教育呈现出国际化的发展趋势,促使高等院校开设专业双语教学课程,培养复合型科技和教育人才。2001年,教育部在《关于加强高等学校本科教学工作提高教学质量的若干意见》中明确提出,高等学校要大力提倡编写、引进和使用先进教材,积极推动使用英语等外语进行教学。我国引进国外优秀生命科学教材进行生物学专业英语的双语教学工作的确能够让学生了解和借鉴国际先进的研究成果和技术,提高学生生物学专业英语阅读、会话、视听和写作等综合语言能力。但是,国外优秀生命科学教材内容很丰富且价格昂贵,有些内容不太符合我国高校教学和学生学习的实际需求,这就需要我们编写能满足我国不同层次大学教学的实际需求且适应师生英语水平的优秀双语教材。因此,我们撰写了《普通生物学专业英语》一书。

本书分为三章:第一章是生物学专业知识与技术,包括生物学介绍、生物大分子、细胞结构和功能、细胞分离、细胞培养与动物克隆、遗传信息传递及其调控、遗传规律与遗传病、动植物微生物及其应用、转基因食品及其生物安全性、生物多样性及其保护、水产养殖技术和应用、生物信息学和基因组学13个单元;第二章是科技英语翻译技巧,包括科技英语行文规范、习惯表达法、翻译原则和实例3个单元;第三章是专业科技论文写作技巧,包括科技论文的定义、类型、特点、基本格式和写作步骤与技巧4个单元。此外,该书附有习题答案、各单元选段的英译汉范例以及主要参考文献等内容。

本书由从事生物学双语教学的周延清教授和从事大学英语教学的陈晓春副教授负责撰写和统稿,中州大学王芳老师负责对附录、部分图片和文字等进行处理(约3万字)。

为了方便读者领会各单元的核心内容,每个单元前都添加了中文导语,且单元后都附有英汉对照词语;为了帮助读者深入理解、复习、掌握所学内容,每章或单元后面都设置了练习题;为了提高读者生物学专业英语阅读、会话、视听和写作等综合语言能力，每隔两单元设计了一个语言表达实践活动。

　　本书的撰写与出版得到了教育部"'普通生物学'国家级双语教学示范课程建设"项目和河南师范大学"生物学英汉双语课程建设与实践"教改项目的资助，得到了中国科学技术大学出版社的支持以及河南师范大学生命科学学院师生员工的关心、支持与帮助。本书参考和使用了国外 *Essential Biology*、*Concepts in Biology*、*Gene Cloning and DNA Analysis* 和 *Ecology：Concepts & Applications* 等生命科学教材和国内一些文献资料以及网站上的文章和图表，在此一并表示衷心的感谢！

　　由于编者水平有限，书中若有不妥之处，敬请同行与读者批评指正。

编　者

2012 年 6 月

Contents
目　　录

Preface ·· (ⅰ)
Chapter 1　Reading Materials of Life Sciences ············· (1)
　Unit 1　Introduction to Biology ································· (1)
　　1.1　The Significance of Biology in Human Life ············ (1)
　　1.2　The History of Biology ···································· (2)
　　1.3　The Characteristics of Living Things ···················· (3)
　　1.4　The Importance of Biology ································ (7)
　　1.5　Future Direcitons in Biology ······························ (8)
　　1.6　Famous Scientists in Biology ······························ (9)
　Unit 2　Biomacromolecules ······································· (11)
　　2.1　Introduction to Biomacromolecules ······················ (11)
　　2.2　Four Classes of Important Biomacromolecules ········· (12)
　Unit 3　Cell Structures and Functions ··························· (26)
　　3.1　Introduction to Cells and Cell Biology ··················· (26)
　　3.2　Basic Cell Structures ·· (27)
　　3.3　Several Important Cell Structures and Their Functions ········ (29)
　Unit 4　Cell Division, Culture and Animal Cloning ············ (44)
　　4.1　Cell Division and Its Functions ···························· (44)
　　4.2　Cell Culture and Its Applications ························· (45)
　　4.3　Cloning ·· (47)
　Unit 5　Transfer of Genetic Information and Its Regulation ········ (57)
　　5.1　The Central Dogma ·· (58)
　　5.2　DNA Replication ··· (59)
　　5.3　DNA Transcription ·· (62)
　　5.4　Translation ·· (64)
　　5.5　Regulation of Gene Expression ···························· (66)
　Unit 6　Genetic Laws and Disorders ····························· (68)
　　6.1　Laws of Genetics ··· (68)

6.2	Genetic Disorders	(74)
Unit 7	Microbes and Their Uses	(84)
7.1	Breif Introduction to Microbes and Microbiology	(84)
7.2	Important Microbes	(85)
7.3	Microbial Uses	(91)
Unit 8	Plants and Their Uses	(96)
8.1	Plants and Botany	(97)
8.2	Main Types of Green Plants and Their Characteristics	(98)
8.3	Uses of Plants	(103)
Unit 9	Animals and Their Uses	(110)
9.1	Animals and Zoology	(111)
9.2	Animal Structures	(112)
9.3	Uses of Animals	(126)
Unit 10	GMF and Biosafety	(132)
10.1	Biotechnology and Its Main Types	(133)
10.2	Genetically Modified Organism (GMO)	(134)
10.3	Genetically Modified Foods (GMF)	(144)
10.4	GMF Biosafety	(145)
Unit 11	Biodiversity and Its Conservation	(153)
11.1	Ecology, Its Branches and Applications	(154)
11.2	Biodiversity	(154)
11.3	Human Benefits from Biodiversity	(161)
11.4	Biodiversity Crisis	(163)
11.5	Biodiversity Conservation and Sustainable Development	(164)
Unit 12	Technologies and Applications of Aquaculture	(170)
12.1	Aquaculture	(170)
12.2	Fish Aquaculture	(171)
12.3	Shrimp Farming	(173)
12.4	Turtle Farming	(176)
12.5	Oyster Farming	(177)
12.6	Algaculture	(179)
Unit 13	Bioinformatics and Genomics	(187)
13.1	Bioinformatics	(187)
13.2	Genomics and Its Main Branches	(190)

Contents   V

Chapter 2 Translation Techniques of English for Science and Technology (EST) ······ (202)

Unit 1 Writing Rules of English Articles for Science and Technology and Examples ······ (202)

1.1 Characteristics of EST Words ······ (202)

1.2 Characteristics of EST Sentences ······ (206)

1.3 Characteristics of EST Discourses ······ (210)

Unit 2 General Idioms and Examples ······ (211)

2.1 Words as Idioms ······ (211)

2.2 Phrases as Idioms ······ (211)

2.3 Sentence Patterns as Idioms ······ (213)

Unit 3 The Translation Rules and Examples of English Articles for Science and Technology ······ (214)

3.1 Translate English into Chinese ······ (215)

3.2 Translate Chinese into English ······ (217)

Chapter 3 Writing Techniques of English Articles for Science and Technology ······ (223)

Unit 1 English Articles for Science and Technology and Their Types ······ (223)

1.1 English Articles for Science and Technology ······ (223)

1.2 The Types of English Articles for Science and Technology ······ (224)

Unit 2 The Characteristics of English Articles for Science and Technology ······ (225)

2.1 Technicality ······ (226)

2.2 Creativity ······ (226)

2.3 Scientificness ······ (227)

2.4 Accuracy ······ (227)

2.5 Popularity and normalization ······ (227)

2.6 Objectivity ······ (228)

2.7 Figures and Tables, Formulae and Signs ······ (229)

Unit 3 Basic Formats of English Articles for Science and Technology ······ (230)

3.1 Basic Formats of English Articles for Bachelor ······ (230)

3.2　Basic Formats of Research Paper ………………………………… (230)
Unit 4　Writing Procedures and Technologies of English Articles for
　　　　Science and Technology ……………………………………… (236)
　4.1　Selected Topic and Title of EST ………………………………… (237)
　4.2　Preparation of EST ……………………………………………… (237)
　4.3　Writing of EST …………………………………………………… (237)
　4.4　Example Analysis ………………………………………………… (237)

Keys …………………………………………………………………………… (243)

Appendix ……………………………………………………………………… (256)

References …………………………………………………………………… (257)

Chapter 1　Reading Materials of Life Sciences

Unit 1　Introduction to Biology

导语　生物是自然界有生命的物质,具有非生命物质所不具有的代谢过程、生殖过程、对环境刺激反应的过程、生长发育、遗传和变异等特征,可分为动物、植物和微生物三大类群。生物学是研究生物的科学,可分为动物学、植物学和微生物学及其多种分支学科。学习和掌握生物学知识、原理和技术有利于我们认识生命现象和规律,分析和解决生物学相关问题,造福于人类。

本单元主要介绍生物学在人类生活中的意义、生命特征、生物学的发展史、学科趋势、领军人物、基本概念等。

1.1　The Significance of Biology in Human Life

Maybe you have heard of the following questions: How does a single cell become a new plant? Can agriculture be revolutionized? How do computer monitors, cell phones, and microwave ovens affect us? Is DNA testing reliable enough to be admitted as evidence in court cases? What pills can be developed by people to control a person's weight? Can scientists manipulate our genes to control certain genetic disease such as red-green blindness? Are human activities really causing the world to get warmer and result in increased incidence of skin cancer? Will people develop a vaccine for AIDS in the near future? Will new, inexpensive, socially acceptable methods of birth control be developed that can slow world population growth? These questions and many others have biological basis. Biology has an enormous impact on our everyday life, and people can not understand many important issues without a basic understanding of life science. It is no wonder that biology is daily news. Whatever your reason for taking this course is, even if only to meet your colleges' requirement, you will soon discover that this is the best time ever to study biology.

1.2　The History of Biology

Biology is the science of life. Specifically, biology is a science that deals with living things and how they interact with their surroundings. Biology is both an old and a vast science that gets bigger every year because of the great discovery explosion.

The history of biology traces back to the study of the living world from ancient to modern times. Our earliest recorded biology comes from the ancient Greeks, but even prehistoric man left beautiful drawings of animals behind in his caves, which seemingly indicate that man has a sensitive awareness of proportion, anatomy and motion. When man existed principally as a hunter, he practiced biology of a sort as he sought out his food, for he had to know the ways of the hunted animal, the ways of those animals that would prey upon him, and the sources of edible plants. When he turned from nomad life to a more stable, agricultural existence, he had to have a greater knowledge of plants and animals before he could domesticate them sufficiently well to provide himself with a ready sources of food. And as he domesticated them, they domesticate him, for he had to adapt himself to their ways of life, and to adapt them to his own. It is from these early beginnings that biology had its start.

Although the concept of biology as a single coherent field arose in the 19th century, the biological sciences emerged from traditions of medicine and natural history in the ancient Greco-Roman world. This ancient work was further developed in the Middle Ages by Muslim physicians and scholars. During the European Renaissance and early modern period, biological thought was revolutionized in Europe by a renewed interest in empiricism and the discovery of many novel organisms. Prominent in this movement were Vesalius and Harvey, who used experimentation and careful observation in physiology, and naturalists such as Linnaeus and Buffon who began to classify the diversity of life and the fossil record, as well as the development and behavior of organisms. Microscopy revealed the previously unknown world of microorganisms, laying the groundwork for cell theory. The growing importance of natural theology, partly a response to the rise of mechanical philosophy, encouraged the growth of natural history. Over the 18th and 19th centuries, biological sciences such as botany and zoology became increasingly professional scientific disciplines. Naturalists such as Alexander von Humboldt investigated the interaction between organisms and their environments, and the ways this relationship depends on geography—laying the foundations for biogeography, ecology and ethology. Naturalists began to reject essentialism and consider the importance of extinction and the mutability of species. Cell theory provided a new perspective on the fundamental basis of life. These developments, as well as the results from embryology and paleontology, were synthesized in Charles Darwin's theory of evolution by natural selection. The end of the 19th century saw the fall of spontaneous generation and the rise of the germ theory of disease, though the mechanism of inheritance remained a mystery.

In the early 20th century, the rediscovery of Mendel's work led to the rapid development of genetics by Thomas Hunt Morgan and his students, and by the 1930s the combination of population genetics and natural selection in the "neo-Darwinian synthesis". New disciplines developed rapidly, especially after Watson and Crick proposed the structure of DNA. Following the establishment of the Central Dogma and the cracking of the genetic code, biology was largely split into between organismal biology—the fields that deal with whole organisms and groups of organisms—and the fields related to cellular and molecular biology. By the late 20th century, new fields like genomics and proteomics were reversing this trend, with organismal biologists using molecular techniques, and molecular and cell biologists investigating the interplay between genes and the environment, as well as the genetics of natural populations of organisms.

1.3 The Characteristics of Living Things

In nature, there are many different types of living things. Some can fly in the sky, some can swim in water, others can run or walk on land, still others can go through soil. However, they are all called living things. Why? For living things have special common abilities and structures or characteristics not typically found in non-living things: ① metabolism, ② reproduction, ③ responsive processes, ④ control processes, ⑤ a unique structural organization, ⑥ heredity and variation, and ⑦ growth and development. It is important to recognize that while these characteristics are typical of all living things, they may not necessarily all be present in each organism at every point in time. For example, some individuals may reproduce or grow only at certain times.

1.3.1 Metabolism

Metabolism is the set of chemical reactions that happen in the cells of living organisms to sustain life. These processes allow organisms to grow and reproduce, maintain their structures, and respond to their environments, and do many other activities, and are controlled and sequenced. Metabolism is usually divided into two types: catabolism and anabolism. The former breaks down organic matter to provide energy and smaller molecules in cellular respiration, while the latter uses energy and smaller molecules to construct certain biomacromolecules including proteins and nucleic acids in cells. There are three essential aspects of metabolism: ① nutrient uptake, ② nutrient processing, and ③ waste elimination. All organisms expend energy to take in nutrients into their cells from their environment to maintain their lives, for example, many animals take them in by eating other organisms. Once inside, nutrients enter a network of chemical reactions. These reactions manipulate nutrients in order to manufacture new parts, make repairs, reproduce, and provide energy for essential activities. However, not all materials entering a living thing are valuable to it. There may be portions of nutrients that are useless or even harmful. Organisms eliminate these portions as waste. These metabolic processes also produce unusable heat energy, which may be considered a waste product.

1.3.2 Reproduction

Reproduction, a fundamental feature of all known life, is the biological process by which new "offspring" individual organisms are produced from their "parents". All over of the world, every individual organism exists as the result of reproduction. Growth and reproduction are directly related to metabolism because neither can occur without gaining and processing nutrients. Since all organisms eventually die, life would cease to exist without reproduction. In general, there are two different ways that various kinds of organisms reproduce and guarantee their continued existence. Some kinds of living things reproduce by sexual reproduction in which two individuals contribute to the creation of a unique, new organism. Asexual reproduction occurs when an individual organism makes identical copies of itself.

1.3.3 Responsive Processes

Organisms also respond to changes within their bodies and in their surroundings in a meaningful way. These responsive processes have been organized into three categories: irritability, individual adaptation, and adaptation of populations, which is also known as evolution.

Irritability is an individual's ability to recognize a stimulus and rapidly respond to it, such as your response to a loud noise, beautiful sunset, or noxious odor. The response occurs only in the individual receiving the stimulus and the reaction is rapid because the structures and processes that cause the response to occur (i.e., muscles, bones, and nerves) are already in place.

Individual adaptation also results from an individual's reaction to a stimulus but is slower because it requires growth or some other fundamental change in an organism. For example, when the days are getting shorter, a weasel responds such that its fur color will change from its brown summer coat to its white winter coat—genes responsible for the production of brown pigment are "turned off" and new white hair grows. Similarly, the response of our body to disease organisms requires a change in the way cells work to attack and eventually destroy the disease-causing organisms. Or the body responds to lower oxygen levels by producing more red blood cells, which carry oxygen. This is why athletes like to train at high elevations. Their ability to transport oxygen to muscles is improved by the increased number of red blood cells.

Evolution involves changes in the kinds of characteristics displayed by individuals within the population. It is a slow change in the genetic makeup of a population of organisms over generations. This process occurs over long periods of time and enables a species to adapt and better survive long-term changes in its environment over many generations. For example, the development of structures that enable birds to fly long distances, allow them to respond to a world in which the winter season presents severe conditions that would threaten survival. Similarly, the development of the human brain and the ability to reason allowed our ancestors to craft and use tools. The use of tools allowed them to survive and be successful in a great variety of environmental conditions.

1.3.4 Control Processes

Control processes are mechanisms that ensure an organism will carry out all metabolic activities in the proper sequence (coordination) and at the proper rate (regulation). All the chemical reactions of an organism are coordinated and linked together in specific pathways. The orchestration of all the reactions ensures that there will be specific stepwise handling of the nutrients needed to maintain life.

1. The molecules responsible for coordinating these reactions are known as enzymes that are able to increase and control the rate at which life's chemical reactions occur, and that regulate the amount of nutrients processed into other forms. The physical activities of organisms are coordinated. When an insect walks, the activities of the muscles of its six legs are coordinated so that an orderly movement results.

Many of the internal activities of organisms are interrelated and coordinated so that a constant internal environment is maintained. This constant internal environment is called homeostasis. For example, when we begin to exercise, we use up oxygen more rapidly, so the amount of oxygen in the blood falls. In order to maintain a "constant internal environment", the body must obtain more oxygen.

2. This involves more rapid contractions of the muscles that cause breathing and a more rapid and forceful pumping of the heart to get blood to the lungs. These activities must occur together at the right time and at the correct rate, and when they do, the level of oxygen in the blood will remain normal while supporting the additional muscular activity.

1.3.5 Unique Structural Organization

Living things also share basic structural similarities. All living things are made up of structural units called cells. Cells have an outer limiting membrane and several kinds of internal structures. Each structure has specific functions. Some living things, like you, consist of trillions of cells while others such as bacteria or yeasts, consist of only one cell. Any unit that is capable of functioning independently is called an organism, whether it consists of a single cell or complex groups of interacting cells. Nonliving materials, such as rocks, water, or gases, do not share a structurally complex common subunit.

1.3.6 Heredity and Variation

The genetic information of each organism is segregated within it and passed from it to its offsprings. This is why offsprings are similar to their parents. However, genetic information does vary somewhat because of crossover and recombination, so there are some dissimilarities between parents and their offsprings.

1.4 The Importance of Biology

We owe our current high standard of living to biological advances in several areas:

(1) Food production. Plant and animal breeders have developed organisms that provide better sources of food than the original varieties. Improvements in yield have been brought about in plants and animals. The improvements in the plants, along with changed farming practices, have led to greatly increased production of food. Animal breeders also have had great successes. The pig, chicken, and cow of today are much different animals from those available even 100 years ago. Chickens lay more eggs, dairy cows give more milk, and beef cattle grow faster. All of these improvements raise our standard of living. One interesting example is the change in the kinds of pigs that are raised. At one time, farmers wanted pigs that were fatty. The fat could be made into lard, soap, and a variety of other useful products. As the demand for the fat products of pigs declined, animal breeders developed pigs that gave a high yield of meat and relatively little fat.

(2) Disease control. There has been fantastic progress in the area of health and disease control. Many diseases, such as polio, whooping cough, measles, and mumps, can be easily controlled by vaccinations. The understanding of how the human body works has led to treatments that can control such diseases as diabetes, high blood pressure, and even some kinds of cancer. Paradoxically, these advances contribute to a major biological problem: the increasing size of the human population.

(3) One of the newest applications of biology is the development of techniques for artificially transferring genes from one organism to another, used for producing

certain medicinal drugs, increasing crop productivity and curing certain human diseases.

(4) Perhaps, the most important application of biology is to help us understand and respond to the environmental problems, for example, global changes in weather and climate, and find the solution to them.

1.5 Future Direcitons in Biology

Although biology has made major advances, many problems remain to be solved. For example, scientists are seeking major advances in the control of the human population and there is a continued interest in the development of more efficient methods of producing food. Some areas that will receive much attention in the future are as follows:

(1) The relationship between genetic information and such diseases as Alzheimer's disease, stroke, arthritis, and cancer. These and many other diseases are caused by abnormal body chemistry, which is the result of hereditary characteristics. Curing certain hereditary diseases is a big job. It requires a thorough understanding of genetics and the manipulation of hereditary information in all of the trillions of cells of the organism.

(2) Ecology. Climate change, destruction of natural ecosystems to feed a rapidly increasing human population, and pollution are all still severe problems. Most people need to learn that some environmental changes may be acceptable and that other changes will ultimately lead to our destruction. We have two tasks. The first is to improve technology and increase our understanding about how things work in our biological world. The second, and probably the more difficult, is to educate, pressure, and remind people that their actions determine the kind of world in which the next generation will live.

(3) Unity of analysis and summary. Comprehensively investigate gene, molecules and cells and how they interact to form complex life system.

(4) Multi-disciplines cross and fusion.

(5) Further elucidation of essence of life.

(6) Unity of basic research and applied research.

In addition, biologists should also make suggestions to politicians and other policy makers about which courses of action are the most logical from a scientific point of view.

1.6 Famous Scientists in Biology

Biology is so vast that it is subdivided into many different subjects such as taxonomy, botany, zoology, microbiology, virology, physiology, ecology, cell biology, biochemistry, biotechnology, evolution, genetics and so on. There are many famous scientists studying living things. For example, ① Taxonomists: Carl von Linne proposing three kingdom system, Whittaker R H putting forward five kingdom system, Oparin Alexander Ivanovich establishing three domain system; ② Geneticists: Gregor Johann Mendel discovering law of segragation and law of independent assortment, Thomas Hunt Morgan discovering law of Linkage and Crossover, Kimura M founding the neutral theory of molecular evolution, Thomas Roderick proposing genomics; ③ Biochemists: Beadle G W and Frederick Sanger putting forward theory of one-gene-one-enzyme and chain termination method, respectively; ④ Molecular Biologist: Cohen S N Kary Mullis, James Watson and Francis Crick Monod J M and Jacob F, Seymour Benzer, Richard Palmiter and Ralph Brinster developing genetic engineering, PCR, DNA double helix model, lactose operon model, cistron and trangenic mouse ("Super" mouse), repectively; ⑤ Zoologists: Jane Goodall, Charles Sutherland Elton; ⑥ Naturalist: Charles Robert Darwin, the founder of evolution theory; ⑦ Famous breeder: Longping Yuan, the father of hybrid rice.

Vocabulary

taxonomy /tæk'sɔnəmi:/ n. 生物分类,分类系统

ethology /i:'θɔlədʒi/ n. 动物行为学,人类行为学

photosynthesis /ˌfəutəu'sinθisis/ n. 光合作用

transplant /træns'pla:nt/ vt. 移植,移种 n. (器官、皮肤、头发等的)移植,移植的器官,移植物

metabolism /mə'tæbəˌlizəm/ n. 新陈代谢

polio /'pəuliˌəu/ n. 骨髓灰质炎,小儿麻痹症

ecosystem /'i:kəsistəm/ n. 生态系统

homeostasis /ˌhəumiəu'steisis/ n. 内环境稳定

toxin /'tɔksin/ n. 毒素

yeast /ji:st/ n. 酵母,发酵物

dipheria /di'fiəriə/ n. 白喉

mumps /mʌmps/ n. 腮腺炎

vaccination /ˌvæksə'neiʃən/ n. 接种疫

苗,种痘,牛痘疤 袭的,承袭的
fungi /'fʌŋgai/ n. 真菌   arthritis /aː'θraitis/ n. 关节炎
pigment /'pigmənt/ n. 色素,颜料   membrane /'mem,brein/ n. 膜,隔膜
hereditary /hi'reditəri/ adj. 遗传的;世   Measles /'miːz(ə)lz/ n. 麻疹

Exercises

1. Translate the following English into Chinese.

(1) Broadly speaking, biology is the study of living things, while, specifically, it is a science that deals with living things and how they interact with their surroundings.

(2) Living things show several characteristics that nonliving things do not display: metabolism, reproduction, response, control, unique structural organization and so on.

(3) The response of our body to disease-causing organisms requires a change in the way by which cells work to attack and eventually destroy them.

(4) Maintaining homeostasis during our exercise involves more rapid contraction of some muscles that cause breathing and a more rapid and forceful pumping of the heart to get blood to the lungs.

2. Fill in the blanks with the appropriate words you have just learned in this unit.

(1) In order to survive, the individuals in a population must _____.

(2) When you are very hungry, urgently looking for food is a response to a _____.

(3) Offsprings resemble their parents in that they inherit a set of _____ materials.

(4) The maintenance of constant internal conditions is called _____.

(5) We owe our current high standard of living to biological advances in several areas such as _____, _____ and so on.

3. Multiple Choice Questions.

(1) Metabolism is divided into two types (　　) and three aspects (　　).

　　A. catabolism　　　　B. injection　　　　C. anabolism

　　D. digestion　　　　　E. waste elimination

(2) Which one(s) belong(s) to responsive process (　　) and control processes (　　), respectively?

　　A. coordination　　　　B. individual adaptation

C. regulation   D. evolution

(3) A characteristic which gives an organism the abilities to acquire resources and cope with the harshness of the physical environment is called (   ).

   A. a stimulus   B. photosynthesis   C. reproduction
   D. an adaptation   E. growth

(4) The essence of the evolutionary process is (   ).

   A. reproduction   B. population size
   C. the survival instinct   D. variability in a population
   E. the change in genetic composition from generation to generation

4. Writing.

Please write a short English letter to your teacher, introducing your preferences for biology.

Unit 2 Biomacromolecules

导语 生物化学是一门研究生命物质的化学组成、结构及生命活动过程中各种化学变化的生物学分支学科。它主要用于研究细胞内各组分，如蛋白质、糖类、脂类、核酸等生物大分子的结构和功能。生物化学与遗传学、分子生物学、细胞学、微生物学、生理学和基因组学等学科关系密切，其广泛应用于工业、农业、医学、环保和国防以及科学研究等方面。

本单元主要介绍糖类、脂类、蛋白质和核酸四类生物大分子的组成、结构、分类、功能和应用。

2.1 Introduction to Biomacromolecules

In cells, there are many molecules, but there are only four classes of important biomacromolecules such as carbohydrates, lipids, proteins and nucleic acids. Cells make most of their large molecules by stringing smaller or identical organic molecules into chains, called polymers. The smaller or identical molecules in polymers are known as monomers, which are usually combined by a dehydration synthesis reaction (de = remove; hydro = water; synthesis = combine). This reaction results in the synthesis or formation of a macromolecule when water is removed from between the two smaller component parts. For example, when a monomer with an-OH group attached to its carbon skeleton approaches another monomer with an available hydrogen, dehydration synthesis can occur. The reverse of a dehydration synthesis reaction is known as hydrolysis (hydro = water; lyse = to split or break). Hydrolysis is the process of splitting a larger organic molecule into two or more component parts by the addition of water. Digestion of food molecules in the stomach is an important example of hydrolysis.

2.2 Four Classes of Important Biomacromolecules

2.2.1 Carbohydrates

Carbohydrates are some macronutrients that provide the body with energy, composed of carbon, hydrogen, and oxygen atoms, and play a number of roles in living things. They serve as an immediate source of energy (sugars), provide shape to certain cells (for example, cellulose in plant cell walls), are components of many antibiotics and coenzymes, and are an essential part of genes (DNA). Carbon, hydrogen, and oxygen atoms are linked together to form monomers called simple sugars or monosaccharides (mono = single; saccharide = sweet, sugar). The empirical formula for a simple sugar is easy to recognize because there are equal numbers of carbons and oxygens and twice as many hydrogens, for example, $C_3H_6O_3$ or $C_5H_{10}-O_5$. We usually describe simple sugars by the number of carbons in the molecule. The ending "-ose" indicates that you are dealing with a carbohydrate. A triose has three carbons, a pentose has five, and a hexose has six. If you remember that the number of carbons equals the number of oxygen atoms and that number of hydrogens is double that number, these names tell you the empirical formula for the simple sugar.

Simple sugars, such as glucose, fructose, and galactose, provide the chemical energy necessary to keep organisms alive. These simple sugars combine with each other by dehydration synthesis to form complex carbohydrates (Fig. 2-1). When two simple sugars bond to each other, a disaccharide (di = two) is formed; when three bond together, a trisaccbaride (tri = three) is formed. Generally, we call a complex carbohydrate which is larger than this a polysaccharide (many sugar units). In all cases, the complex carbohydrates are formed by the removal of water from between the sugars. Some common examples of polysaccharides are starch and glycogen. Cellulose is an important polysaccharide used in constructing the cell walls of plant cells. Humans cannot digest this complex carbohydrate, so we are not able to use it as an energy source. On the other hand, animals known as ruminants (e.g., cows and sheep) and termites have microorganisms within their digestive tracts that do digest cellulose, making it an energy source for them. Fiber is an important addition to the diet because it helps control weight, reduce the risk of colon cancer, and control constipation and diarrhea.

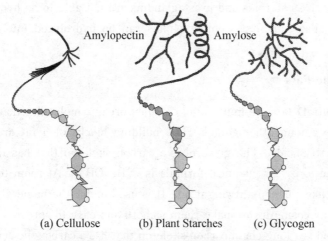

(a) Cellulose   (b) Plant Starches   (c) Glycogen

Fig. 2-1 Polysaccharides or complex carbohydrates
(Eldon D E, Frederick C R, 2004)

(a) cellulose; (b) plant starch including amylose and amylopectin; (c) glycogen, sometimes called aminal starch, in muscle cells. They are all polymers of simple sugars, but differ from one another in how they are joined together. While many organisms can digest the bonds found in glycogen and plant starch molecules, few are able to break those that link the monosaccharides of cellulose together.

Simple sugars can be used by the cell as components in other, more complex molecules. Sugar molecules are a part of other, larger molecules such as DNA, RNA, or ATP. The ATP molecule is important in energy transfer. It has a simple sugar (ribose) as part of its structural makeup. The building blocks of the genetic material (DNA) also have a sugar component.

2.2.2 Lipids

Lipids are also one of three macronutrients that provide the body with energy. We generally call them fats. However, there are three different types of lipids: true fats (pork chop fat or olive oil), phospholipids (the primary component of cell membranes), and steroids (most hormones). In general, lipids are large, nonpolar, organic molecules that do not easily dissolve in polar solvents such as water. They are soluble in nonpolar substances such as ester or acetone. Just like carbohydrates, the lipids are also composed of carbon, hydrogen, and oxygen. Simple lipids such as steroids and prostaglandins are not able to be hydrolyzed into smaller and similar subunits. Complex lipids can be hydrolyzed into smaller and similar units.

2.2.2.1 True Fats

True (neutral) fats are important, complex organic molecules that are used to provide energy among other things. The building blocks of a fat are a glycerol molecule and fatty acids. The glycerol is a carbon skeleton that has three alcohol groups attached to it. Its chemical formula is $C_3H_5(OH)_3$. At room temperature, glycerol looks like clear, lightweight oil. It is used under the name glycerin as an additive to many cosmetics to make them smooth and easy to spread.

A fatty acid is a long-chain carbon skeleton that has a carboxylic acid functional group. If the carbon skeleton has as much hydrogen bonded to it as possible, we call it saturated. The saturated fatty acid is stearic acid, a component of solid meat fats such as mutton tallow. Saturated fats are generally found in animal tissues —they tend to be solids at room temperatures. Some examples of saturated fats are butter, whale blubber, suet, lard, and fats associated with such meats as steak or pork chops. If the carbons are double-bonded to each other at one or more points, the fatty acid is said to be unsaturated. The occurrence of a double bond in a fatty acid is indicated by the Greek letter "ω" (omega) followed by a number, for example, oleic acid.

2.2.2.2 Steroids

Steroids are characterized by their arrangement of interlocking rings of carbon. They often serve as hormones that aid in regulating body processes. We have already mentioned one steroid molecule, cholesterol, that you are probably familiar with. Although serum cholesterol has been implicated in many cases of atherosclerosis, this steroid is made by your body for use as a component of cell membranes. It is also used by your body to make bile acids. These products of your liver are channeled into your intestine to emulsify fats. Cholesterol is also necessary for the manufacture of vitamin D. Cholesterol molecules in the skin react with ultraviolet light to produce vitamin D, which assists in the proper development of bones and teeth. A large number of steroid molecules are hormones. Some of them regulate reproductive processes such as egg and sperm production; others regulate such things as salt concentration in the blood.

2.2.3 Proteins

Proteins are also one of three macronutrients that provide the body with energy. They are polymers constructed with amino acid monomers. An amino acid is a short carbon skeleton that contains an amino group on one end of the skeleton and a carboxyl group at the other end. In addition, the carbon skeleton may have one of several different side chains. These vary in their composition and are generally noted as the amino acid's R-group. About 20 common amino acids are important to cells and each differs from one another in the nature of its attached R-group. The amino acids can bond together by dehydration synthesis reactions. When two amino acids form a bond by removal of water, the nitrogen of the amino group of one is linked to the carbon of the carboxyl group of another. This covalent bond is termed a peptide bond. Any amino acid can form a peptide bond with any other amino acid. They fit together in a specific way, with the amino group of one bonding to the carboxyl group of the next. You can imagine that by using 20 different amino acids as building blocks, you can construct millions of different combinations. Each of these combinations is termed a polypeptide chain. A specific polypeptide is composed of a specific sequence of amino acids bonded end to end. The specific sequence of amino acids in a polypeptide is controlled by the genetic information of an organism. Genes are specific messages that tell the cell to link particular amino acids in a specific order; that is, they determine a polypeptide's primary structure. The kinds of side chains on these amino acids influence the shape that the polypeptide forms.

One protein consists of one or more polypeptide chains folded into a unique shape. The specific shape that determines a protein's function comprises four successive levels of structure such as primary structure, secondary structure, tertiary structure and quaternary structure.

(1) Primary structure. Primary structure is the sequence of amino acids forming its polypeptide chain(s).

(2) Secondary structure. The string of amino acids in a polypeptide chain coils or folds into regular patterns or particular shapes called secondary structure, such as an alpha helix or a pleated sheet, whereas other portions remain straight. For example, at this secondary level some proteins (e.g., hair) take the form of an alpha helix, a shape like that of a coiled telephone cord. The helical shape is maintained by hydrogen bonds formed between different amino acid side chains at different locations in the polypeptide. Remember that these forces of attraction do not form molecules but result in the orientation of one part of a molecule to another part within the same molecule. Other polypeptides form hydrogen bonds that cause them to make several flat folds that resemble a pleated skirt. This is called a beta pleated sheet. The way a particular protein folds is important to its function. In Alzhenmer's, Bovine spongiform encephalitis (mad cow disease), and Creutzfelts-Jakob's diseases, protein structures are not formed correctly. This results in characteristic nervous system symptoms.

(3) Tertiary structure. Tertiary structure refers to the overall, three dimensional shapes of a polypeptide. A good example of tertiary structure can be seen when a coiled phone cord becomes so twisted that it folds around and back on itself in several places. The oxygen-holding protein, found in muscle cells and myoglobin, displays tertiary structure; it is composed of a single (153 amino acids) helical molecule folded back and bonded to itself in several places.

(4) Quaternary structure. frequently several different polypeptides, each with its own tertiary structure, twist around each other and chemically combine. The larger, globular structure formed by these interacting polypeptides is called the protein's quaternary (fourth-degree) structure. The individual polypeptide chains are bonded to each other by the interactions of certain side chains, which can form disulfide covalent bonds. Quaternary structure is displayed by the protein molecules called immunoglobulins or antibodies, which fight diseases such as mumps and chicken pox, and the protein portion of the hemoglobin molecule (globin is globular in shape).

The structure of a protein is closely related to its function. Any changes in the arrangement of amino acids within a protein can have far-reaching effects on its function. For example, normal hemoglobin found in red blood cells consists of two kinds of polypeptide chains called the alpha and beta chains. The beta chain is composed of 146 amino acids. If just one of these amino acids is replaced by a different one, the hemoglobin molecule may not function properly. A classic example of this results in a condition known as sickle-cell anemia. In this case, the sixth amino acid in the beta chain, which is normally glutamic acid, is replaced by valine. This minor change causes the hemoglobin to fold differently, and the red blood cells that contain this altered hemoglobin assume a sickle shape when the body is deprived of an adequate supply of oxygen.

Every one of us has tens of thousands of different kinds of proteins. There are seven major classess of proteins.

(1) Structural proteins. They are important for maintaining the shape of cells and organisms. They make up the cell membrane, muscle cells, blood cells, the silk of spinders, the hair of mammals and the fibers that make up our tendons and ligaments. Collagen provides shape and support.

(2) Enzymes. Catalysts speed the rate of chemical reactions.

(3) Signal proteins. Some hormones such as insulin and oxytocin. Insulin is produced by the pancreas and controls the amount of glucose in the blood. If insulin production is too low, or if the molecule is improperly constructed, glucose molecules are not removed from the bloodstream at a rate fast enough. The excess sugar is then eliminated in the urine. Other symptoms of excessive sugar in the blood include excessive thirst and even loss of consciousness. The disease caused by improperly functioning insulin is known as diabetes. Oxytocin stimulates the contraction of the uterus furing childbirth. It is also an example of an organic molecule that has been produced artificially (e.g., pitocin) and is used by physicians to induce labor. These enzymes and some hormones are called regulator proteins, which can help determine what activities will occur in the organism.

(4) Carrier or transport proteins. They pick up and deliver molecules at one place and transport them to another. For example, proteins regularly attach to cholesterol entering the system from the diet-forming molecules called lipoproteins, which are transported through the circulatory system. The cholesterol is released at a distance from the digestive tract and the proteins return

to pick up more entering dietary cholesterol; Hemoglobins conveys oxygen from our lungs to other parts of our bodies.

(5) Storage proteins. Ovalbumin and prolamins and glutelins of cereal endosperm proteins. Ovalbumin serves as a source of amino acids for developing embryos.

(6) Defense proteins. They fight infections of dangerous microbes and chemicals (e.g., antibodies in the blood).

(7) Contractile proteins. They provide muscular movement.

2.2.4 Nucleic Acids

The last class of biomacromolecules is the nucleic acids. Nucleic acids are complex polymeric molecules that store and transfer information within a cell. There are two types of nucleic acids, DNA (deoxyribonucleic acid) and RNA (ribonucleic acid). DNA serves as genetic material while RNA plays a vital role in the manufacture of proteins. All nucleic acids are constructed of fundamental monomers known as nucleotides. Each nucleotide is composed of three parts: ① a 5-carbon simple sugar molecule that may be ribose or deoxyribose, ② a phosphate group, and ③ a nitrogenous base. The nitrogenous bases may be one of five types. Two of the bases are the larger, double ring molecules Adenine and Guanine. The smaller bases are the single ring bases Thymine, Cytosine, and Uracil. Nucleotides (monomers) are linked together in long sequences (polymers) so that the sugar and phosphate sequence forms a "backbone" and the nitrogenous bases stick out to the side. DNA has deoxyribose sugar and the bases A, T, G, and C, while RNA has ribose sugar and the bases A, U, G, and C.

DNA is composed of two strands to form a ladderlike structure, thousands of bases long. The two strands are attached between their protruding bases according to the base pair rule, that is, Adenine protruding from one strand always pairs with Thymine protruding from the other (in the case of RNA, Adenine always pairs with Uracil). Guanine always pairs with Cytosine. One strand of DNA is called the coding strand because it has a meaningful genetic message written using the nitrogenous bases as letters (e.g., the base sequence CATTAGACT). If these bases are read in groups of three, they make sense to us (i.e., "cat", "tag", and "act"). This is the basis of the genetic code for all organisms. The opposite strand is called non-coding since it makes no "sense" but protects the coding strand from chemical and physical damage. Both strands are twisted into a helix. Strands of helical DNA may contain tens or thousands of base pairs (AT and GC combinations) that an organism reads as a sequence of chapters in a book. Each chapter is a gene. Just as chapters in a book are identified by beginning and ending statements, different genes along a DNA strand have beginning and ending signals. They tell when to start and when to stop reading a particular gene. Human body cells contain 46 strands (books) of helical DNA, each containing thousands of genes (chapters). These strands are called chromosomes when they become super coiled in preparation for cellular reproduction. Before cell reproduction, the DNA makes copies of the coding and non-coding strands ensuring that the offspring or daughter cells will each receive a full complement of the genes required for their survival.

RNA is found in three forms. Messenger RNA (mRNA) is a single strand copy of a portion of the coding strand of DNA for a specific gene. When mRNA is formed on the surface of the DNA, the base pair rule (A pairs with U and G pairs with C) applies. After mRNA is formed and peeled off, it moves to ribosomes where the genetic message can be translated into a protein molecule. Ribosomes contain another type of RNA, ribosomal RNA (rRNA). rRNA is also an RNA copy of DNA, but after being formed, it becomes twisted and covered in protein to form a ribosome. The third form of RNA, transfer RNA (tRNA), is also an RNA copy of different segments of DNA, but when peeled off the surface of the DNA, each takes the form of a cloverleaf. tRNA molecules are responsible for transferring specific amino acids to the ribosome where all three forms of RNA come together and cooperate in the manufacture of protein molecules.

Vocabulary

monomer /ˈmɔnəmə/ n. 单体
macromolecule /ˌmækrəuˈmɔlikjuːl/ n. 巨大分子，高分子
carbohydrate /ˌkɑːbəuˈhaidreit/ n. 碳水化合物，糖类
pentose /ˈpentəus/ n. 戊糖
hexose /ˈheksəus/ n. 己糖
polysaccharide /ˌpɔliˈsækəraid/ n. 多糖，聚糖，多聚糖

diarrhea /ˌdaiəˈriːə/ n. 痢疾，腹泻
lipid /ˈlipid, ˈlaipid/ n. 脂质，油脂（脂肪，乳酪）
phospholipid /ˌfɔsfəuˈlipid/ n. 磷脂
glycerol /ˈglisərɔl/ n. 甘油，丙三醇
steroid /ˈstiərɔid/ n. 类固醇
cholesterol /kɔˈlestərɔl, kɔˈlestərəl/ n. 胆固醇
dehydration /ˌdiːhaiˈdreiʃən/ n. 脱水

acetyl /'æsitil/ n. 乙酰基，醋酸基
pesticide /'pestisaid/ n. 杀虫剂
myoglobin /'maiəgləuobin/ n. 肌红蛋白
pitocin /pit'əusin/ n. 催产素
ovalbumin /ˌəuvæl'bjuːmən/ n. 卵白蛋白，卵清蛋白

collagen /'kɔlədʒən/ n. 胶原蛋白
acetone /'æsitəun/ n. 丙酮
prostaglandin /ˌprɔstə'glændin/ n. 前列腺素
glycerin /'glisərin/ n. 甘油

Exercises

1. Multiple Choice Questions.

(1) A glucose molecule is to starch as (   ).
　A. a steriod is to a lipid
　B. a protein is to an amino acid
　C. a nucleic acid is to a polypeptide
　D. a nucleotide is to a nucleic acid
　E. an amino acid is to a nucleic acid

(2) What makes a fatty acid an acid? (   )
　A. It does not dissolve in water.
　B. It is capable of bonding with other molecules to form a fat.
　C. It has a carhydroxyl group that donates a hydrogen ion to a solution.
　D. It contains only two atoms.
　E. It is a polymer made of many smaller subunits.

(3) Where would you be most likely to find a hydrophobic amino acid R group in the three-dimensional structure of a protein? (   )
　A. At both ends of the polypeptide chain.
　B. On the outside, in the water.
　C. Covalently bonded to another R group.
　D. On the inside, away from water.
　E. Covalently bonded to the amino group of the next amino acid.

(4) Pancreatic amylases can attach to starch molecules and help break them down to disacharides, but they can not decompose celluloses. Why not? (   )
　A. Cellulose is a kind of fat, not a carbohydrate like starch.
　B. Cellulose molecules are much too large.
　C. Starch is made of glucose while cellulose is made of other sugars.
　D. The bonds between sugars in cellulose are much stronger.
　E. The simple sugars in cellulose bond differently, giving cellulose a different shape.

(5) A shortage of phosphorus in the soil would make it especially difficult for a plant to manufacture (   ).

    A. DNA   B. fatty acids   C. proteins   D. sucrose   E. cellulose

(6) Lipids differ from other large biological molecules in that they (   ).

    A. are much large   B. are not truly polymers

    C. do not have specific shapes   D. do not contain carbon

    E. contain nitrogen atoms

(7) Carbohydrates, lipids, nucleic acids, and proteins are all (   ).

    A. inorganic chemicals   B. inorganic molecules

    C. inorganic polymers   D. biochemicals   E. biological monomers

(8) Which can describe phospholipids? (   )

    A. Phospholipids are solubale in water.

    B. Phospholipids are not solubale in water because their phosphates "heads" make them hydrophobic.

    C. Their fatty asic tails are solubale in water.

    D. Phospholipids consist of a glycerol covalently bonded to two fatty acid chains and a phosphate group.

    E. Their phosphates "heads" make them hydrophobic.

(9) The process by which small molecular subunits are bonded together to form macromolecules is called (   ).

    A. condensation   B. monomerization   C. hydrolysis

    D. organization   E. assembly

(10) The process by which macromolecules are disassembled into individual monomers is called (   ).

    A. monomerization   B. condensation   C. hydrolysis

    D. polymerization   E. disorganization

(11) In living systems, carbohydrates function as (   ).

    A. the ultimate director of metabolism

    B. foundation for membranes

    C. waterproofing agents

    D. energy storehouses and building materials

    E. thermal insulators and shock absorbers

(12) Bemard discovered that the liver chemically converts various foods, such as proteins, to glucose, which it then stores as glycogen; and that when the body needs sugar for fuel, the stored glycogen is transformed back into glucose and released into the

bloodstream to satisfy glucose-depleted tissues. Bemard used the balance between glycogen formation and breakdown to formulate the concept of (   ).

    A. hydrolysis   B. catabolism   C. metabolism

    D. respiration   E. homeostasis

(13) Animals digest cellulose (   ).

    A. after it goes through the process of homeostasis

    B. easily because it is made of glucoses

    C. after it is decomposed by microorganisms in their digestive tracts

    D. after it is polymerized by organisms in their digestive tracts

    E. after it is broken down by an enzyme produced by their own bodies

(14) Which cellular function is shared by proteins and lipids? (   )

    A. Both have representatives which act as hormones.

    B. Both can be used as antibodies by vertebrates to combat foreign materials.

    C. Both can act as enzymes.

    D. Both are used in oxygen transport in the blood.

    E. Both are involved in forming the contractile machinery of skeletal muscle.

(15) Which group of the following is responsible for regulating gene expression, oxygen transport and metabolism? (   )

    A. Proteins.   B. Lipids.   C. Carbohydrates.

    D. Steriods.   E. Polysaccharides.

(16) The subunits of nucleic ascids are (   ).

    A. DNAs   B. RNAs   C. nucleotides

    D. polymers   E. proteins

(17) Which can best describe the flow of hereditary information in a cell? (   )

    A. The sequence of nucleotides in a molecule of RNA determines the sequence of amino acids in a protein, which in turn determines the sequence of DNA.

    B. The sequence of amino acids in a protein determines the sequence of nucleotides in a molecule of RNA, which in turn determines the sequence of DNA.

    C. The sequence of DNA determines the sequence of nucleotides in a molecule of RNA, which in turn determines the sequence of amino acids in a protein.

    D. The sequence of amino acids in a protein determines the sequence of DNA, which in turn determines the sequence of nucleotides in a molecule of RNA.

2. True or False.

(1) The sugars circulating in your blood are primarily disaccharides. (　)

(2) Genes are composed of DNA. (　)

(3) The bormine testosterone is a steriod, a type of protein. (　)

(4) When amino acids are linked to form a polypeptide, water is produced as a by-product. (　)

(5) When a protein is denatured, its primary structure is the level of the structure most likely to be disrupted. (　)

(6) Fat molecules store energy in cells. (　).

(7) Users of anabolic steriods can experience reduced sex drive and infertility. (　)

3. Answer the following questions in English.

(1) How can a cell make so many different kinds of proteins out of only 20 animo acids?

(2) Briefly state the functions of proteins in a cell.

4. Think and answer the following questions.

When you eat candies, their sucroses are broken down into two monosaccharides such as glucose and fructose in your intestine, which one is then absorbed into your blood?

5. Comprehensive Reading.

In any cell, many kinds of enzymes are sensitive to changing environmental conditions such as pH and temperature. In order for a cell to stay alive in the environment, innumerable biochemical reactions must be controlled to ensure that an organism will carry out all metabolic activities in the proper sequence (coordination) and at the proper rate (regulation). Coordination of enzymatic activities in a cell results when specific reactions occur in a given sequence, for example, $A \rightarrow B \rightarrow C \rightarrow D \rightarrow E$. This ensures that a particular nutrient will be converted to a particular end product necessary to the survival of the cell. Should a cell not be able to coordinate its reactions, essential products might be produced at the wrong time or never be produced at all, and the cell would die. Regulation of biochemical reactions refers to how a cell controls the amount of chemical product. For example, if a cell manufactures too much lipid, the presence of those molecules could interfere with other life sustaining reactions, resulting in the death of the cell. On the other hand, if a cell does not produce enough of an essential molecule, such as a digestive enzyme, it might also die.

Any one substrate may be acted upon by several different enzymes. Although all these different enzymes may combine with the same substrate, they do not have the same chemical effect on the substrate because each converts the substrate to different end products. For instance, acetyl is a substrate that can be acted upon by citrate synthetase, fatty acid synthetase, and malate synthetase. Which Enzyme has the greatest success depends on the number of each type of enzyme available and the suitability of the environment for the enzyme's operation. Whenever several different enzymes may combine with a given substrate, enzymatic competition will happen. For example, the use a cell makes of the substrate molecule acetyl is directly controlled by the amount and kinds of enzymes it prodices. The number and kind of enzymes produced are regulated by the cell's genes. It is the job of chemical messengers (called gene-regulator proteins) to inform the genes as to whether specific enzyme-producing genes should be turned on or off or whether they should have their protein-producing activities increased or decreased. Gene-regulator proteins that decrease protein production are called gene-repressor proteins, whereas those that increase protein production are gene-activator proteins. If the cell is in need of protein, the acetyl could be metabolized to provide one of the building blocks for the construction of protein by turning up the production of the enzyme maltase. If the cell requires energy to move or grow, more acetyl can be metabolized to release this energy by producing more citrate synthetases. When the enzyme fatty acid synthesize outcompetes the other two, the acetyl is used in fat production and storage. Negative-feedback inhibition controls the synthesis of many molecules within a cell, which occurs within an enzyme-controlled reaction sequence. As the number of end products increases, some product molecules feed back to one of the previous reactions and have a negative effect on the enzyme controlling that reaction; that is, they inhibit or prevent that enzyme from performing at its best.

In addition, the operation of enzymes can be influenced by the presence of other molecules. An inhibitor is a molecule that attaches itself to an enzyme and interferes with its ability to form an enzyme-substrate complex. One of the early kinds of pesticides used to spray fruit trees contained arsenic. The arsenic attached itself to insect enzymes and inhibited the normal growth and reproduction of insects. Organophosphates are pesticides that inhibit several enzymes necessary for the operation of the nervous system. When they are incorporated into nerve cells, they disrupt normal nerve transmission and cause the death of the affected organisms. In humans, death due to pesticides is usually caused by uncontrolled muscle contractions, resulting in breathing failure.

We use enzyme inhibition to control disease. The sulfa drugs are used to control a variety of bacteria, such as the bacterium *streptococcus pyogenes*, causing strep throat and scarlet fever. The drug resembles one of the bacterium's necessary substrates and so prevents some of the cell's enzymes from producing an essential cell component. As a result, the bacterial cell dies because its normal metabolism is not maintained. Those that survive become the grandparents of a new population of drug-resistant bacteria. Antibiotics act as agents of natural selection favoring those cells that have the genetic ability to withstand the effects of the drug. Since one essential life characteristic is evolution, the prevention of drug resistance is impossible. The development of resistance can only be slowed, not stopped. Microbes may become resistant to antibiotics in four ways: ① they can stop producing the molecule that is the target of the drug; ② they can modify the target; ③ they can become impermeable to the drug; ④ they can release enzymes that inactivate the antibiotic.

Questions for Discussion:

(1) How must biochemical reactions in cells be controlled to ensure that an organism will carry out all metabolic activities?

(2) which factors regulate the number and kind of enzymes used in a set of cellular reactions?

(3) How are new antibiotics-resistant microorganisms transformed from antibiotics-sensitive ones by resistance selection?

6. Conversation in Groups.

In this part, first divide students into small groups, and then each group makes up a short conversation about vegetables (celery, cauliflower, cucumber), food (rice, noodle, dumpling, sesame seed cake), fruits and meats (beef, pork, mutton and chicken). After that each member of the group plays a role in the conversation (e.g., Member A, Member B and so on).

Tips: 1. Talking about meals one likes or dislikes;
    2. Talking about cooking, for example, making a healthy meal or nutritious dishes;
    3. Talking about planting vegetables;
    4. Comparing the nutritious ingredients in different vegetables and food;
    5. Inviting someone to have delicious food (vegetables, meat and so on).

Unit 3 Cell Structures and Functions

导语 细胞是生命结构和功能的基本单位,细胞的特殊性决定了生物个体的特殊性,因此,对细胞的研究是揭开生命奥秘、改造生命和征服疾病的关键。细胞分为原核细胞和真核细胞两大类。原核细胞具有细胞壁、细胞膜、细胞质及其内的拟核、质粒和核糖体等结构;真核细胞具有细胞壁(如植物细胞)、细胞膜、细胞质及其中的细胞器和细胞核等结构。细胞生物学是研究细胞的结构、功能和各种生命规律的一门生物学分支学科。

本单元介绍细胞的概念及其共同特性,细胞生物学的概念及其分支学科,细胞类型,细胞膜和细胞质及其内的内质网、溶酶体、线粒体、叶绿体和细胞核等结构与功能。

3.1 Introduction to Cells and Cell Biology

Cell is the functional basic unit of life in cytology. The cell theory, first developed in 1839 by Matthias Jakob Schleiden and Theodor Schwann, states that all organisms are composed of one or more cells, that all cells come from preexisting cells, that vital functions of an organism occur within cells, and that all cells contain the hereditary information necessary for regulating cell functions and for transmitting information to the next generation of cells. Up to date, most biologists recognize two major cell types, prokaryotes and eukaryotes. All of the cell have certain things in common: ① cell membranes, ② cytoplasm, ③ genetic material, ④ energy currency, ⑤ enzymes and coenzymes. Cell biology is the subdiscipline of biology that studies cells. It deals with all aspects of cells including their anatomy, physiological properties, interactions with their environment, cell division and cell processes such as cell respiration, and cell death and so on, and is closely related to other areas of biology such as zoology, botany, microbiology, genetics, molecular biology, immunology, and developmental biology and biochemistry. Modern biology is rooted in an understanding of the molecules within cells and of the interactions between cells that allow construction of multicellular organisms. The more we learn about the structure, function, and development of different organisms, the more we recognize that all life processes exhibit remarkable similarities. Molecular Cell Biology concentrates on the macromolecules and reactions studied by biochemists, the processes described by cell biologists, the gene control pathways identified by molecular biologists and geneticists. In this millennium, genomics and proteomics will reshape molecular cell biology. Some techniques will be used to study cells such as microscope, cell culture, immunostaining, computational genomics, DNA microarrays, gene knockdown, in situ hybridization, PCR and cloning, ect.

However, viruses are not cellular in nature but a core of nucleic acid and a surrounding coat or capsid composed of protein. For this reason, the viruses are called acellular or noncellular.

3.2 Basic Cell Structures

3.2.1 Prokaryotic Cell Structures

Most sinlge-celled organisms such as bacteria are prokaryotic cells. Prokaryotic cells do not have true nucleus, so the DNA is not contained within a membrane but is coiled up in a region of the cytoplasm called the nucleoid. For example, bacterial cells have the following structures (Fig. 3-1, (a)): ① Capsule. The additional outer covering of some bacteria protects the cell when engulfed by other organisms, assists in retaining moisture, and helps the cell adhere to surfaces and nutrients. ② Cell wall. Outer covering of most cells that protects the bacterial cell and gives it shape. ③ Cytoplasm. A gel-like substance composed mainly of water that also contains enzymes, salts, cell components, and various organic molecules. ④ Cell Membrane or Plasma Membrane. Surrounds the cell's cytoplasm and regulates the flow of substances in and out of the cell. ⑤ Ribosomes. Cell structures responsible for protein production. ⑥ Nucleoid. Area of the cytoplasm that contains the single bacterial DNA molecule. ⑦ Plasmids. Gene carrying, circular DNA structures. ⑧ Flagella. Long, whip-like protrusion that aids in cellular locomotion. ⑨ Pili. Hair-like structures on the surface of the cell that attach to other bacterial cells. Shorter pili called fimbriae help bacteria attach to surfaces.

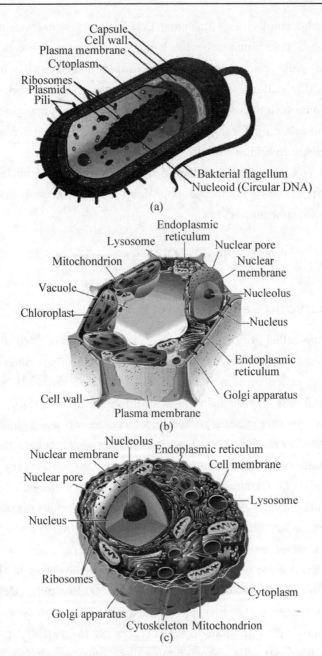

Fig. 3-1 Cell types and their structures (Eldon, Frederick, 2004)
(a) Cell structures of a bacterium from *Wikipedia* and eukaryotic cells; (b) a plant cell; (c) an animal cell.

3.2.2 Eukaryotic Cell Structures

Except bacteria and archaebacteria, all other living things such as kingdoms Protista (algae and protozoa), Fungi, Planate (plants), and Animalia (animals) are all comprised of eukaryotic cells. Eukaryotic cells, having evolved from a prokaryote-like predecessor, are more complex than prokaryotic cells. Multicellular eukaryotic organisms, such as plants and animals, and single-celled eukaryotes, including paramecium, amoeba and yeasts are composed of eukaryotic cells. Their basic structures of animal and plant cells (Fig. 3-1, (b) and (c)) are as follows: ① plant cell wall, a complex polysaccharidic network and mainly consists of cellulose, hemicellulose, and pectins. ② Plasma membrane, the structure separating the inside from the outside of the cell. ③ Cytoplasm, a mixture of organic and inorganic materials; the fluid portion called cytosol, in which there are some organelles (specialized subunit within a cell that has a specific function, and is usually separately enclosed within its own lipid bilayer) such as mitochondria, chloroplasts, ribosomes, endoplasmic reticulum, lysosome, Golgi apparatus, central vacuole, cytoskeleton. ④ Nucleus, a double membrane-bound control center separating the genetic material, DNA, from the rest of the cell.

3.3 Several Important Cell Structures and Their Functions

3.3.1 Cell Membranes

One feature common to all cells and many of the organelles eukaryotic cells contain is a thin layer of material called membrane including cell membrane and organelles' membrane. Membrane can be folded and twisted into many different structures, shapes, and forms. The particular arrangement of membrane of an organelle is related to its functions. This is similar to the way a piece of fabric can be fashioned into a pair of pants, a shirt, sheets, pillowcases, or a rag doll. All cellular membranes have a fundamental molecular structure that allows them to be fashioned into a variety of different organelles. Cell membrane primarily consists of the phospholipid bilayer with embedded proteins, which is selectively permeable to ions and organic molecules and controls the movement of substances in and out of cells. Cell membranes are involved in a variety of cellular processes such as cell adhesion, ion conductivity and cell signaling and serve as the attachment surface for the extracellular glycocalyx and cell wall and intracellular cytoskeleton.

The current hypothesis of how membranes are constructed is known as the fluid mosaic model (Fig. 3-2), which proposes that the various molecules of the membrane are able to flow and move about. The membrane maintains its form because of the physical interaction of its molecules with its surroundings. The phospholipids molecules of the membrane have one hydrophilic end (the glycerol portion) that is soluble in water and one hydrophobic end that is not water soluble,

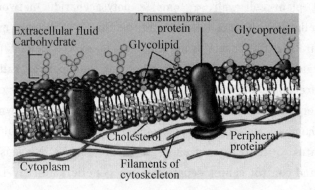

Fig. 3-2　The fluid mosaic membrane structure

comprised of fatty acids. We commonly represent this molecule as a balloon with two strings. The inflated balloon represents the glycerol and negatively charged phosphate; the two strings represent the uncharged fatty acids. Consequently, when phospholipids molecules are placed in water, they form a double-layered sheet, with the water soluble portions of the molecules facing away from each other. This is commonly referred to as a phospholipid bilayer. If phospholipid molecules are shaken in a glass of water, the molecules will automatically form double-layered membranes. It is important to understand that the membrane formed is not rigid or stiff but resembles a heavy olive oil in consistency. The component phospholipids are in constant motion as they move with the surrounding water molecules and slide past one another. The typical membrane structure consists of a phospholipid bilayer with a number of proteins scattered throughout, along with some carbohydrates (glycoproteins), glycolipids and sterols, similar to the way one does a mosaic tile, hence the name. The protein component of cellular membranes can be found on either surface of the membrane, or in the membrane among the phospholipid molecules. Many of the protein molecules are capable of moving from one side to the other. Some of these proteins help with the chemical activities of the cell. Others aid in the movement of molecules across the membrane by forming channels through which substances may travel or by acting as transport molecules. Some protein molecules found on the outside surfaces of cellular membranes have carbohydrates or fats attached to them. In addition, cholesterol is found in the middle of the membrane, in the hydrophobic region, because it is not water soluble. It appears to play a role in stabilizing the membrane and keeping it flexible. Carbohydrates are usually found on the outside of the membrane, where they are bound to proteins or lipids. They appear to play a role in cell-to-cell interactions and are involved in binding with regulatory molecules.

If a cell is to stay alive, it must meet the characteristics of life. This includes taking nutrients in and eliminating wastes and other by-products of metabolism. Several mechanisms allow cells to carry out the characteristic of life. They include:

(1) Passive transport, such as diffusion, dialysis, osmosis and facilitated diffusion.

① Diffusion is defined as the net movement of a kind of molecule from a place where it is in higher concentration to another place where it is scarce. When a kind of molecule is completely dispersed, and movement is equal in all directions, we say that the system has reached a state of dynamic equilibrium. The rate of diffusion is related to the kinetic energy and size of the molecules. Because diffusion only occurs when molecules are unevenly distributed, the relative concentration of the molecules is important in determining how fast diffusion occurs. The difference in concentration of the molecules is known as a concentration gradient or diffusion gradient. When the molecules are equally distributed, no such gradient exists. Diffusion can take place only as long as there are no barriers to the free movement of molecules. In the case of a cell, the membrane permits some molecules to pass through, whereas others are not allowed to pass or are allowed to pass more slowly. Whether a molecule is able to pass through the membrane also depends on its size, electric charge, and solubility in the phospholipids membrane. The direction of diffusion is determined by the relative concentration of specific molecules on the two sides of the membrane, and the energy that causes diffusion to occur is supplied by the kinetic energy of the molecules themselves. Diffusion is an important means by which materials are exchanged between a cell and its environment. Because the movement of the molecules is random, the cell has little control over the process; thus, diffusion is considered a passive process. For example, animals are constantly using oxygen in various chemical reactions. Consequently, the oxygen concentration in cells always remains low. The cells, then, contain a lower concentration of oxygen than the oxygen level outside the cells. This creates a diffusion gradient, and the oxygen molecules diffuse from the outside of the cell to the inside of the cell. Another characteristic of all membranes is that they are selectively permeable. Selectively permeable means that a membrane will allow certain molecules to pass across it and will prevent others from doing so. Molecules that are able to dissolve in phospholipids, such as vitamins A and D, can pass through the membrane rather easily; however, many molecules cannot pass through at all. In certain cases, the membrane differentiates on the basis of molecular size; that is, the membrane allows small molecules, such as water, to pass through and prevents the passage of larger molecules. The membrane may also regulate the passage of ions.

② Dialysis. We make use of diffusion across a selectively permeable membrane when we use a dialysis machine to remove wastes from the blood. If a kidney is unable to function normally, blood from a patient is diverted to a series of tubes composed of selectively permeable membranes. The toxins that have concentrated the blood diffuse into the surrounding fluids in the dialysis machine, and the cleaned blood is returned to the patient. Thus the machine functions in place of the kidney.

③ Osmosis. The net movement (diffusion) of water molecules through a selectively permeable membrane is known as osmosis. A proper amount of water is required if a cell is to function efficiently. Too much water in a cell may dilute the cell contents and interfere with the chemical reactions necessary to keep the cell alive. Too little water in the cell may result in a buildup of poisonous waste products. As with the diffusion of other molecules, osmosis is a passive process because the cell has no control over the diffusion of water molecules. This means that the cell can remain in balance with an environment only if that environment does not cause the cell to lose or gain too much water. If cells contain a concentration of water and dissolved materials equal to that of their surroundings, the cells are said to be isotonic to their surroundings. For example, the ocean contains many kinds of dissolved salts. Organisms such as sponges, jellyfishes, and protozoa are isotonic because the amount of material dissolved in their cellular water is equal to the amount of salt dissolved in the ocean's water. Under normal conditions, when we drink small amounts of water the cells of the brain swell a little, and signals are sent to the kidneys to rid the body of excess water. By contrast, marathon runners may drink large quantities of water in a very short time following a race. This rapid addition of water to the body may cause abnormal swelling of brain cells because the excess water can not be gotten rid of rapidly enough. If this happens, the person may lose consciousness or even die because the brain cells have swollen too much.

④ Facilitated diffusion. Some molecules move across the membrane by combining with specific carrier proteins. When the rate of diffusion of a substance is increased in the presence of a carrier, we call this facilitated diffusion (Fig. 3-3). Because this is diffusion, the net direction of movement is in accordance with the concentration gradient. Therefore, this is considered a passive transport method. One example of facilitated diffusion is the movement of glucose molecules across the membranes of certain cells. In order for the glucose molecules to pass into these cells, specific proteins are required to carry them across the membrane. The action of the carrier does not require an input of energy other than the kinetic energy of the molecules.

(2) Active transport. When molecules are moved across the membrane from an area of low concentration to an area of high concentration, the cell must expend energy. The process of using a carrier protein to move molecules up a concentration gradient is called active transport (Fig. 3-4). Active transport is very specific: only certain molecules or ions are able to be moved in this way, and they must be carried by specific proteins in the membrane. The action of the carrier requires an input of energy other than the kinetic energy of the molecules; therefore, this process is termed active transport. For example, sodium and potassium ions are actively pumped across cell membranes. Sodium ions are pumped out of cells up a concentration gradient. Potassium ions are pumped into cells up a concentration gradient.

(3) Endocytosis and exocytosis. In addition to active transport, materials can

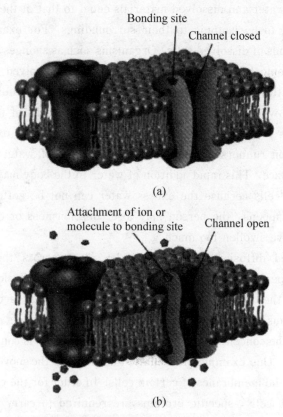

Fig. 3-3 Facilitated Diffusion (Ruth Bernstein, Stephen Bernstein, 1996)

(a) A channel protein is closed unless stimulated; (b) The channel protein opens for diffusion in response to attachment by a particular molecule or ion to receptor protein. Sometimes receptor protein and channel protein are the same molecule, as shown here, and sometimes separate molecules in the membrane. Although the process is helped (facilitated) by a particular membrane protein, no chemical-bond energy in the form of ATP is required for this process.

be transported into a cell by endocytosis and out by exocytosis. Phagocytosis is another name for one kind of endocytosis that is the process cells use to wrap membrane around a particle (usually food) and engulf it. This is the process leukocytes use to surround invading bacteria, viruses, and other foreign materials. Because of this, these kinds of cells are called phagocytes. Many types of cells use phagocytosis to acquire large amounts of material from their environments. If a cell is not surrounding a large quantity of material but is merely engulfing some molecules dissolved in water, the process is termed pinocytosis. The processes of phagocytosis and pinocytosis differ from active transport in that the cell surrounds large amounts of material with a membrane rather than taking the material in molecule by molecule through the membrane.

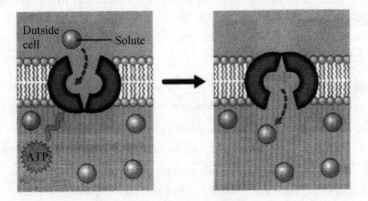

Fig. 3-4 Active transport (Campbell, Reece, 2002)

Transport proteins or carrier proteins are specific in their recongnition of molecules, each of which has a binding site that accepts only a certain solute. Using energy from ATP, this transport protein pumps the solute against a concentration gradient.

3.3.2 Cytoplasm

The cytoplasm is a gel-like substance residing between the cell membrane and the nucleus, which has three major elements, such as the cytosol, organelles and inclusions. In prokaryotic cells, all the material inside the plasma membrane is cytoplasm without organelles. Cytosol makes up about 70% of the cell volume and is composed of water, salts and organic molecules. The cytoplasm also contains the protein filaments that make up the cytoskeleton, soluble proteins and small structures such as ribosomes, proteasomes, and the mysterious vault complexes. The inner, granular and more fluid portion of the cytoplasm is referred to as endoplasm. Cytoplasmic inclusions are small particles of insoluble substances suspended in the cytosol. For example, calcium oxalate or silicon dioxide and lipid droplets, which are composed of lipids, such as fatty acids and sterols, and proteins. The cytoplasm provides support to the internal structures by being a medium for their suspension, maintains the shape and consistency of the cell, stores many chemicals, works as the site of vital metabolic reactions like anaerobic glycolysis and protein synthesis. Exchange of chemicals between the organelles is also one among the cytoplasm functions in a cell. Exchange of materials with the extra cellular fluid is common for both plant cell cytoplasm functions and animal cell cytoplasm functions too.

3.3.2.1 Endoplasmic Reticulum

The endoplasmic reticulum (ER) is a eukaryotic organelle that forms an interconnected network of tubules, vesicles, and cisternae within cells. The endoplasmic reticulum manufactures, processes, and transports a wide variety of biochemical compounds for use inside and outside of the cell. Endoplasmic reticula are divided into two basic types: rough endoplasmic reticula (RER) (Fig. 3-5) and smooth endoplasmic reticula (SER). Rough endoplasmic reticula synthesize

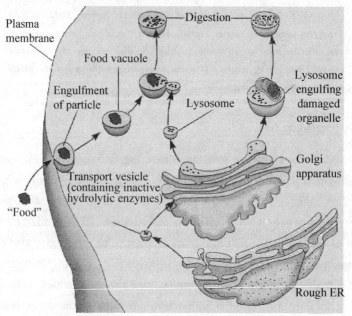

Fig. 3-5 The functions and structures of ER, Golgi apparatus and lysosome

proteins, because their surfaces are covered with ribosomes, which is involved mainly in the production and processing of proteins, which may be either transmembrane proteins or water-soluble proteins. However, smooth endoplasmic reticula synthesize lipids and steroids, metabolize carbohydrates and steroids (but not lipids), and regulate calcium concentration, drug metabolism (the smooth ER is the site at which some drugs are modified by microsomal enzymes), and attachment of receptors on cell membrane proteins. Sarcoplasmic reticula solely regulate calcium levels, which is a special type of smooth ER found in smooth and striated muscle. The only structural difference between this organelle and the SER is the medley of proteins they have. In addition, the endoplasmic reticulum serves as many general functions, including the facilitation of protein folding, the transport of synthesized proteins (e.g., secretory proteins, mostly glycoproteins, which also involves), the attachment of oligosaccharides, insertion of proteins into the endoplasmic reticulum membrane: integral membrane, disulfide bond formation and rearrangement, drug metabolism.

3.3.2.2 Lysosome

Lysosome is a membrane-bounded organelle, which contains digestive enzymes. Lysosomes break down cellular waste products, fats, carbohydrates, proteins, and other macromolecules into simple compounds, which are then returned to the cytoplasm as new cell-building materials (Fig. 3-5). The lysosomes use some 40 different types of hydrolytic enzymes, manufactured in the endoplasmic reticulum and modified in the Golgi apparatus. Lysosomes are often budded from the membrane of the Golgi apparatus, but in some cases they develop gradually from late endosomes, which are vesicles that carry materials brought into the cell by a process known as endocytosis. The membrane of lysosomes is a single layer membrane, and protects the rest of the cell from the digestive enzymes contained in the lysosomes, which would otherwise cause significant damage. The cell is further safeguarded from exposure to the biochemical catalysts present in lysosomes by their dependency on an acidic environment. With an average pH of about 4.8, the lysosomal matrix is favorable for enzymatic activity, but the neutral environment of the cytosol renders most of the digestive enzymes inoperative, so even if a lysosome is ruptured, the cell as a whole may remain uninjured.

Some human diseases are caused by lysosome enzyme disorders. Tay-Sachs disease, for example, is caused by a genetic defect that prevents the formation of an essential enzyme that breaks down ganglioside lipids. An accumulation of undigested ganglioside damages the nervous system, causing mental retardation and death in early childhood. Some studies have provided important insights into the relationship of lysosomes to disease processes and other aspects of cellular development. When silicon dioxide particles are inhaled into lungs, they are taken up by phagocytes in the tissue. These cells die, releasing the silica which can be ingested by other phagocytes with the same result. Repeated phagocytic deaths ultimately lead to stimulation of fibroblast deposition of nodules of collagen fibers which decrease lung elasticity and thus impair lung function and eventually lead to silicosis. The development of fibrous tissues in the lungs of people who have been exposed to asbestos fibers is one symptom of asbestosis, a disease similar in many ways to silicosis related to silica exposure.

3.3.2.3 Mitochondrion and Chloroplast

Mitochondrion and chloroplast are energy-converting organelles. They are chemically different and are incapable of interconversion, but they are associated with energy conversion reactions in the cell. The mitochondrion is an organelle resembling a small bag. These inner folded surfaces are known as the cristae. Located on the surface of the cristae are particular proteins and enzymes involved in aerobic cellular respiration. Aerobic cellular respiration is the series of reactions involved in the release of usable energy from food molecules, which requires the participation of oxygen molecules. Enzymes that speed the breakdown of simple nutrients are arranged in a sequence on the mitochondrial membrane. The average human cell contains upwards of 10,000 mitochondria. Cells involved in activities that require large amount of energy, such as muscle cells, contain many more mitochondria. The mitochondria have the following roles: ① production of ATP through respiration, ② regulation of cellular metabolism, ③ storage of calcium ions. (The concentrations of free calcium in the cell can regulate an array of reactions and is important for signal transduction in the cell. Mitochondria can transiently store calcium, a contributing process for the cell's homeostasis of calcium), ④ regulation of the membrane potential, ⑤ apoptosis-programmed cell death, ⑥ Calcium signaling (including calcium-evoked apoptosis), ⑦ cellular proliferation regulation, ⑧ steriod synthesis and certain heme synthesis reactions, and ⑨ some fuctions in specific types of cells. For example, mitochondria in liver cells contain enzymes that allow them to detoxify ammonia, a waste product of protein metabolism. A mutation in the genes regulating any of these functions can result in mitochondrial diseases.

The chloroplast is a membranous, saclike organelle containing chlorophyll and is only found in plants and other eukaryotic organisms. Some cells contain only one large chloroplast; others contain hundreds of smaller chloroplasts. The chloroplast has a envelope composed of inner membrane and outer membrane, intermembrane space and stroma including some molecules such as proteins, DNA, RNA and ribosomes, and grana (stacks of thylakoids). The basic function of the chloroplast is photosynthesis which actually takes place on the membrane of the thylakoid in grana. Photosynthesis is the process of converting sunlight energy to chemical-bond energy in chloroplasts, which synthesizes carbohydrates from water and carbon dioxide and releases oxygen. In addition, the chloroplast is the origin of all of the food (sugar) used by the other organelles of the plant or algae. Most of the sugars created in the chloroplast are converted by the plants into starch stored in the plastids.

3.3.3 Nucleus

The nucleus is a membrane-enclosed organelle found in eukaryotic cells, whose membrane is not composed of phospholipids and proteins arranged in cellular membranes. It contains most of the cell's genetic material, nuclear envelope and pores, nucleolus and nucleoplasm. A nucleolus is the site of ribosome manufacture. After being produced in the nucleolus, ribosomes are exported to the cytoplasm where they translate mRNA. Nucleoli are composed of specific granules and fibers in association with the cell's DNA used in the manufacture of ribosomes. Nucleoplasm is a colloidal mixture composed of water and the molecules used in the construction of ribosomes, nucleic acids, and other nuclear material. The nuclei's functions are cell compartmentalization, gene expression and processing of pre-mRNA.

Vocabulary

prokaryote /prəuˈkæriːəut/ n. 原核细胞   eukaryote /juˈkæriəut/ n. 真核细胞

cytoplasm /ˈsaitəuplæzm/ n. 细胞质
fluid mosaic model 流动镶嵌模型
hydrophilic /ˌhaidrəuˈfilik/ adj. 亲水的，吸水的
phagocytosis /ˌfægəsaiˈtəusis/ n. 噬菌作用
osmosis /ɔzˈməusis/ n. 渗透作用
dialysis /daiˈælisis/ n. 透析（作用）
sponge /spʌndʒ/ n. 海绵，海绵体，海绵状物，棉球，纱布
hypertonic /haipəˈtɔnik/ adj. 张力亢进的，高渗的
endocytosis /ˌendəusaiˈtəusis/ n. 内吞作用
pinocytosis /painəusaiˈtəusis/ n. 胞饮（作用），饮液（作用），吞饮（作用）
nucleoplasm /ˈnjuːkliəplæzm/ n. 核质，核浆
mitochondrion /maitəuˈkɔndriən/ n. 线粒体
chloroplast /ˈklɔ(ː)rəplæst/ n. 叶绿体
thylakoid /ˈθailəkɔid/ n. 类囊体
granum /ˈgreinəm/ n. 叶绿体基粒
stroma /ˈstrəumə/ n. 叶绿体的基质
nucleolus /njuːˈkliːələs/ n. 核仁
heterotroph /ˈhetərəutrɔf/ n. 异养生物
adrenal /əˈdrinəl/ adj. 肾上腺的 n. 肾上腺
silicosis /ˌsiliˈkəusis/ n. 矽肺，矽肺病
asbestosis /ˌæsbesˈtəusis/ n. 石绵肺症
centrosome /ˈsentrəsəum/ n. 中心体
compartmentalization /kɔmpɑːtˌmentləlaiˈzeiʃən/ n. 分隔成区

Exercises

1. Construct a concept map to show relationships among the following concepts.

Aerobic cellular respiration	Osmosis
Carbon dioxide	Oxygen
Chloroplast	Sugar
Facilitated diffusion	Water
Mitochondrion	Cell membrane
Carrier	Energy (ATP or Sunlight)
Photosynthesis	

2. Reading Comprehension.

All living organisms require energy to sustain life. The source of this energy comes from the chemical bonds of molecules. Burning wood is an example of a chemical reaction that results in the release of energy by breaking chemical bonds. The organic molecules of wood are broken and changed into the end products of ash, gas (CO_2), water (H_2O), and energy (heat and light). Living organisms are capable of carrying out these same types of reactions but in a controlled manner. By controlling energy-releasing reactions, they are able to use the energy to power activities such as reproduction, movement, and growth. These reactions form a biochemical pathway when they are linked to one another. The products of one reaction are used as the reactants for the next.

Within eukaryotic cells, certain biochemical pathways are carried out in specific organelles. Chloroplasts are the sites of photosynthesis, and mitochondria are the site of most of the reactions of cellular respiration. Organisms such as green plants, algae, and certain bacteria are capable of trapping sunlight energy and holding it in the chemical bonds of molecules such as carbohydrates. The process of converting sunlight energy to chemical-bond energy, called photosynthesis, is a major biochemical pathway. Photosynthetic organisms produce food molecules, such as carbohydrates. Cellular respiration, a second major biochemical pathway, is a chain of reactions during which cells release the chemical-bond energy and convert it into other usable forms. All organisms must carry out cellular respiration if they are to survive. Whether organisms manufacture food or take it in from the environment, they all use chemical-bond energy. Organisms that are able to make energy-containing organic molecules from inorganic raw materials by using basic energy sources such as sunlight are called autotrophs. All other organisms are called heterotrophs. Heterotrophs get their engrgy from the chemical bonds of food molecules such as fats, carbohydrates, and proteins.

Because prokaryotic cells lack mitochondria and chloroplasts, they carry out photosynthesis and cellular respiration within the cytoplasm or on the inner surfaces of the cell or other special membranes.

Questions for Discussion:

(1) Where do bacteria carry out cellular respiration?

(2) What does the energy that all living organisms require to sustain life come from?

(3) What are the differences of photosynthesis from respiration?

3. Please analyse how clenbuterol（瘦肉精）may enter pig cells based on plasma membrane characteristic(s).

4. Matching Questions.

The numbered term on the left best matches the letter of the phrase on the right. Use each only once.

(1) mitochondria   a. convert energy stored in some organic molecules into ATP

(2) ribosome   b. the site of protein synthesis
(3) nucleus   c. a cell's genetic control center
(4) chloroplast   d. the site of photosynthesis
(5) organelle   e. specialized compartments inside the cell
(6) cell membrane   f. the bilayer feet between the cell and the outside world
(7) plasmolysis   g. the shrinking of a plant cell away from its cell wall when it is put in a hypertonic solution
(8) active transport h. the transport of only certain ions or molecules cross the plasma membrane into cells with the help of carrier proteins and ATP
(9) chlorophyll   i. major light-absorbing pigment of photosynthesis
(10) autotroph   j. an organism that manufactures its own food from inorganic molecules

5. Multiple Choice Questions.

(1) Which of the following describes the process of aerobic respiration? (   )
   A. Use sunlight energy.
   B. Results in the incomplete oxidation of glucose.
   C. Takes place in the presence of oxygen.
   D. Takes place in chloroplast.
   E. Release oxygen.

(2) Which is released as a byproduct of photosynthesis? (   )
   A. H_2.   B. O_2.   C. H_2O.   D. CO_2.

(3) Why do you perceive chlorophyll as being green? Because it (   ).
   A. is green   B. absorbs green light   C. reflects green light
   D. reflects blue light   E. absorbs red light

(4) Which would you expect to increase the rate of photosynthesis? (   )
   A. Increasing the O_2 concentration.
   B. Increasing the CO_2 concentration.
   C. Decreasing the duration of exposure to red light.
   D. Decreasing the intensity of exposure to red light.
   E. Increasing the intensity and duration of exposure to X-rays.

(5) Which is best describes the function of a cell's selectively permeable membrane?
(   )

A. It controls the movement of selected substances across the membrane and out of a cell.

B. It can make a cell import and accumulate essential molecules in concentrations high enough for normal metabolism.

C. It can block most molecules' entry into a cell based primarily on their insolubility in lipid.

D. It contains some proteins.

(6) What is the source of energy for passive transport? (   )

A. Water.　　　　　　　B. Protein

C. Carbohydrate.　　　　D. The kinetic energy of the molecules.

(7) Water always moves across a membrane by osmosis from the (   ).

A. hypertonic compartment to the hypotonic one

B. hypotonic compartment to the hypertonic one

C. low water to the high water concentration

D. high to the low solute concentration

(8) In phagocytosis, (   ).

A. large molecules are expelled from the cell

B. liquid materials are engulfed

C. liquid materials are expelled from the cell

D. cellular energy is required

(9) Cell theory (   ).

A. only applies to animals

B. only applies to eukaryotic single-cell microbe

C. applies to all living things composed of cells

D. distinguish the cells of the plants and animals

(10) Lysosomes (   ).

A. play an important role in the building of the body tissue

B. are assembled in the cell nucleus

C. contains powerful digestive enzymes

D. pass through the cytoplasm and are excreted outside the cell

Unit 4 Cell Division, Culture and Animal Cloning

导语 细胞工程是在细胞水平上通过细胞融合、核移植（无性繁殖、克隆动物）、染色体或基因移植以及组织和细胞培养等方法，快速繁殖和培养出新物种或者产品的技术。它是现代生物技术和生物学研究的重要组成部分，广泛应用于农、林、园艺和医学等领域中。其主要技术领域有动植物细胞与组织培养、细胞融合、细胞核移植、染色体工程、胚胎工程、干细胞工程、转基因生物与生物反应器等方面。

本单元主要介绍细胞分裂及其作用，细胞培养技术及其应用，克隆的概念，动物克隆的技术、应用和进展以及争论。

4.1 Cell Division and Its Functions

Cell division is the process by which a *parent cell* divides into two or more *daughter cells*. Cell division is usually a small segment of a larger cell cycle and divided into three types such as amitosis, mitosis and meiosis (Fig. 4-1). Amitosis is cell division without nuclear envelope breakdown and formation of well-visible mitotic spindle and condenced chromosomes. Mitosis is the process by which an eukaryotic cell separates the chromosomes in its cell nucleus into two identical sets, in two separate nuclei. Mitosis is named after spindles or the formation and appearance of chromosomes are involved in it. Mitosis is important for the maintenance of the chromosomal set. Meiosis is the name for the special type of cell division that produces gametes. It is proceded by an interphase stage during which DNA replication occurs, composed of two parts: meiosis I and meiosis II. In meiosis I, members of homologous pairs of chromosomes divide into two complete sets. This is sometimes called a reduction division in which daughter cells get only half the chromosomes from the parent cell. The division begins with replicated chromosomes composed of two chromatids. The sequence of events in meiosis I is artificially divided into four phases: prophase I, metaphase I, anaphase I and telophase I. Meiosis II includes four phases: prophase II, metaphase II, anaphase II, and telophase II. The two daughter cells formed during meiosis I continue through meiosis II so that, usually, four cells result from the two divisions. Meiosis II is similar to mitosis. The roles of meiosis mainly are heredity, variation and evolution. The several important functions of cell division are as follows: increase the body and sex cells, maintain the body and repair damaged tissues, replace dead cells with new ones, and slows living organisms to grow.

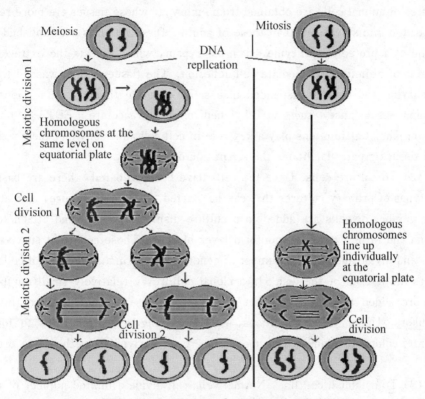

Fig. 4-1 Comparison of mitosis and meiosis

4.2 Cell Culture and Its Applications

Cell culture is the cultivation of cells derived from multicellular eukaryotes, especially animal cells. However, there are also cultures of plants, fungi and microbes. Cells grown in culture usually require very special conditions such as specific pH, temperature, nutrients, growth factors and so on.

The procedure for cell culture is the following:

(1) To obtain the cell. In most cases, one need only remove a vial of frozen, previously cultured cells from a tank of liquid nitrogen, thaw the vial, and transfer the cells to the waiting medium. A culture of this type is called a secondary culture because the cells are derived from a pervious culture. In a primary culture, on the other hand, the cells are obtained directly from the organism. Most primary cultures of animal cells are obtained from embryos, whose tissues are more readily dissociated into single cell than those of adults. Dissociation is accomplished with the aid of a proteolytic enzyme, such as trypsin, which digests the extracellular domains of proteins that mediate cell adhesion. The tissue is then washed free of the enzyme and usually suspended in a saline solution that lacks Ca^{2+} ions and contains a substance, such as ethylenediamine tetraacetate (EDTA), binding calcium ions. Calcium ions play a key role in cell-cell adhesion, and their removal from tissues greatly facilitates the separation of cells.

(2) To culture cells. Once the cells have been prepared, there are basically two types of primary cultures that can be started. In a mass culture, a relatively large number of cells are added to a culture dish; they settle and attach to the bottom and form a relatively uniform layer of cells. Those cells that survive will grow and divide and, after a number of generations, form a monolayer of cells that covers the bottom of the dish. In a clonal culture, a relatively small number of cells are added to a dish, so that each cell resides at some distance from its neighbors. Under these conditions, each surviving cell proliferates to form a separate colony or clone whose members are all derived from the same original cell.

(3) To establish cell line. Normal cells can divide a limited number of times (typically 50 to 100) before they undergo senescence and death, so many of the cells commonly used in tissue culture studies have undergo genetic modification that allow them to grow indefinitely. Cells of this type are referred to as a cell line, and they typically grow into malignant tumors when injected into susceptible laboratory animals. The frequency with which a normal cell growing in culture spontaneously transforms into a cell line depends on the organism from which it was derived. For example, mouse cells transform at a relatively high frequency, while human cells transform only rarely.

The majority of the articles in cell biology deal with cultured cells in that ① cultured cells can be obtained in large quantity; ② most cultures contain only a single type of cell; ③ many different cellular activities, including endocytosis, cell movement, cell division, membrane trafficking, and macromolecular synthesis, can be studied in cell culture; ④ cell can differentiate in culture; ⑤ cultured cells respond to treatment with drugs, hormones, growth factors, and other active substances.

Cell culture is also very important to biotechnology processes because most research programs depend on the ability to grow cells outside the parent animal. Mass culture of animal cell lines is fundamental to the manufacture of viral vaccines and other products of biotechnology. For instance, vaccines for polio, measles, mumps, rubella, and chickenpox are currently made in cell cultures. Recombinant DNA technology produced enzymes, synthetic hormones, immunobiologicals (monoclonal antibodies, interleukins, lymphokines), and anticancer agents in animal cell cultures. Moreover, more complex proteins currently must be made in animal cells. An important example of such a complex protein is the hormone erythropoietin. The cost of growing mammalian cell cultures is high, so research is underway to produce such complex proteins in insect cells or in higher plants, use of single embryonic cell and somatic embryos as a source for direct gene transfer via particle bombardment, transient gene expression and confocal microscopic observation is one of its applications. It also offers to confirm single cell origin of somatic embryos and the asymmetry of the first cell division. In addition, cell culture also has the following applications: ① Cell culture in two dimensions. Research in tissue engineering, stem cells and molecular biology primarily involves cultures of cells on flat plastic dishes, known as two-dimensional (2D) cell culture. ② Tissue culture and engineering. Cell culture is a fundamental component of tissue culture and tissue engineering. The major application of human cell culture is in stem cell industry, where mesenchymal stem cells can be cultured and cryopreserved for future use.

4.3 Cloning

4.3.1 Clone

Clones are genetically identical individuals, which have exactly the same genetic make-up as another individual, of the same species. Clones can derive from a number of processes both natural and artificial. A replica of a DNA sequence or a gene is produced by genetic engineering. In the case of simple organisms, a group of genetically identical cells descended from a single common ancestor, such as a bacterial colony whose members arose from a single original cell as a result of binary fission. Yeast offsprings are budded off from the parent to create "daughters" which are genetically identical to the parent. In animals and plants, a clone is identical with the original animal or plant. Plant clones are the result of asexual or vegetative propagation by plant tissue culture. Animal clones are a group of animals asexually produced from a single animal parent.

4.3.2 Animal Cloning Methods and Characteristics

Cloning is the most attractive story of the new biotechnologies and the one which causes the most heated discussion over its worth. Cloning is the creation of cells or whole animals using DNA from a single "parent", bypassing the normal reproductive process. The clone has the same DNA as the parent. Identical twins are naturally occurring clones, but it is also possible to produce artificial clones by using certain cloning techniques. Generally, there are several important types of artificial cloning technology:

(1) cell nuclear transfer or transplantation including ① embryo cell nuclear transplantation, also called embryo cloning, by which mouse, rabbit, goat, sheep, pig, cattle and monkey were cloned, ② embryo stem cell nuclear transplantation, and ③ somatic cell nuclear transplantation, by which Dolly was cloned.

(2) Embryo bisection or splitting, by which mouse, rabbit, goat, sheep, pig, cattle and horse were cloned.

(3) Chimeric Embryo. Here, we only introduce two types of them.

4.3.2.1 Somatic Cell Nuclear Transfer

Somatic cell nuclear transfer is the process most often used in animal cloning. It refers to the transfer of the nucleus from a somatic cell to an egg cell. A somatic cell is any cell of the body other than a germ (sex) cell. In this process, the nucleus of a somatic cell is removed and inserted into an unfertilized egg that has had its nucleus removed. The egg with its donated nucleus is then nurtured and divides until it becomes an embryo. The embryo is then placed inside a surrogate mother and develops inside the surrogate. This technique has some disadvantages:

① Very low efficiency, less than 1%-10% of cloned mammalian embryos result in offspring, for example, to create Dolly (Fig. 4-2), it took 277 trails. ② Very

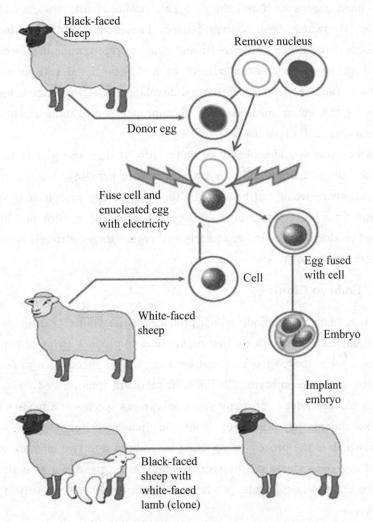

Fig. 4-2 The cloning process of a sheep named Dolly by somatic cell neclear transfer

high chance of abnormal offspring. The success and failure of cloning have generated heated debate in many countries, particularly as some scientists have suggested cloning human. Multiple gene defects can be found in cloned mice. When 10,000 genes were screened, 4% were shown to be functioning incorrectly.

Cloned animals suffer from developmental abnormalities including extended gestation, large birth weight, inadequate formation of planceta, and histological defects in most organs such as kidney, brain, cardiovascular system and muscle. ③ A tendency toward obesity, liver failure, pneumonia, and premature death. These effects may be due to ① inefficient nuclear reprogramming, which is the reversal of the gene expression pattern of a differentiated cell to one that is totipotent and capable of directing normal development, ② cellular aging because of the age of the donor nucleus, and ③ improper segregation of chromosomes during embryonic cell divisions.

Human cloning would probably be more difficult than sheep or cattle cloning, because the cells of human embryos start producing proteins at a relatively early stage. Thus, there would not be as much time for the egg cytoplasm to reprogram a transplanted nucleus. However, the successful cloning of mice in 1998, which also started producing proteins at an early embryonic stage, strongly indicated that this problem can be overcome in humans.

4.3.2.2 Embryo Cloning

This is a medical technique which produces monozygotic (identical) twins or triplets. It duplicates the process that nature uses to produce twins or triplets. One or more cells are removed from a fertilized embryo and encouraged to develop into one or more duplicate embryos. Twins or triplets are thus formed, with identical DNA. This has been done for many years on various species of animals; only very limited experimentation has been done on humans. For example, artificial twinning, which is the process of splitting an embryo into two or more embryos:

① An egg cell is fertilised by sperm, then left to grow into an embryo;

② The embryo is split into two or more embryos when it is still in the early cell stage;

③ The split embryos are nurtured into new embryos, all genetically identical, then implanted into surrogate mothers to grow.

This process is not the same as nuclear transfer, as the born animal has biological parents, and is a clone of its brothers and sisters. In nuclear transfer, the born animal is a clone of its parent.

4.3.3 Applications of Cloning by Nuclear Transfer

There are a number of commercial and medical interests in cloning by nuclear transfer. These include ① cloning transgenic animals, that is, to rapidly produce herds of transgenic or gene-targeted farm animals that produce valuable human proteins such as human clotting factor IX in cloned sheep milk, ② cloning prize farm animals (e.g., cows with high milk production) or race horses, ③ cloning wildlife and endangered species for conservation, ④ cloning pets and ⑤ cloning for stem cells, which would involve creating an embryo by transferring the nucleus from a patient's cell into a human egg cell stripped of its own nucleus to produce stem cells. The hope is to develop technique of growing the ES cells into specific cell types to treat such conditions as Parkinson's disease, diabetes or spinal cord injury. There would in theory, be no problem with human immune rejection in using grafts derived from these cells to repair diseased or damaged tissues, since they originated from the patient's own cells.

4.3.4 Animal Cloning Advances

The first animal cloning experiments were conducted in 1950s with the frog, *Rana pipiens* to test the question "Does cell differentiation depend on changes in gene expression or changes in the content of the genome?". In 1960s, John Gurdon and co-workers used the nuclei from intestinal epithelial cells of the South African clawed frog tadpoles for nuclear transfer and approximately 1% of the embryos developed into normal, fertile adult frogs. Their findings established the basic principle that the process of cell differentiation does not necessarily require any stable change to the genetic make-up of a cell. Cell differentiation depends on changes in the expression of the genome. Confirming these findings in mammalian cells took another 30 years.

A major challenge in performing somatic cell nuclear transfer in mammals is the small size of the mammalian egg, which is less than 0.1% the volume of a frog egg. The techniques for micromanipulation, enucleation and fusion of an egg with a single somatic cell were developed in the late 1960s and early 1970s, but transfer of nuclei from very early embryos into enucleated sheep eggs were not successfully performed until 1986. This success was followed by cloning of rabbits, pigs, mice, cows, and monkeys using donor nuclei from very early embryos. Cloning nonhuman primates have proved difficult. Neti and Ditto are the only successfully cloned rhesus monkeys to date. In 1996, Keith Campbell and Ian Wilnut developed this technique further and performed the transfer of nuclei from an established embryonic stem cell line from day 9 embryo to enucleated sheep eggs. These nuclear transfers resulted in two healthy cloned sheep named Megan and Morag. In 1997, Dolly was cloned from the udder cell of an adult sheep in Scotland by Wilmut, Campbell and coworkers. Dolly was the first mammal cloned from an adult cell. The cloning of Dolly confirmed the two key principles of genetic equivalence. First, differentiated animal cells on their own are unable to develop into complete animals but the nuclei of the most differentiated cells retain all the necessary genetic information. Second, transfer of a nucleus from a differentiated cell to the environment of the enucleated egg reprograms the nucleus and allows the full development of a viable animal that is genetically identical to the donor of the somatic cell.

Since Dolly, many other mammals have been successfully cloned from adult donor cell nuclei. These include cows, pigs, mice, domestic cats, horses, a mule, goats, dogs and rabbits (Fig. 4-3). The efficiency of mammalian nuclear transfer-

Fig. 4-3 **Other cloned mammals**
(a) a cloned rabbit and its mother; (b) three cloned pigs; (c) a cloned horse and its mother; (d) cloned monkeys.

experiments is very similar to that obtained from frogs. Less than 1% of all nuclear transfers from adult differentiated cells result in normal-appearing offspring.

4.3.5 Controversies over Cloning and Cloned Food

In 2008, the United States Food and Drug Administration concluded "meat and milk from cattle, swine, and goat clones or their offspring are as safe to eat as food we eat from those species now". In 2009, the Food Safety Commission of Japan concluded that foods derived from somatic cell nuclear transfer, cloned cattle and pigs and their offspring, would have equivalent safety as those derived from cattle and pigs produced by the conventional technologies. However, cloning remains a very controversial topic. Genetic improvements allow producers to potentially lower prices, increase the quality of meat and milk products, and possibly increase resistance to diseases. Nevertheless, many have expressed concern over the technology and outrage over the use of meat and milk from cloned animal and their offspring. These consumers and animal welfare organizations oppose the technology due to moral and ethical objections and concerns about food safety and potential harm to the cloned animal and their surrogate mothers. The consumers' concerns related to food derived from cloned animal included food safety, benefits of animal cloning, welfare of animal used for cloning, and trust in governmental food agencies. In bioethics, the ethics of cloning refers to a variety of ethical positions regarding the practice and possibilities of cloning, especially human cloning. While many of these views are religious in origin, the questions raised by cloning are faced by secular perspectives as well. As the science of cloning continues to advance, governments have dealt with ethical questions through legislation. Another concern is that cloning used on animals may someday be used on humans. Some people may be more open to the idea of cloning of animals because most western countries have passed legislation against cloning humans, yet only a few countries passed legislation against cloning animals.

Vocabulary

amitosis /ˌæmiˈtəusis/ n. （细胞之）无丝
分裂

mitosis /miˈtəusis/ n. 有丝分裂
meiosis /maiˈəusis/ n. 减数分裂

gamete /ˈgæmiːt/ n. 配子
interphase /ˈintə(ː)feiz/ n. 分裂间期
chromosome /ˈkrəuməsəum/ n. 染色体
fungi /ˈfʌŋgai/ n. 真菌（fungus 的复数）
embryo /ˈembriəu/ n. 胚胎
proteolytic /ˌprəutiəˈlitik/ adj. 蛋白水解的
trypsin /ˈtripsin/ n. 胰蛋白酶
ethylenediamine tetraacetate /ˈtetrəˈsiːteit/ （EDTA) n. 乙二胺四乙酸
senescence /siˈnesəns/ n. 衰老
trafficking /ˈtræfikiŋ/ n. 运输
immunobiological /ˌimjunəbaiˈɔlədʒikəl/ n. 免疫生物产品
lymphokine /ˈlimfəukain/ n. 淋巴因子，淋巴激活素
erythropoietin /iˌriθrəˈpɔiətin/ n. 红细胞生成素
somatic /səuˈmætik/ adj. 体细胞的
mesenchymal /mesˈenkiməl/ adj. 间叶细胞的，微囊的
polio /ˈpəuliːəu/ n. 小儿麻痹症
measles /ˈmiːzəlz/ n. 麻疹
mumps /mʌmps/ n. 腮腺炎
rubella /ruːˈbelə/ n. 风疹
chickenpox /ˈtʃikinˌpɔks/ n. 水痘
placenta /pləˈsentə/ n. 胎盘，胎座
pneumonia /njuːˈməunjə/ n. 肺炎
enucleate /iˈnjuːklieit/ vt. 去核
mammal /ˈmæməl/ n. 哺乳动物
nuclear transfer 核移植
hollowed-out adj. 挖空的；掏空的
artificial twinning 人工孪生技术

Exercises

1. Matching Questions.

The numbered terms on the left match the letters on the right.

（1）daughter cell　　a. cell formed from the division of a mother cell that contains a copy or one-half of the mother cell's DNA

（2）gamete　　b. mature haploid cell that functions during sexual reproduction

（3）mother cell　　c. a diploid dividing cell

（4）cell division　　d. the process by which the number of cells will be increased

（5）somatic cell　　e. the cells that make up the body of an organism

（6）meiosis　　f. the process of cell division which produces gametes

（7）zygote　　g. the cell resulting from the union of egg and sperm

（8）cross over　　h. the some segment exchange between non-sister chromatids in reduction division

(9) independent assortment   i. the separation of the two members of a pair of homologous chromosome from each other independently of other homologous chromosome pairs in anaphase

(10) nuclear transfer   j. the transfer of DNA or nucleus from the outside to the inside of one receipt cell

2. Fill in the blanks with the appropriate words you have just learned in this unit.

(1) Each of the four cells produced by reduction division has _____ as many chromosomes as their mother cell.

(2) Cell culture is the cultivation of cells derived from multicellular _____ including animal and plant cells.

(3) In a _____, the cells undergo genetic modification that allow them to grow indefinitely.

(4) Animal cell culture can produce anticancer agents and _____ for some human diseases.

(5) The methods of animal cloning are divided into two types such as _____ and _____ cloning according to the donor cell type.

(6) There are a number of commercial and medical interests in cloning by _____.

(7) Cytokinesis can happen _____ times during reduction division in a single cell.

(8) The production of sex cells in preparation for sexual reproduction is a function of _____.

(9) Less than 1% of all nuclear transfers from _____ result in normal-appearing offspring.

(10) _____ is the process of splitting an embryo into two or more embryos.

3. Multiple Choice Questions.

(1) (   ) forms a continuous link between parents and their offsprings.
　　A. Gametes   B. Mother cell   C. Cytokinesis   D. Genetic material

(2) Homologous chromosomes are identical in size, shape, function and appearance, but they (   ).
　　A. may have different versions of a particular gene
　　B. always have a particular gene in different locations
　　C. determine different traits

D. have different DNA molecule(s)

(3) If one of 23 pairs of chromosomes in certain person doesn't separate from each other during anaphase I of meiosis I, the consequence would be the production of four cells (   ).

    A. two with 22 chromosomes and two with 24 ones

    B. each with 23 chromosomes

    C. two with 45 chromosomes and two with 47 ones

    D. one with 23 chromosomes and three with 25 ones

(4) (   ) doesn't belong to the applications of animal cloning by nuclear transfer.

    A. The development of transgenic animals

    B. Cloning prize farm animals or race horses

    C. Wildlife and endangered species conservation

    D. Somatic hybridization

4. Assume that corn plants have a diploid number of only 2, please draw one figure, in which the male plant's chromosomes are diagrammed on the left, and those of the female are diagrammed on the right.

5. Reading Comprehension.

Serial Cloning

Serial cloning by somatic cell nuclear transfer has been successfully achieved in four species of mammals to date. Mice were cloned for up to six generations, pigs for three generations, and bulls and cats for two generations. All these reports except one indicated that serial cloning efficiency decreased as the round of cloning increased. Similarly, in multiple generational embryo cloning, the developmental capacity of bovine cloned embryos greatly decreased with the increase of cloning generation. Intriguingly, when different types of nuclear donors were used in serial pig cloning (i.e., G1 clones were derived from fetal fibroblasts, while G2 and G3 clones were derived from salivary gland progenitor cells), no significant difference among G1, G2 and G3 pigs was detected. The extension of cloning studies to serial cloning had a practical application in transgenic animal production. Somatic cell cloning technology was applied to produce transgenic animals with greater efficiency compared with other transgenic methods, such as pronuclear microinjection. However, the finite lifespan of primary cells limited multiple genetic modifications in a cell line. For example, bovine fetal fibroblast cells, commonly used to make transgenic cattle, had 30 – 50 population doublings (PDs) before senescence, while one genetic modification required 30 – 45 PDs. Although multiple genetic modifications could be done in embryonic stem cells, no reliable embryonic stem cells of livestock have been obtained to date. The serial cloning technique could be used to increase the PD number of a cell line for multiple genetic modifications. Usually, bovine transgenic cloned embryos derived from transgenic fetal fibroblasts were transferred into surrogates, and fetuses were retrieved by caesarian section during early gestation (30 – 70 days), from which fetal fibroblasts were rederived. The rejuvenated fetal fibroblast line is then used for further genetic modification. Therefore, serial cloning paved the way to produce transgenic animals with multiple genetic modifications.

Questions for Discussion:

(1) Which species of mammals have been cloned with Serial cloning by somatic cell nuclear transfer up to date?

(2) Is the decrease of serial cloning efficiency with the increase of the round of cloning similar to that of the developmental capacity of bovine cloned embryos with the increase of cloning generation in multiple generational embryo cloning?

(3) Does somatic cell cloning technology have the greater efficiency of the production of transgenic animals compared with other transgenic methods?

(4) Can serial cloning technique not increase the population doublings number of a cell line for multiple genetic modifications?

6. English poster in international academic conferences.

Poster is a sign posted in a public place as one kind of academic achievement's presentations. Suppose you attend an international academic meeting and you are asked to make a poster in English including title, name and address of the author, abstract, materials, methods, tables and figures, results, etc. Now choose one topic in biology (e.g., a plant, an animal) and make a poster by yourself after class. In the following class, post it on blackboard, stand beside it, trying to introduce it to your classmates in English.

Unit 5   Transfer of Genetic Information and Its Regulation

导语   分子生物学是在分子水平上研究生物大分子的结构和功能、研究生命活动的普遍规律、阐明生命现象的本质的学科，是当代生物科学的重要分支。分子生物学和生物化学、生物物理学、遗传学、微生物学等学科关系十分密切。分子生物学的主要内容包括核酸和蛋白质的结构，遗传信息的复制、转录与翻译、修复与突变，基因表达调控，基因组学和生物信息学等。遗传信息传递的中心法则是其理论体系的核心。

本单元主要介绍中心法则，DNA 的复制和转录，蛋白质合成以及基因表达调控。

5.1 The Central Dogma

DNA and RNA relate to inheritance, cell structure, and cell activities. The modified central dogma can explain the flow of genetic information through the cell. It is most easily written in this form:

```
                (replication)        (transcription)        (translation)
         DNA ←────────────── [DNA] ──────────────→ RNA ──────────────→ proteins
                                       ↑         │
                                       │ (retrotranscription)
                                       └─────────┘
```

in which at the center of DNA (genetic information), it goes to the left to reproduce itself, a process called DNA replication. Going to the right, DNA supervises the manufacture of RNA (a process known as transcription), which in turn is involved in the production of protein molecules, a process known as translation. In retroviruses, going to the left, RNA supervises the manufacture of DNA (a process known as retrotranscription). DNA replication occurs in cells in preparation for the cell division processes of mitosis and meiosis. Without replication, daughter cells would not receive the library of information required to sustain life. The transcription process results in the formation of a strand of RNA that is a copy of a segment of the DNA on which it is formed. Some of the RNA molecules become involved in various biochemical processes; others are used in the translation of the RNA information into proteins. Structural proteins are used by cell as building materials (feathers, collagen, hair), while others are used to direct and control chemical reactions (enzymes or hormones) or carry molecules from place to place (hemoglobin). Enzymes made from the DNA blueprints by transcription and translation are used as tools to make exact copies of the genetic material. More blueprints are made so that future generations of cells will have the genetic materials necessary to manufacture their own regulatory and structural proteins. Without DNA, RNA, and enzymes, life would not occur.

5.2 DNA Replication

The first major function of DNA is to store genetic information like a library. DNA replication is the process of duplicating the genetic material. The major form of DNA replication is semidiscontinuous and semiconservative DNA replication in the nuclear DNA of eukaryotes, some viruses (e.g., SV40) and bacteria. In this form, the DNA synthesis occurs from 5' to 3', DNA polymerases catalyze DNA synthesis, leading strand synthesis is continuous, while lagging strand synthesis is discontinuous. The DNA replication process (Fig. 5-1) is the following:

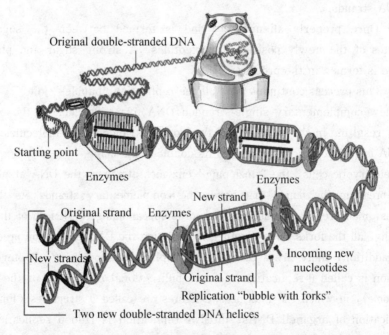

Fig. 5-1 DNA replication summary (Eldon, Frederick, 2004)

(1) It begins as an enzyme breaks the attachments between the two strands of DNA. In eukaryotic cells, this occurs in hundreds of different spots along the length of the DNA.

(2) Moving along the DNA, the enzyme "unzips" the halves of the DNA, and a new nucleotide pairs with its complementary base and is covalently bonded between the sugar and phosphate to the new backbone.

(3) Proceeding in opposite directions on each side, the enzyme attaching new DNA nucleotides into position.

(4) The enzyme that speeds the addition of new nucleotides to the growing chain works along with another enzyme to make sure that no mistakes are made. If the wrong nucleotide appears to be headed for a match, the enzyme will reject it in favor of the correct nucleotide. If a mistake is made and a wrong nucleotide is paired into position, specific enzymes have the ability to replace it with the correct one.

(5) Replication proceeds in both directions, appearing as "bubbles".

(6) The complementary molecules pair with the exposed nitrogenous bases of both DNA strands.

(7) Once properly aligned, a bond is formed between the sugars and phosphates of the newly positioned nucleotides. A strong sugar and phosphate backbone is formed in the process.

(8) This process continues until all the replication "bubbles" join.

A new complementary single-stranded DNA forms on each of the old DNA strands, resulting in the formation of two double-stranded DNA molecules. As the new DNA is completed, it twists into its double-helix shape.

In eukaryotic cells, the "unzipping" enzymes attach to the DNA at numerous points, breaking the bonds that bonds the complementary strands. As the DNA replicates, many replication bubbles and forks appear along the length of the DNA. Eventually, all the forks come together, completing the DNA replication process.

In addition, there are a few of DNA replication models: ① Bacterial DNA replication is called θ-replication. (e.g., bidirectional replication of the *E. coli* chromosome), in which the intermediate figures are called θ structures (Fig. 5-2). ② Replication of organell DNAs. mtDNA replication is D-loop replication, also called the strand displacement model. This replication is unidirectional around the circle and there is one replication fork for each strand. One strand is light strand (L) and the other the heavy one (H). The difference of H from L arose from their different buoyant densities in denaturing CsCl density gradients because of a strand bias in base composition. Replication of cpDNA remains a subject of debate. So far, there are three models: D-loop replication, D-loop for the formation of θ-replication structure and its conversion to a rolling circle replication, and recombination-dependent replication. ③ Rolling circle replication. For example, phage Φ × 174 replication. ④ Replication of linear DNA. In this replication, DNA polymerase requires a short RNA primer and proceeds only 5' to 3'. When the final primer is removed from the lagging strand at the end of a chromosome, one 8-12 nt region is left unreplicated. This causes chromosomes to get shorter with each round of replication. Moreover, progressive shortening of chromosomes (telomers) would lead to chromosome instability and cell or organismal death. Telomerase can prevents constant loss of important DNA from chromosome ends, for telomerase is a reverse transcriptase that carries its own RNA molecule, which is used as a template when it elongates telomeres, which are shortened after each replication cycle.

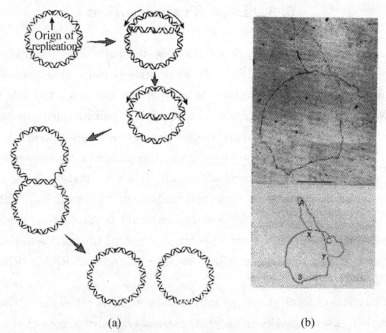

Fig. 5-2 Bacterial DNA replication (Lizabeth A Allison, 2008)
(a) Bidirectional replication of *E. coli* chromosome. The intermediate figures are called theta (θ) structures. (b) Autoradiograph of *E. coli* DNA during replication. A, B and C indicate three loops, created by the existence of two replication forks, X and Y, in the DNA.

The completion of the DNA replication process yields two double helices that are identical in their nucleotide sequences. Half of each is new, half is the original parent DNA molecule. The DNA replication process is highly accurate. It has been estimated that there is only one error made for every 2×10^9 nucleotides. A human cell contains 46 chromosomes consisting of about 3,000,000,000 (3 billion) base pairs. This averages to about five errors per cell. Don't forget that this figure is an estimate, whereas some cells may have five errors per replication, others may have more, and some may have no errors at all. It is also important to note that some errors may be major and deadly, whereas others are insignificant. Because this error rate is so small, DNA replication is considered by most to be essentially error-free. Following DNA replication, the cell now contains twice the amount of genetic information and is ready to begin division.

5.3 DNA Transcription

The second major function of DNA is to make these single-stranded, complementary RNA copies of DNA. This operation is called transcription, which means to transfer data from one form to another. In this case, the data is copied from DNA language to RNA language. The same base pairing rules that control the accuracy of DNA replication apply to the process of transcription. Using this process, the genetic information stored as a DNA chemical code is carried in the form of an RNA copy to other parts of the cell. It is RNA that is used to guide the assembly of amino acids into structural and regulatory proteins. Without the process of transcription, genetic information would be useless in directing cell functions. Although many types of RNA are synthesized from the genes, the three most important are messenger RNA (mRNA), transfer RNA (tRNA), and ribosomal RNA (rRNA).

Transcription begins in a way that is similar to DNA replication. The double-stranded DNA is separated by an enzyme, exposing the nitrogenous-base sequences of the two strands. However, unlike DNA replication, transcription occurs only on one of the two DNA strands, which serves as a template for the synthesis of RNA. This side is also referred to as the coding strand of the DNA. But which strand is copied? Where does it start and when does it stop? Where along the sequence of thousands of nitrogenous bases does the chemical code for the manufacture of a particular enzyme begin and where does it end? If transcription begins randomly, the resulting RNA may not be an accurate copy of the code, and the enzyme product may be useless or deadly to the cell.

5.3.1 Prokaryotic Transcription

Each bacterial gene is made of attached nucleotides that are transcribed in order into a single strand of RNA. This RNA molecule is used to direct the assembly of a specific sequence of amino acids to form a polypeptide. This system follows the pattern of:

One DNA gene⟶one RNA⟶one polypeptide

The beginning of each gene on a DNA strand is identified by the presence of a region known as the promoter, just ahead of an initiation code that has the base sequence TAC. The gene ends with a terminator region, just in back of one of three possible termination codes: ATT, ATC, or ACT. These are the "start reading here" and "stop reading here" signals. The actual genetic information is located between start codon and stop codon:

Promoter:::start codon:::gene:::stop codon:::terminator region

When a bacterial gene is transcribed into RNA, the DNA is "unzipped", and an enzyme known as RNA polymerase attaches to the DNA at the promoter region. It is from this region that the enzymes will begin to assemble RNA nucleotides into a complete, single-stranded copy of the gene, including initiation and termination codes. Triplet RNA nucleotide sequences complementary to DNA codes are called codons. Remember that there is no thymine in RNA molecules; it is replaced with uracil. Therefore the initiation code in DNA (TAC) would be base-paired by RNA polymerase to form the RNA codon AUG. When transcription is complete, the newly assembled RNA is separated from its DNA template and made available for use in cell; the DNA recoils into its original double-helix form.

5.3.2 Eukaryotic Transcription

The transcription system is different in eukaryotic cells (Fig. 5-3). A eukaryotic gene begins with a promoter region and an initiation code, and ends with a termination code and region. However, the intervening gene sequence contains patches of nucleotides that apparently have no meaning but do serve important roles in maintaining the cell. If they were used in protein synthesis, the resulting proteins would be worthless. To remedy this problem, eukaryotic cells prune these segments from the mRNA after transcription. When such split genes are transcribed, RNA polymerase synthesizes a strand of pre-mRNA that initially includes copies of both exons (meaningful mRNA coding sequences) and introns (meaningless mRNA coding sequences). Soon after its manufacture, this pre-mRNA molecule has the meaningless introns clipped out and the exons spliced together into the final version, or mature mRNA, which is used by the cell. In humans, it has been found that the exons of a single gene may be spliced together in three different ways resulting in the production of three different mature messenger RNAs. This means that a single gene can be responsible for the production of three different proteins. Learning this information has lead geneticists to revise their estimate of the total number of genes found in the human genome from 100,000 to an estimated 300,000.

5.4 Translation

mRNA is a molecule of RNA encoding a chemical "blueprint" for a protein product, and carries coding information to ribosomes, the sites of protein synthesis. In mRNA as in DNA, genetic information is encoded in the sequence of nucleotides arranged into codons consisting of three bases each. Each codon encodes for a specific amino acid, except the stop codons. This process is called translation (Fig. 5-3), which is the process of the conversion of nucleic acid language to protein language, requiring two other types of RNA: tRNA and rRNA. tRNA mediates recognition of the codon and provides the corresponding amino acid, whereas rRNA is a central component of ribosomes. To translate mRNA language to protein language, a dictionary is necessary. The protein language has 20 words in the form of 20 common amino acids. Thus, there are more than enough nucleotide words for the 20 amino acid molecules because each nucleotide triplet codes for an amino acid.

Notice that more than one mRNA codon may code for the same amino acid. such "synonyms" can have survival value. If, for example, the gene or the mRNA becomes damaged in a way that causes a particular nucleotide base to change to another type, the chances are still good that the proper amino acid will be read into its proper position. But not all such changes can be compensated for by the codon

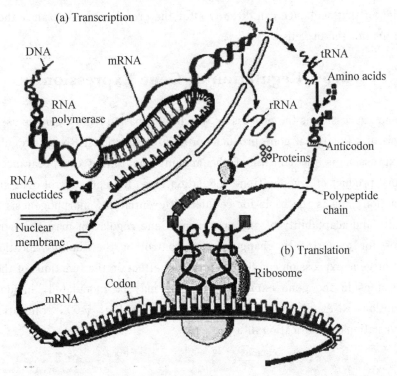

Fig. 5-3 Transcription and translation in a eukaryotic cell

system, and an altered protein may be produced. Changes can occure that cause great harm. Some damage is so extensive that the entire strand of DNA is broken, resulting in improper protein synthesis, or a total lack of synthesis. Any change in DNA is called a mutation. The mRNA moves through the ribosomes, its specific codon sequence allows for the chemical bonding of a specific sequence of amino acids. Remember that the DNA originally determined the sequence of bases in the RNA. Each protein has specific sequence of amino acids that determines its three-dimensional shape. This shape determines the activity of the protein which may be a structural component of a cell or a regulatory prorein, such as an enzyme. Any changes in amino acids or their order changes the action of the protein molecule. The protein insulin, for example, has a different amino acid sequence from the digestive enzyme trypsin. Both proteins are essential to human life and must be produced constantly and accurately. The amino acid sequence of each is detemined by a different gene. Each gene is a particular sequence of DNA nucleotides. Any alteration of that sequence can directly alter the protein structure and, therefore, the survival of the organism.

5.5 Regulation of Gene Expression

Gene expression is the process by which information from a gene is used in the synthesis of a functional gene product (protein or functional RNA). Regulation of gene expression is the control of the amount and timing of appearance of the functional product of a gene. Gene regulation gives the cell control over structure and function, and is the basis for cellular differentiation, morphogenesis and the versatility and adaptability of any organism. Gene regulation may also serve as a substrate for evolutionary change, since control of the timing, location, and amount of gene expression can have a profound effect on the functions of the gene. Several steps in the gene expression process may be modulated, including the transcription, RNA splicing (Fig. 5-4) and editing (Fig. 5-5), translation, and post-translational modification of a protein.

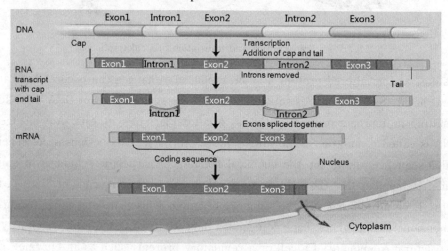

Fig. 5-4 RNA splicing

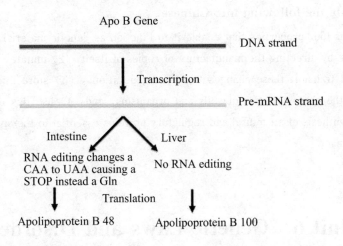

Fig. 5-5 RNA editing

Vocabulary

central dogma /ˈdɔgmə/ n. 中心法则
replication /ˌrepləikeiʃən/ n. 复制
transcription /trænˈskripʃən/ n. 转录
translation /trænsˈleiʃən/ n. 翻译，蛋白质合成
retrotranscription /ˈretrəutrænˈskripʃən/ n. 逆转录
nucleotide /ˈnjuːkliətaid/ n. 核苷酸
duplicate /ˈdjuːplikit/ vt. 复制，使加倍，使成双
hemoglobin /ˈhiːməuˌgləubin/ n. 血红蛋白
nucleoprotein /ˌnjuːkliəuˈprəutiːn/ n. 核蛋白质
covalent bond /kəuˈveilənt bɔnd/ n. 共价键
phosphate /ˈfɔsfeit/ n. 磷酸盐
polymerase /ˈpɔliməˌreis/ n. 聚合酶
complementary /ˌkɔmpləˈmentəriː/ adj. 补充的，补足的，互补于……的
nitrogenous /naiˈtrɔdʒinəs/ adj. 氮的，含氮的
promoter /prəˈməutə/ n. 启动子
triplet code /ˈtriplit kəud/ n. 三联体密码
mutation /mjuː(ː)ˈteiʃən/ n. 突变
telomerase /teˈləməreis/ n. 端粒酶

Exercises

1. Briefly state the Central Dogma in English, please.
2. Concisely explain Fig. 5-3 in English.

3. Translate the following into Chinese.

DNA has four properties that enable it to function as genetic material. It is able to (1) replicate by directing the manufacture of copies of itself, (2) mutate, or chemically change, and transmit these changes to future generations, (3) store information that determines the characteristics of cells and organisms, and (4) use this information to direct the synthesis of structural and regulatory proteins essential to the operation of the cell or organism.

Unit 6   Genetic Laws and Disorders

导语   遗传学是研究生物的遗传与变异及其规律的一门生物学分支科学。它有很多分支学科，如经典遗传学、分子遗传学、医学遗传学(研究遗传性疾病的遗传规律和本质)和临床遗传学(研究遗传病的诊断和预防)。掌握遗传学知识、原理和技术对人类的生物养殖和育种、遗传病的诊治和产品研发等至关重要。

本单元主要介绍了遗传学之父孟德尔的分离定律和自由组合定律及其修饰与补充(如不完全显性、共显性和环境影响)、连锁遗传、伴性遗传和细胞质遗传，遗传病及其类型、检测和咨询。

6.1   Laws of Genetics

6.1.1   What is Genetics?

Genetics is the field of biology studying heredity and variation as well as their laws. Heredity is the similarities of organisms' individuals between parents and offsprings. Variation is the differences of organisms' offsprings from their parents.

6.1.2   Mendel's Laws

The father of genetics is Gregor Mendel, who performed experiments concerning the inheritance of certain characteristics in garden pea (*Pisum satium*) plants. From his work, Mendel concluded which traits were dominant and which were recessive, and formulated several genetic laws to describe how characteristics are passed from one generation to the next and how they are expressed in an individual. For example, ① Mendel's law of segregation. When gametes are formed by a diploid heterozygote, the alleles that control a trait separate from each other into different gametes, retaining their individuality, and gametes combine randomly in forming offsprings (Fig. 6-1). ② Mendel's law of independent assortment. Two members of one allele pair separate from each other independently of the members of non-allele pairs (Fig. 6-2), while the members of non-allele pairs combine randomly into different gametes during the formation of gametes by a diploid heterozygote.

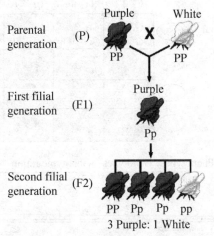

Fig. 6-1 Mendel's law of segregation

6.1.3 Modification of Mendelian Ratios

Mendelian segregation of alleles can be disguised by a variety of factors so that Mendelian ratios are modified. For example, codominance, incomplete dominance, environmental effects, epistasis, continuous variation, pleiotropic effects, lethal gene and so on.

6.1.3.1 Incomplete Dominance

Incomplete dominance is the phenomenon that F1 hybrids have an appearance between the phenotypes of the two parents. For example, when red four o'clock plants or snapdragons are crossed with white ones, all the F1 hybrids have pink

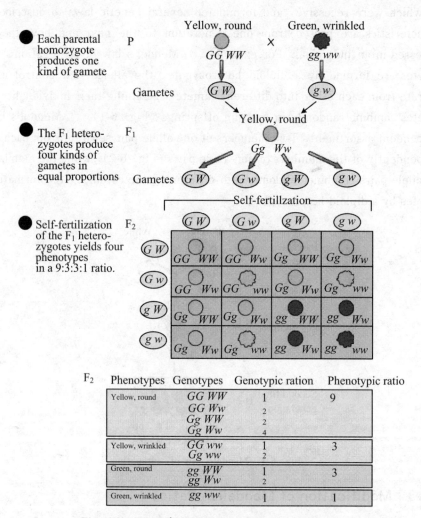

Fig. 6-2 Mendel's law of independent assortment

A pea with yellow and round seeds X a pea plant with green and wrinkled seeds produces offsprings.

flowers, and in F2, the genotypic ratio and phenotypic ratio are the same: 1 : 2 : 1(Fig. 6-3). Because there are two alleles for the color of these flowers, red and white, but there are three phenotypes, red, white, and pink. Both the red-flower allele and the white-flower allele partially express themselves when both are present, and this results in pink. Because neither allele is dominant, the genotypic ratio is identical to phenotypic ratio.

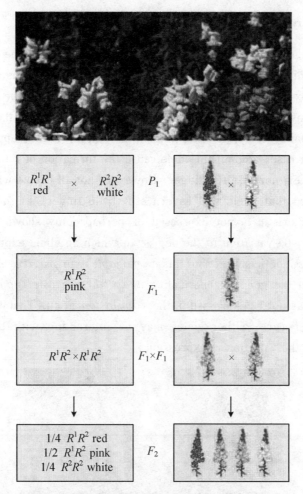

Fig. 6-3 Incomplete dominance shown in the flower color of snapdragons (William, Michael, 2002)

6.1.3.2 Codominance

In cases of dominance and recessiveness, one of a pair of alleles clearly overpowers the other. Although this is common, it is not always the case. In some combinations of alleles, there is a codominance. This is a situation in which both alleles in a heterozygous condition express themselves. For instance, $L^M L^N$ blood type in the MN blood group and $I^A I^B$ blood type in the ABO blood group, heterozygotes, express an intermediate, blended phenotype.

6.1.3.3 Environmental Influences on Gene Expression

Maybe you assumed that the dominant allele would always be expressed in a heterozygous individual. It is not so simple, there are exceptions. For example, the allele for six fingers (*polydactylism*) is dominant over the allele for five fingers in humans (Fig. 6-4). Some people who have received the allele for six fingers have a fairly complete sixth finger; in others, it may appear as a little stub. In another case, a dominant allele cause the formation of a little finger that can't be bent like a normal little finger. However, not all people who are believed to have inherited that allele will have a stiff little finger. In some cases, this dominant characteristic is not expressed or perhaps only shown on one hand. Thus, there may be variation in the degree to which an allele expresses itself *in an individual*. Geneticists refer to this *as variable expressivity*. A good example of this occurs in the genetic abnormality *neurofibromatosis typy* 1 (NF1). In some cases it may not be expressed in the *population* at all. This is referred to as a *lack of penetrance*. Other genes may be interacting with these dominant alleles, causing the variation in expression.

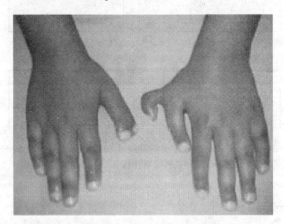

Fig. 6-4 Six fingers (*polydactylism*)
(Eldon, Frederick, 2004)

Both internal and external environmental factors can influence the expression of genes. For example, at conception, a male receives genes that will eventually determine the pitch of his voice. However, these genes are expressed differently after puberty. At puberty, male sex hormones are released. This internal environmental change results in the deeper male voice. A male who does not produce these hormones retains a higer-pitched voice in later life. Another characteristic whose expression is influenced by internal gene-regulating mechanisms is that of male-pattern baldness.

A comparable situation in females occurs when an abnormally functioning adrenal gland causes the release of large amounts of male hormones. This results in a female with a deeper voice. Also recall the genetic disease PKU. If children with *phenylketonuria* (*PKU*) are allowed to eat foods containing the amino acid phenylalanine, they will become mentally retarded. However, if the amino acid phenylalanine is excluded from the diet, and certain other dietary adjustments are made, the person will develop normally. Neutral sweet is a phenylalanine-based sweetener, so people with this genetic disorder must use caution when buying products that contain it.

Diet is an external environmental factor that can influence the phenotype of an individual. *Diabetes mellitus*, a metabolic disorder in which glucose is not properly metabolized and is passed out of the body in the urine, has a genetic basis. Some people who have a family history of diabetes are thought to have inherited the trait for this disease. Evidence indicates that they can delay the onset of the disease by reducing the amount of sugar in their diet. This change in the external environment influences gene expression in much the same way that sunlight affects the expression of freckles in humans (Fig. 6-5).

Fig. 6-5 The environment and gene expression (Eldon, Frederick, 2004)
The allele for freckles expresses itself more fully when a person is exposed to sunlight.

6.1.4 Linkage Genetics

Genetic linkage is the tendency of certain loci or alleles to be inherited together. Genetic loci that are physically close to one another on the same chromosome tend to stay together during meiosis, and are thus genetically linked. Famous geneticist, Thomas Hunt Morgan put forward Law of linkage and crossover.

6.1.5 Sex-linked Inheritance

Sex linkage is the phenotypic expression of an allele related to the chromosomal sex of the individual. This mode of inheritance is in contrast to the inheritance of traits on autosomal chromosomes, where both sexes have the same probability of inheritance. For example, the X-linked inheritance of white eyed mutation in fruit flies and the X-linked inheritance of red-green blindness in human beings.

6.1.6 Cytoplasmic Inheritance

Extranuclear inheritance is the transmission of genes that occur outside the nucleus. It is found in most eukaryotes and is commonly known to occur in cytoplasmic organelles such as mitochondria and chloroplasts or from cellular parasites like viruses or bacteria. One of the earliest and best known examples of cytoplasmic inheritance is that discovered by Correns in a variegated variety of the four o'clock plant *Mirabilis jalapa*. Variegated plants have some branches which carry normal green leaves, some branches with variegated leaves (mosaic of green and white patches) and some branches which have all white leaves.

6.2 Genetic Disorders

6.2.1 Genetic Disorders and Their Types

A genetic disorder is an illness caused by abnormalities in genes or chromosomes. Most genetic disorders are quite rare and affect one person in every several thousands or millions. Some genetic disorders are caused by a mutation in a gene or group of genes in a person's cells. These mutations can occur randomly or because of an environmental exposure such as cigarette smoking. Others are inherited. A mutated gene is passed down through a family and each generation of children can inherit the gene that causes the disease. Still others are due to problems with the number of chromosomes. In Down syndrome, for example, there is an extra copy of chromosome 21. However, the same disease, such as some forms of cancer, may be caused by an inherited genetic condition in some people, by new mutations in other people, and by non-genetic causes in still other people.

There are several types of genetic disorders: chromosomal abnormalities, single gene defects, multifactorial problems and teratogenic problems. The most common genetic type of diseases are Down's syndrome, autistic disorders, and color-blindness.

(1) Chromosomal abnoramalities. Chromosomal abnormalities in the baby may be inherited from the parent or may occur with no family history. The following chromosomal problems are the most common: aneuploidy—more or fewer chromosomes than the normal number, including Down syndrome (trisomy 21) and Turner syndrome (one of the two sex chromosomes is not transferred, leaving a single X chromosome, or 45 total), and deletion (part of a chromosome is missing, or part of the DNA code is missing), and inversion (when a chromosome breaks and the piece of the chromosome turns upside down and reattaches itself. Inversions may or may not cause birth defects depending upon their exact structure), and translocation (a rearrangement of a chromosome segment from one location to another, either within the same chromosome or to another), including balanced translocation (the DNA is equally exchanged between chromosomes and none is lost or added. A parent with a balanced translocation is healthy, but he/she may be at risk for passing unbalanced chromosomes in a pregnancy), Robertsonian translocation (a balanced translocation in which one chromosome joins the end of another), and mosaicism (the presence of two or more chromosome patterns in the cells of a person, resulting in two or more cell lines (i. e., some with 46 chromosomes, others with 47).

(2) Single gene disorders. Single gene disorders are also known as Mendelian inheritance disorders. In them, a single gene is responsible for a defect or abnormality. Single gene disorders usually have greater risks of inheritance. they can be: ① dominant (an abnormality occurs when only one of the genes from one parent is abnormal. If the parent has the disorder, the baby has a 50 percent

chance of inheriting it), for example, achondroplasia (imperfect bone development causing dwarfism) and Marfan syndrome (a connective tissue disorder causing long limbs and heart defects). Dominant genetic disorders continuously show up in individuals homozygous and heterozygous for the dominant allele in a pedigree (Fig. 6-6). ② recessive (an abnormality only occurs when both parents have abnormal genes. If both parents are carriers, a baby has a 25 percent chance of having the disorder), for examples, cystic fibrosis (a disorder of the glands causing excess mucus in the lungs and problems with pancreas function and food absorption), sickle cell disease, albinism (Fig. 6-7) and Tay Sachs disease (an inherited autosomal recessive condition that causes a progressive degeneration of the central nervous system which is fatal (usually by age 5). Some types of recessive gene disorders confer an advantage in the heterozygous state in certain environments. Recessive genetic disorders discontinuously show up in individuals homozygous for the recessive allele in a pedigree. ③ X-linked (the disorder is determined by genes on the X chromosome. Males are mainly affected and have the disorder. Daughters of men with the disorder are carriers of the trait and have a one in two chance of passing it to their children. Sons of women who are carriers each have a one in two chance of having the disorder), for examples, Duchenne muscular dystrophy (a disease of muscle wasting) and hemophilia (a bleeding disorder caused by low levels, or absence of, a blood protein that is essential for clotting).

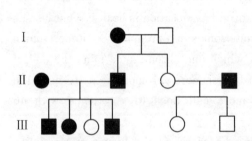

Fig. 6-6 Pedigree of one autosomal dominant genetic disease

Fig. 6-7 An example of albinism

(3) Multifactorial problems. Some birth defects do not follow a single gene or chromosomal abnormality pattern. They may be due to several problems, or a

combined effect of genes and the environment. It is difficult to predict inheritance of abnormalities caused by multiple factors. Examples include heart defects, cleft lip or cleft palate, and neural tube defects (defects in the spine or brain).

(4) Teratogenic problems. Certain substances are known to cause abnormalities in babies. Many birth defects occur when the fetus is exposed to teratogens (substances that cause abnormalities) during the first trimester of pregnancy when organs are forming. Some known teratogens include the following: certain medications (always consult your physician before taking any medications during pregnancy), alcohol, high level radiation exposure, lead and certain infections (such as rubella).

6.2.2 Genetic Testing

If you know that you have a genetic problem in your family, you can have genetic testing to see if your baby could be affected. Genetic testing is defined as "the analysis of human DNA, RNA, chromosomes, proteins and certain metabolites in order to detect heritable disease-related genotypes, mutations, phenotypes or karyotypes for clinical purposes". Genetic tests are tests on blood and other tissue to find genetic disorders. About 900 such tests are available. Doctors use genetic tests for several reasons:

① Finding possible genetic diseases in unborn babies;

② Finding out if people carry a gene for a disease and might pass it on to their children;

③ Screening embryos for disease;

④ Testing for genetic diseases in adults before they cause symptoms;

⑤ Confirming a diagnosis in a person who has disease symptoms.

There are five different types of genetic testing, which are the carrier identification, prenatal diagnosis, newborn screening, late-onset disorder, and predictive gene testing. The varying types of gene tests are utilized to look for abnormalities in the entire chromosomes, in the protein products of genes, or in short stretches near the genes or within the DNA. ① In Carrier identification test, it includes the genetic tests utilized by couples having families with a history of recessive genetic disorders, and who are planning to have children. To date, there are three genetic disorders, namely cystic fibrosis, Tay-Sachs and sickle-cell anemia, which can be tested by patients. Couples who use this test shall learn whether they carry recessive allele for inherited diseases which can be carried on to their children. ② The Prenatal diagnosis is the genetic test done on fetuses. This test is helpful in determining whether the child may have carried genes linked to physical deterioration or mental retardation. An example of disease for prenatal diagnosis is Down syndrome. Included in this test are biochemical, DNA-based and chromosomal tests. ③ In Newborn Screening, the tests are done for Phenylketonuria, and congenital hypothyroidism in newly born infants for preventative health action. The test documents the absence of a protein which is useful in functionality. ④ The Late-onset disorders, the test can detect presence of more serious diseases such as cancer and heart disease. The tests may suggest vulnerability or predisposition for diseases which are complex and have environmental and genetic component. Either way, the Late-onset disorders may help in early detection, and thus, early treatment and more chances of fast recovery. ⑤ In preventive gene testing, the test identifies people who may be at risk of contracting a disease before any of the signs begin to appear. According to the recent information, there are already more than two dozens of diseases which can be tested in patients (http://www.charlesempire.com).

6.2.3 Genetic Counseling

The way in which the disorder is inherited can help determine the risks it will have on a pregnancy and the risk it will recur in future children. Risks for having a baby with a birth defect from a genetic abnormality may be increased when

① the parents have another child with a genetic disorder;

② there is a family history of a genetic disorder;

③ one parent has a chromosomal abnormality;

④ the fetus has abnormalities seen on ultrasound.

If you are expecting a baby or planning to have a baby, your doctor can run many tests to help assess the health of both you and your baby. Your doctor may also refer you for genetic counseling. Genetic counseling provides information and support to people who have, or may be at risk for genetic disorders. There are many reasons to seek genetic counseling. You may consider it if you

① Have an inherited disorder;

② Are pregnant or planning to be pregnant after age 35 (Fig. 6-8);

③ Already have a child with a genetic disorder or birth defect;

④ Have had two or more pregnancy losses or a baby who died;
⑤ Have had ultrasound or screening tests that suggest a possible problem.

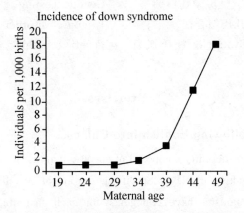

Fig. 6-8 The correlation between incidence of Down syndrome and age of mother

Frequency of Down syndrome is about 1 in 750 children. However, it is much more common among children of older women.

Vocabulary

offspring /'ɔfspriŋ/ n. 后代
overshadow /,əuvə'ʃædəu/ vt. 遮暗，掩盖
allele /ə'li:l/ n. 等位基因
genotype /'dʒenətaip/ n. 基因型
phenotype /'fi:nətaip/ n. 表现型
codominance /,kəu'dɔminəns/ n. 共显性
snapdragon /'snæp,drægən/ n. 金鱼草
Law of independent assortment 独立分配定律
polydactylism /pɔli'dæktilisəm/ n. 多指
neurofibromatosis /,njuərəufai,brəumə'təusis/ n. 神经纤维瘤病
phenylketonuria /,fenəl,ki:tə'njuəriə/ n. 苯丙酮尿症
the pros and cons n. 利弊

epistasis /i'pistəsis/ n. 基因上位(作用)
pleiotropic /,plaiəu'trɔpik/ adj. 多效性的
freckle /'frekəl/ n. 雀斑
Law of linkage and crossover 连锁互换定律
autosomal /,ɔ:təu'səuməl/ adj. 常染色体的
Down syndrome 唐氏综合症状，先天愚型
homozygous /,hɔmə'zaigəus/ adj. 纯合的
heterozygous /,hetərəu'zaigəs/ adj. 杂合的
pedigree /'pedi,gri:/ n. 家谱，系谱
achondroplasia /ei,kɔndrə'pleʒiə/ n. 软骨发育不全

cystic fibrosis 囊胞性纤维症
albinism /ˈælbənizəm/ n. 白化病
Tay Sachs disease 家族性黑蒙性白痴
Marfan syndrome 马凡氏综合征
Duchenne muscular dystrophy 杜氏肌营养不良

cleft lip 唇裂，兔唇
teratogen /təˈrætədʒən/ n. 致畸原
Genetic Testing 遗传检测
late-onset disorder 迟发性遗传病
genetic counseling 遗传咨询

Exercises

1. Translate the following English into Chinese.

Genes are units of heredity composed of specific lengths of DNA that determine the characteristics an organism displays. Specific genes are at specific loci on specific chromosomes. Diploid organisms have two genes for each characteristic. The alternative forms of genes for a characteristic are called alleles. There may be many different alleles for a particular characteristic. Some alleles are dominant over other alleles that are said to be recessive. Organisms with two identical alleles are homozygous for a characteristic; those with different alleles are heterozygous. The phenotype displayed by an organism is the result of the effect of the environment on the ability of the genes to express themselves.

2. Fill in the blanks with the appropriate words you have just learned in this unit.

(1) There are several types of genetic disorders: _____, _____, _____ and _____.

(2) Single gene disorders are divided into two types such as _____ and _____.

(3) Five different types of genetic testing are _____, _____, _____, _____ and _____.

(4) Genetic counseling provides _____ and support to people who have, or may be at risk for _____.

(5) Each strand of DNA acts as a _____ for the construction of a new, complementary strand during DNA replication.

(6) In eukaryotic cells, only the _____ strand of DNA is transcribed.

3. Reading Comprenhesion.

Passage 1 Nondisjunction and Chromosomal Abnormalities

In the normal process of meiosis, diploid cells have their number of chromosomes reduced to haploid. This involves segregating homologous chromosomes into separate cells during Meiosis I. Occasionally, a pair of homologous chromosomes does not segregate properly during gametogenesis and both chromosomes of a pair end up in the same gamete. This kind of division is known as nondisjunction, in which two cells are missing a chromosome. This usually results in the death of the cells. The other cells have a double dose of one chromosome. Apparently, the genes of an organism are balanced against one another. A double dose of some genes and a single dose of others results in abnormalities that may lead to the death of the cell. Some of these abnormal cells, however, do live and develop into sperm or eggs. If one of these abnormal sperm or eggs unites with a normal gamete, the offspring will have an abnormal number of chromosomes. There will be three or one of the kinds of chromosomes instead of the normal two, a condition referred to as trisomy $(2n+1)$ or monosomy $(2n-1)$. Should the other cell survive and become involved in fertilization, it will only have one of the pair of homologous chromosomes, a condition referred to as monosomy. All the cells that develop by mitosis from such zygotes will be either trisomic or monosomic. It is possible to examine cells and count chromosomes. One example of the effects of nondisjunction is Down syndrome. The frequency of occurrence of Down syndrome in women increases very rapidly after age 37, so many physicians encourage couples to have their children in their early midtwenties and not in their late thirties or early forties. Physicians normally encourage older women who are pregnant to have the cells of their fetus checked to see if they have the normal chromosome number. It is important to know that the male parent can also contribute the extra chromosome 21. However, it appears that this occurs less than 30% of the time.

Sometimes a portion of chromosome 14 may be cut out and joined to chromosome 21. The transfer of a piece of one nonhomologous chromosome to another is called a chromosomal translocation. A person with this 14/21 translocation is monosomic and has only 45 chromosomes; one 14 and one 21 are missing and replaced by the translocated 14/21. Statistically, about 15% of the children of carrier mothers inherit the 14/21 chromosome and have Down syndrome. Fewer of the children born to fathers with translocation inherit the abnormal chromosome and are Downic.

Whenever an individual is born with a chromosomal abnormality such as a monosomic or a trisomic condition, it is recommended that both parents have a karyotype in an attempt to identify the possible source of the problem. This is not to fix blame but to provide information on the likelihood that a next pregnancy would also result in a child with a chromosomal abnormality.

Questions for Discussion:

(1) What is non-disjunction?

(2) What is the correlation between the frequency of Down syndrome in women and their ages?

(3) What is chromosomal translocation?

Passage 2 Sickle-cell Disease

The two recessive alleles for sickle-cell hemoglobin (Hb^s and Hb^s) can result in abnormally shaped red blood cells. This occurs because the hemoglobin molecules are synthesized with the wrong amino acid sequence. These abnormal hemoglobin molecules tend to attach to one another in long, rodlike chains when oxygen is in short supply, that is, with exercise, pneumonia, emphysema. These rodlike chains distort the shape of the red blood cells into a sickle shape. When these abnormal red blood cells change shape, they clog small blood vessels. The sickled red cells are also destroyed more rapidly than normal cells. This results in a shortage of red blood cells, a condition known as anemia, and an oxygen deficiency in the tissues that have become clogged. People with sickle-cell anemia may experience pain, swelling, and damage to organs such as the heart, lungs, brain, and kidneys.

Sickle-cell anemia can be lethal in the homozygous recessive condition. In the homozygous dominant condition ($Hb^A Hb^A$), the person has normal red blood cells. In the heterozygous condition ($Hb^A Hb^S$), patients produce both kinds of red blood cells. When the amount of oxygen in the blood falls below a certain level, those able to sickle will distort. However, when this occurs, most people heterozygous for the trait do not show severe symptoms. Therefore, these alleles are related to one another in a codominant fashion. However, under the right circumstances, being heterozygous can be beneficial. A person with a single sickle-cell allele is more resistant to malaria than a person without this allele.

Genotype	Phenotype
$Hb^A Hb^A$	Normal hemoglobin and nonresistance to malaria
$Hb^A Hb^S$	Nomal hemoglobin and resistance to malaria
$Hb^S Hb^S$	Resistance to malaria but death from sickle-cell anemia

Originally, sickle-cell anemia was found at a high frequency in parts of the world where malaria was common, such as tropical regions of Africa and South America. Today, however, this genetic disease can be found anywhere in the world. In the United States, it is most common among black populations whose ancestors came from equatorial Africa.

Questions for Discussion:
   (1) What genetic pattern is Sickle-cell anemia?
   (2) What results in Sickle-cell anemia?
   (3) In what condition can Sickle-cell anemia be lethal?

4. Multiple Choice Questions.

   (1) Which describes transcription? (   )
   A. It is the process used to make DNA.
   B. Only one copy of rRNA is ever made from a particular gene.
   C. It is the process used to make rRNA, tRNA, and mRNA.
   D. Two strands of DNA for a particular gene are transcribed.
   E. Only one copy of mRNA is ever made from a particular gene.

   (2) Which describes protein synthesis? (   )
   A. Translocation of the ribosome exposes a new codon for base pairing with an anticodon.
   B. DNA is directly involved in translation.
   C. RNA polymerase is the enzyme responsible for transcription.
   D. One amino acid is always carried by more than one tRNA.
   E. Each tRNA with a anticodon always carries a different amino acid.

   (3) Which of the following describes the function of DNA polymerase? (   )
   A. It moves along each template strand of the open helix, keeping the strands separate and joining segments of DNA together.
   B. It moves along each template strand of the open helix, reading the nucleotide in the template, covalently joining the completemenary nucleotide onto the end of the new strand, and unwinding the helix.
   C. It moves along each template strand of the open helix, keeping the nucleotide in the template, and covalently joining the completemenary nucleotide onto the end of the new strand.
   D. It moves along each template strand of the open helix, keeping the nucleotide in the template, unwinding the helix, keeping the strands separate, and

joining segments of DNA together.

E. It moves along each template strand of the open helix, reading the nucleotide in the template, covalently joining the completemenary nucleotide onto the end of the new strand, unwinding the helix, and keeping the strands separate.

(4) The stop codon (   ).

A. is the last amino acid in the chain

B. is the next to the last amino acid in the chain

C. specifies the last amino acid in the chain

D. indicates the previous amino acid is the last in the chain

E. can occur more than once in any given chain

5. English-Reading Report.

You are asked to search for some current English articles on general biology on line and carefully read them to find out their main points and write your own short English reading report. Afterthat, you will introduce it to your classmates in English.

Unit 7　Microbes and Their Uses

　　导语　微生物一般是指个体微小、结构简单、人的肉眼看不见的微小生物，主要包括原核类的细菌、放线菌、立克次氏体、支原体、衣原体、蓝细菌、古细菌和真核类的真菌、酵母菌以及非细胞类的病毒和亚病毒。微生物学是生物学的分支学科之一，是研究微生物生命活动规律的一门学科。它的基本内容包括微生物细胞的结构和功能、微生物的进化和多样性、微生物生态学规律、微生物同人类的关系。

　　本单元主要介绍微生物的一般特征，微生物学及其分支学科，以及细菌、真菌和病毒的结构、组成与特点及其对人类的利与弊。

7.1　Breif Introduction to Microbes and Microbiology

A microorganism or microbe is an organism that is cellular or non-cellular. Microorganisms include bacteria, fungi, archaea, viruses and so on. The majority of them are small and cannot be seen without some type of magnification. Members of the bacteria, protista, and fungi share several characteristics that set them apart from plants and animals. They rely primarily on asexual reproduction. Some microbes are autotrophic, whereas many others are heterotrophic. Microorganisms live in all parts of the biosphere such as water, soil, hot springs, on the ocean floor, atmosphere and deep inside rocks within the Earth's crust. Microorganisms as decomposers are critical to nutrient recycling in ecosystems. As some microorganisms can fix nitrogen, they are a vital part of the nitrogen cycle, and recent studies indicate that airborne microbes may play a role in precipitation and weather. Microbes are also exploited by people in traditional food and beverage preparation. However, pathogenic microbes also have inflicted great distress to human, animal and plant populations through disease, spoilage of crops, foods and the fouling and degradation of man-made structures. More recently, microorganisms have been used as terrorist weapons.

Microbiology is the study of microorganisms, divided into many sub-disciplines which include bacteriology, mycology, phycology, parasitology, virology, microbial ecology, microbial physiology, microbial genetics and molecular biology. Our need to control infectious diseases has brought about the fields of pathology and immunology. Bioinformatics is a new area of research in microbiology.

7.2 Important Microbes

7.2.1 Bacteria

Bacteria are single-celled prokaryotes that lack an organized nucleus and other complex organelles, also called germs, beloging to the Domains Archaea and Eubacteria. Some unusual bacteria (the Archaea) have the genetic ability to function in extreme environments such as sulfur hot springs, on glaciers, and at the openings of submarine volcanic vents. there are approximately five million (5×10^{30}) bacteria on Earth. Bacteria are divided into different groups based on such features as their staining properties, ability to form endospores, shape (morphology), motility, metabolism, and reproduction. For example, bacteria are divided into five groups: coccus, bacillus, spirillum, vibrio and spirochaete (Fig. 7-1) based on bacterial shapes or morphology.

The word bacteria usually brings people to mind tiny things that cause diseases; however, the majority are free living and not harmful. Their roles in the ecosystem include those of decomposers, nitrogen fixers, and other symbionts. It is true that some diseases are caused by bacteria, but only a minority of bacteria are pathogens, microbes that cause infectious diseases.

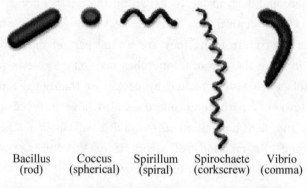

Bacillus　　Coccus　　　Spirillum　Spirochaete　Vibrio
(rod)　　(spherical)　　(spiral)　(corkscrew)　(comma)

Fig. 7-1　The groups of bacteria based on their shapes

Many forms of bacteria are beneficial to humans. Some forms of bacteria decompose dead material, sewage, and other wastes into simpler molecules that can be recycled. Organisms that function in this manner are called saprophytic. The food industry uses bacteria to produce cheese, yogurt, sauerkraut, and many other foods. Alcohols, acetones, acids, and other chemicals are produced by bacterial cultures. The pharmaceutical industry employs bacteria to produce antibiotics and vitamins. Some bacteria can even metabolize oil and are used to clean up oil spills.

There are also mutualistic relationships between bacteria and other organisms. Some intestinal bacteria benefit humans by producing antibiotics that inhibit the development of pathogenic bacteria. They also compete with disease-causing bacteria for nutrients, thereby helping keep the pathogens in check. They aid digestion by releasing various nutrients. They produce and release vitamin K. Mutualistic bacteria establish this symbiotic relationship when they are ingested along with food or drink. When people travel, they consume local bacteria along with their food and drink, and may have problems establishing a new symbiotic relationship with these foreign bacteria. Both the host and the symbionts have to make adjustments to their new environment, which can result in a very uncomfortable situation for both. Some people develop traveler's diarrhea as a result. Animals do not produce the enzymes needed for the digestion of cellulose.

Methanogens, bacteria that obtain metabolic energy by reducing carbon dioxide (CO_2) to methane (CH_4), digest the cellulose consumed by herbivorous animals, such as cows, thereby permitting the cow to obtain simple sugars from the otherwise useless cellulose. There is a mutualistic relationship between the cow and the methanogens. Some methanogens are also found in the human gut and are among the organisms responsible for the production of intestinal gas. In some regions of the world methanogens are used to digest organic waste, and the methane is used as a source of fuel. Certain types of bacteria have a symbiotic relationship with the roots of bean plants and other legumes. These bacteria are capable of converting atmospheric nitrogen into a form that is usable to the plants.

Photosynthetic, colonial blue-green bacteria release significant quantities of oxygen. Colonies of blue-green bacteria are found in aquatic environments, where they form long, filamentous strands commonly called pond scum. Some of the larger cells in the colony are capable of nitrogen fixation and convert atmospheric nitrogen, N_2, to ammonia, NH_3. This provides a form of nitrogen usable to other cells in the colony—an example of division of labor.

Some pathogenic bacteria may be associated with an organism yet do not cause disease. For example, streptococcus pneumoniae may grow in the throats of healthy people without any pathogenic effects. But if a person's resistance is lowered, as after a bout with viral flu, streptococcus pneumoniae may reproduce rapidly in the lungs and cause pneumonia; the relationshop has changed from commensalistic to parasitic.

Bacteria may invade the healthy tissue of the host and cause disease by altering the tissus's normal physiology. Bacteria living in the host release a variety of enzymes that cause the destruction of tissue. Examples are the infectious diseases including strep throat, syphilis (Fig. 7-2,(a)), pneumonia, tuberculosis, and leprosy (Fig. 7-2,(b)). Many other bacterial illnesses are caused by toxins or poisons produced by bacteria that may be consumed with food or drink. In this case, disease can be caused even though the pathogens may never enter the host. For example, botulism is an extremely deadly disease caused by the presence of bacterial toxins in food or drink. Some other bacterial diseases are the result of toxins released from bacteria growing inside the host tissue; tetanus (Fig 7-2, (c)) and diphtheria are examples. In general, toxins may cause tissue damage, fever, aches and pains.

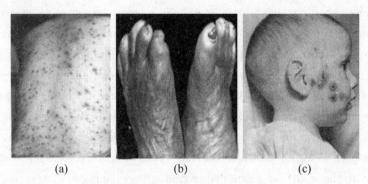

Fig. 7-2 Three bacterial diseases caused by *Treponema Pallidun*,
leprosy bacillus and clostridium tetani, respectively
(a) syphilis; (b) leprosy; (c) tetanus

Bacteria pathogens are also important factors in certain plant diseases. Bacteria are the causative agents in many types of plant blights, wilts, and soft rots. Apples and other fruit trees are susceptible to fire blight, a disease that lowers the fruit yield because it kills the tree's branches. Citrus canker, a disease of citrus fruits that causes cancerlike growths, can generate widespread damage. In a three-year period, Florida citrus growers lost $ 2.5 billion because of this disease.

Because bacteria reproduce so rapidly, a few antibiotic resistant cells in a population can increase to dangerous levels in a very short time. This requires the use of stronger doses of antibiotics or new types of antibiotics to bring the bacteria under control. Furthermore, these resistant strains can be transferred from one host to another. For example, sulfa drugs and penicillin, once widely used to fight infections, are now ineffective against many strains of pathogenic bacteria. As new antibiotics are developed, natural selection encourages the development of resistant bacterial strains. Therefore, humans are constantly waging battles against new strains of resistant bacteria.

7.2.2 Fungus

A fungus is a member of a large group of eukaryotic organisms that includes microorganisms such as yeasts, molds and mushrooms (Fig. 7-3). Fungus is the common name for members of the kingdom Fungi, which has been estimated at around 1.5 million species, with about 5% of these having been formally classified. The majority of fungi are nonmotile, nonphotosynthetic and multicellular. They have a rigid, thin cell wall, which is not composed of cellulose but chitin. In the multicellular fungi the basic structural unit is a network of multicellular filaments. Because all of these organisms are heterotrophy, they must obtain nutrients from organic sources. Most are saprophytes and secrete enzymes that digest large molecules into smaller units that are absorbed. They are very important as decomposers in all ecosystems. They feed on a variety of nutrients ranging from dead organisms to such products as shoes, food-stuffs, and clothing. Most synthetic organic molecules are not readily attacked by fungi; this is why plastic bags, foam cups, and organic pesticides are slow to decompose.

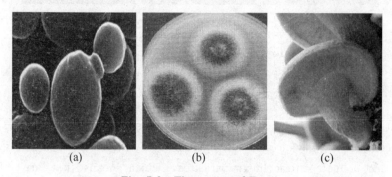

(a)　　　　　　　　　(b)　　　　　　　　　(c)

Fig. 7-3　Three types of Fungi

(a) yeasts; (b) aspergillus flavus; (c) mushrooms

Some fungi are parasitic, whereas others are mutualistic. Many of the parasitic fungi are important plant pests. Some attack and kill plants (chestnut blight, Dutch elm disease); others injure the fruit, leaves, roots, or stems and sible for athlete's foot (Fig. 7-4, (a)), vaginal yeast infections, valley fever, "ringworm" (Fig. 7-4, (b)) and other disease. Mutualistic fungi are important in lichens and in combination with the roots of certain kinds of plants.

The human use of fungi for food preparation or preservation and other purposes is extensive and has a long history. Mushroom farming and mushroom gathering are large industries in many countries. Because of the capacity of this group to produce an enormous range of natural products with antimicrobial or other biological activities, many species have long been used or are being developed for industrial production of antibiotics, vitamins, and anti cancer and cholesterol-lowering drugs. More recently, methods have been developed for metabolic engineering of fungal species. For example, GM yeast species, easily growing at fast rates in large fermentation vessels, has opened up ways of pharmaceutical production.

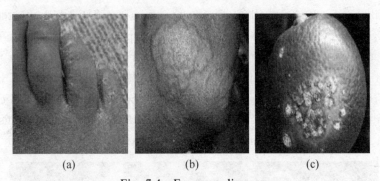

Fig. 7-4 Funguous diseases
(a) athlete's foot; (b) Ringworm; (c) a citrus funguous disease

7.2.3 Non-cell Microbes

Non-cell microbes are divided into three types such as virus, prion and viroid. A virus consists of a nucleic acid core surrounded by a coat of protein (Fig. 7-5). Viruses are obligate intracellular parasites, which means they are infectious particles that can function only when inside a living cell. Viruses are typically host-specific, which means that they usually attack only one kind of cell. Viruses can

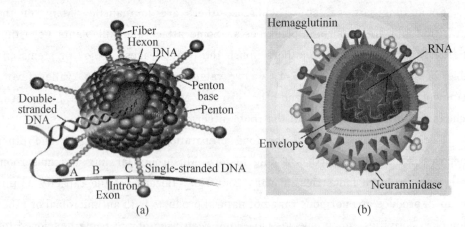

Fig. 7-5 The structures of viruses
(a) Adenovirus; (b) An influenza virus. Neuraminidase and hemagglutinin are proteins found on the envelope, or coat, of the virus that help the virus to lock on to and invade its target cells.

infect only those cells that have the proper receptor sites to which the virus can attach. This site is usually a glycoprotein molecule on the surface of the cell membrane. For example, the virus responsible for measles attaches to the membranes of skin cells, hepatitis viruses attach to liver cells, and mumps viruses attach to the cells in the salivary glands. Host cells for the HIV virus include some types of human brain cells and several types of the cells belonging to the immune system. Once it has attached to the host cell, the virus either enters the cell intact or it injects its nucleic acid into the cell. If it enters the cell, the virus loses its protein coat, releasing the nucleic acid. Once released into the cell, the nucleic acid of the virus may remain free in the cytoplasm or it may link with the host's genetic material.

7.3 Microbial Uses

Microorganisms are vital to humans and the environment, for they are used in
(1) Food. For example, brewing(Fig. 7-6), winemaking, baking, pickling and other food-making processes, and controlling the fermentation process in the production of cultured dairy products such as yogurt and cheese. The cultures also provide flavour and aroma, and inhibit undesirable organisms. For instance, Stilton cheese veined with *Penicillium roqueforti* (Fig. 7-7) is blue.

Fig. 7-6 Kriek, a variety of beer brewed with cherries

Fig. 7-7 Stilton cheese veined with Penicillium roqueforti

(2) Water treatment. Specially cultured microbes are used in the biological treatment of sewage and industrial waste effluent.

(3) Energy. Microbes are used in fermentation to produce ethanol, and in biogas reactors to produce methane, of which algae are used to produce liquid fuels, and bacteria to convert various forms of agricultural and urban waste into usable fuels.

(4) Science. Microbes are also essential tools in biotechnology, biochemistry, genetics, molecular biology, genomics and proteomics. The yeasts are important model organisms in science. Microbes can be harnessed for uses such as creating steroids and treating skin diseases. Scientists are also considering using microbes as a solution for pollution.

(5) Warfare. In the Middle Ages, diseased corpses were thrown into castles during sieges. Individuals near the corpses were exposed to the deadly pathogen and were likely to spread that pathogen to others.

(6) Human health. ① Human digestion: microorganisms can form an endosymbiotic relationship with other, larger organisms. For example, the bacteria that live within the human digestive system contribute to gut immunity, synthesise vitamins such as folic acid and biotin, and ferment complex indigestible carbohydrates. ② Diseases and immunology: microorganisms are the cause of many infectious diseases. They include pathogenic bacteria, causing diseases such as plague, tuberculosis and anthrax; protozoa, causing diseases such as malaria, sleeping sickness and toxoplasmosis; and also fungi causing diseases such as ringworm and candidiasis. However, other diseases such as influenza, yellow fever

or AIDS are caused by pathogenic viruses.

(7) Importance in ecology. Microbes are critical to the processes of decomposition required to cycle nitrogen and other elements back to the natural world.

(8) Hygiene. Hygiene is the avoidance of infection or food spoiling by eliminating microorganisms from the surroundings. There are several methods for investigating the level of hygiene in a sample of food, drinking water, equipment etc. Water samples can be filtrated through an extremely fine filter. This filter is then placed in a nutrient medium. Microorganisms on the filter then grow to form a visible colony. Harmful microorganisms can be detected in food by placing a sample in a nutrient broth designed to enrich the organisms in question. Selective media or PCR, can then be used for detection. The hygiene of hard surfaces, such as cooking pots, can be tested by touching them with a solid piece of nutrient medium and then allowing the microorganisms to grow on it. In addition, in food preparation microorganisms are reduced by preservation methods (such as the addition of vinegar), clean utensils, short storage periods or cool temperatures. If complete sterility is needed, the two most common methods are irradiation and the use of an autoclave.

Vocabulary

protist /'prəutist/ n. 原生生物
planarian /plə'neəriən/ n. 涡虫
plankton /'plæŋktən/ n. 浮游生物
inflict /in'flikt/ vt. 遭受，使吃苦头
symbiont /'simbaiənt/ n. 共生生物
effluent /'eflu:ənt/ n. 污水，工业废水
corpse /kɔ:ps/ n. 死尸，尸体
siege /si:dʒ/ n. 围攻，围困
nonillion /nəu'niljən/ n. ① [英][德]100万的9次方 ② [美][法]1 000 的 10次方
saprophyte /'sæprəufait/ n. 腐生物
yogurt /'jəugət/ n. 酸奶，优格
sauerkraut /'sauəkraut/ n. 酸白菜

diarrhea /ˌdaiə'ri:ə/ n. 痢疾，拉肚子
pond scum /skʌm/ n. 绿藻类层
pathogen /'pæθədʒ(ə)n/ n. 病菌，病原体
pneumonia /nju(:)'məunjə/ n. 肺炎
tuberculosis /tju,bə:kjə'ləusis/ n. 肺结核
syphilis /'sifəlis/ n. 梅毒
tetanus /'tetənəs/ n. 破伤风
diphtheria /dif'θiəri:ə/ n. 白喉
virus /'vaiərəs/ n. 病毒
parasite /'pærəsait/ n. 寄生虫
heterotrophic /ˌhetərəu'trɔfik/ adj. 异养的
aspergillus flavus 黄曲霉
athlete's foot 脚气，香港脚

prion *n*. 阮病毒
measles /'mi:zəlz/ *n*. 麻疹
mumps /mʌmps/ *n*. 腮腺炎
toxoplasmosis /'tɔksəplæz'məusis/ *n*. 弓形体病
candidiasis /ˌkændi'daiəsəs/ *n*. 念珠菌病

Exercises

1. Matching Questions.

Write the letter of the phrase that best matches the numbered on the left. Use each only once.

(1) nucleiod a. some organisms which are small and can not be seen by human naked eyes

(2) prion b. one antibiotic produced by one mold

(3) microbes c. unicellular prokaryotes that lack a true nucleus and other complex organelles such as mitochondria and ER.

(4) retrovirus d. the irregularly shaped region in bacterial cells in which DNA is concentrated but not bound by a membranne

(5) bacteria e. viruses which direct a cell to use a viral RNA genomes as a template to transcribe DNA (reverse transcription)

(6) fungui f. caused by a virus that remains present and dormant in the host after the symptoms of the disease disappeas

(7) penicillin g. some nonphotosynthetic and nonmotile eukaryotic organisms

(8) latent infection h. a neurological disease agent believed to consist solely of protein

2. Fill in the blanks with the appropriate words you have just learned in this unit.

(1) All members of the kingdom _____ are prokaryotes.

(2) Viruses are noncellular and obligate intracellular _____.

(3) Most bacteria are _____ and obtain their carbon and energy from dead organic matter.

(4) HIV stands for _____ which is the causative agent of AIDS.

(5) Viruse have only one kind of _____ acid and a protein coat.

(6) An extracellular _____ help some bacteria avoid phagocytosis.

(7) HIV belongs to a group of viruses called _____.

(8) Yeasts are _____ fungi.

(9) Some bacteria survive a hostile environment by forming _____ that are

resistant to drying, chemicals, and radiation.

3. Multiple Choice Questions.

(1) How is "athlete's foot" caused? (　　)

　A. Infectious bacteria.　　B. Parasitic organism.　　C. Viruses.

　D. Ringworm fungus.　　E. Burn.

(2) What is the function of the fungal antibiotics in natural environments? (　　)

　A. Blocks the growth of microorganisms, especially bacteria.

　B. Works as fungal metabolites.

　C. Kills insects.

　D. Inhibits viruses.

　E. Beautifies natural environments.

(3) In what way do bacteria differ from the eukaryotes? (　　)

　A. Bacteria have a true nucleus.

　B. Bacteria have chloroplasts.

　C. Bacteria have ribosomes.

　D. Bacteria lack membrane-bound organelles.

　E. Bacteria are composed of different group of chemicals.

(4) Bacteria may survive catastrophic change because of their (　　).

　A. rapid reproduction rate

　B. complex internal systems

　C. resistance to genetic change

　D. lack of genetic diversity

　E. limited number of habitats

(5) Which describes obligate anaerobes? (　　)

　A. They thrive only when oxygen is abundant.

　B. They are killed by oxygen.

　C. They cannot survive under water.

　D. They cannot survive inside the human intestine.

　E. They thrive with or without oxygen.

(6) In what way are archaeobacteria and eubacteria similar? (　　)

　A. Both can survive in extremely low pH habitats.

　B. Both have the same shape.

　C. Both lack a true nucleus.

　D. Both have the same materials in their cell walls.

E. Both have identical biochemical processes.

(7) Which describes a virus? (　　)

   A. It has cytoplasm and a nucleus.

   B. It is composed of nucleic acid and protein.

   C. It can reproduce outside a host cell.

   D. It has a ribosome.

   E. It has organelles.

(8) In what way are viruses and their host cells similar? (　　)

   A. Both are about the same size.

   B. Both contain RNA and DNA.

   C. Both engage in activities leading to the production of offspring.

   C. Both can be crystallized and still retain their ability to reproduce.

   E. Both are able to independently perform all necessary biological functions.

(9) Infection by an influenza virus does not transfer life-long immunity because (　　).

   A. the virus periodically alters its surface antigens

   B. the virus attacks the cells of the immune system

   C. the virus produces a latent infection

   D. the virus is not an obigate intracellular parasite

   E. there are over 100 strains of influenza virus; immunity to one strain does not mean immunity to all strains

(10) Which describes all viral diseases? (　　)

   A. They are always fatal.

   B. They are never fatal.

   C. Vaccines offer no protection.

   D. Antibiotic drugs do not hasten their recovery.

   E. Viruses that attack one species do not attack any other.

Unit 8　Plants and Their Uses

导语　植物是生物界中的一大类生物，包括藻类、蕨类、苔藓植物和种子植物

(分为裸子植物和被子植物)。植物学是生物学的一个分支学科,是研究植物及其生活与发展规律的科学。其主要研究内容包括植物形态解剖、生长发育、生理生态、系统进化、分类及其与人类的关系。植物学现已分支出许多学科,如植物形态学、植物分类学、植物生理学、植物遗传学、植物生态学和植物资源学等。

本单元主要介绍植物及其基本特征,绿色植物中主要类群的形态、结构和生殖,植物在食品、产品、美学和科学文化方面的应用以及对人类和其他生物的危害。

8.1 Plants and Botany

8.1.1 Plants

Plants are living organisms belonging to the kingdom Plantae, including familiar organisms such as trees, flowers, herbs, bushes, grasses, vines, ferns, mosses, and green algae (Fig. 8-1, (a) - (c)). the term "plant" implies an association with certain traits, such as being multicellular, possessing cellulose, and having the ability to carry out photosynthesis. In 2010, it is estimated that there are 300 - 315 thousand species of plants on Earth, of which some 260 - 290 thousand are seed plants. Plants are mainly divided into several groups such as land plants, green plants (land plants plus green algae) and Archaeplastida (green plants plus red algae, cyanobacteria and glaucophyte algae). Green plants obtain most of their energy from sunlight via photosynthesis using chlorophyll contained in chloroplasts, which gives them their green color. Plants range in size from tiny floating duckweed, the size of your pencil eraser, to giant sequoia trees as tall as the length of a football field. A wide range of colors stand out against the basic green we associate with plants. Bright spots of color are often flowers and fruit, where the colors may serve as attractants for animals. Plants are adapted to live in just about any environment. There are plants that eat animals (Fig. 8-1, (d)), plants that are parasites, plants that don't carry on photosynthesis, and plants that strangle other plants. They show a remarkable variety of form, function, and activity.

Most plants have common criteria:

① They are anchored to soil, rocks, bark, and other solid objects;

② They have hard, woody tissues that support the plants and allow them to stand upright;

③ They are green and carry on photosynthesis.

Fig. 8-1 Several kinds of plants
(a) lotus flowers; (b) a peony flower; (c) pines; (d) the Venus flytrap, a species of carnivorous plant

8.1.2 Botany

Botany, also called plant science, or plant biology is a branch of biology that involves the scientific study of plant life. It covers a wide range of scientific disciplines including structure, growth, reproduction, metabolism, development, diseases, chemical properties, and evolutionary relationships among taxonomic groups. It is related to many disciplines such as plant physiology, plant genetics, plant cell engineering, plant gene engineering, plant ecology, plant cell biology and so on.

8.2 Main Types of Green Plants and Their Characteristics

Green plants are composed of land plants and green algae. Land plants (embryophytes) are divided into non-vascular plants (bryophytes) and vascular plants (tracheophytes). Here, land plants are introduced.

8.2.1 Non-vascular Plants (Bryophytes)

There are three types of bryophytes: mosses, liverworts and hornworts (Fig. 8-2). Mosses grow as a carpet composed of many parts. Each individual moss plant is composed of a central stalk less than 5 centimeters tall with short, leaflike structures that are sites of photosynthesis. If you look at the individual cells in the leafy portion of a moss, you can distinguish the cytoplasm, cell wall, and chloroplasts. You may also distinguish the nucleus of the cell. This nucleus is haploid(n), meaning that it has only one set of chromosomes. In fact, every cell in the moss plant body is haploid.

They shows primitive or ancestral characteristics, and have several things in common:

① They are small, compact, slow-growing, green plants with motile sperm that swim to eggs.

② There are no well-developed vascular tissues and no mechanism that would provide support to large, upright plant parts such as stems.

③ They do not have true leaves or roots as are found in more highly evolved plants.

④ Nutrients are obtained from the surfaces upon which they grow or from rainwater.

⑤ Their life cycle consists of two stages. The gametophyte (gamete-producing plant) dominates the sporophyte (spore-producing plant).

(a)　　　　　　　(b)　　　　　　　(c)

Fig. 8-2　Non-vascular plants (bryophytes)
(a) liverworts; (b) hornworts; (c) mosses

8.2.2　Vascular Plants (Tracheophytes)

Vascular plants are those plants that have vascular tissue, a specialized conducting system consisting mostly of phloem (food-conducting tissue) and xylem (water-conducting tissue) and cambium. Xylem tissue is the innermost part of the tree trunk or limb, and phloem is outside the cambium. The cambium is positioned between the xylem and the phloem. Cambium cells go through a mitosis, and two cells form. One cell remains cambium tissue, and the other specializes to form vascular tissue. If the cell is on the inside of the cambium ring, it becomes xylem;

if it is on the outside of the cambium ring, it becomes phloem. As cambium cells divide again and again, one cell always remains cambium, and the other becomes vascular tissue. Thus, the tree constantly increases in diameter. Vascular plants have true stems (Fig. 8-3), leaves, and roots.

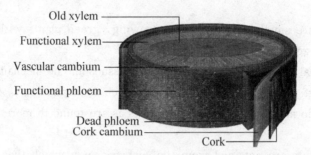

Fig. 8-3 A cross section of the woody stem of a tree (Ruth Bernstein, Stephen Bernstein, 1996)

Xylem makes up most of what we call wood, the approximate age of a tree can be determined and something about the enviroment can be learned from the growth rings on the cut surface. Wide rings indicates good growth years with high rainfall, whereas narrow rings indicate poor growth and low rainfall.

8.2.2.1 Non-Seed-Producing Vascular Plants

Today, the non-seed producing vascular plants are limited to ferns and fern-like plants. They have vascular tissue, being evolutionary links between the nonvascular bryophytes and the highly successful land plants. These plants display many common features:

① Their diploid sporophytes produce haploid spores by meiosis, which develop into gametophytes. The gametophytes produce sperm and egg in antheridia and archegonia. Sperms require water through which they swim in order to reach eggs.

② Fertilization results in a multicellular embryo that gets its nutrients from the gametophyte. The embryo eventually grows into the sporophyte.

③ The sporophyte generation is more dominant in the life cycle than the gametophyte and is usually highly branched.

④ All have well-developed vascular tissue to transport water and nutrients.

⑤ Many have the ability to support upright, above-ground plant parts, for example, leaves.

8.2.2.2 Seed-Producing Vascular Plants

Seed-producing vascular plants are divided into two types such as gymnosperms and angiosperms.

(1) Gymnosperms

The gymnosperms are a group of naked seed-bearing plants, also called perennials, which mean "naked seed" plants, whose seeds are produced on the bare surface of woody, leaflike structures (the female cone). For example, conifers are cone-bearing plants such as pine trees (Fig. 8-1). Cones are reproductive structures. The male cone produces pollen grains. Each of these small dust-like particles contains a sperm nucleus. The female cone is usually larger than the male cone and produces eggs. The process of getting the pollen from the male cone to the female cone is called pollination. Fertilization occurs when the sperm cell from the pollen unites with the egg cell in the archegonium. This may occur months or even years following pollination. The fertilized egg develops into an embryo within the seed. Producing seeds out in the open makes this very important part of the life cycle vulnerable to adverse environmental influences, such as attack by insects, birds, and other organisms. The gymnosperms have true roots, stems, leave and seeds.

(2) Angiosperms

The angiosperms (flowering plants), which mean that the seeds are enclosed within the surrounding tissues of the ovary. The ovary and other tissues mature into a protective structure known as the fruit. Many of the foods we eat are the seed-containing fruits of angiosperms, for example, green beans, melons, tomatoes, and apples. The angiosperms are also called flowering plants. They have true roots, stems, leaves, flowers and fruits. Almost all the trees around us are flowering plants. You can probably recognize some plants from their flowers or fruits. In colder parts of the world, most angiosperms lose all their leaves during the fall. Such trees (Fig. 8-1) are said to be deciduous. However, the majority of angiosperms are not trees; they are small plants like grasses, weeds, vines, houseplants, garden plants, wildflowers, and green houseplants (Fig. 8-1).

The flower of an angiosperm is the structure that produces sex cells and other structures that enable the sperm cells to get to egg cells. The important parts of the flower are the female pistil (composed of the stigma, style, and ovary) and the male stamen (composed of the anther and filament). Any flower that has both male and female parts is called a perfect flower (Fig. 8-4); a flower containing just female or just male parts is called an imperfect flower. Any additional parts of the flower are called accessory structures such as sepals and petals, because fertilization can occur without them. Sepals form the outermost whorl of the flower and serve a protective function. Petals increase the probability of fertilization. Before the sperm cell in the pollen can join with the egg cell inside the ovary, it must somehow get to the egg. This is the process called pollination. Some flowers with showy petals are adapted to attracting insects, which unintentionally carry the pollen to the pistil. Others have become adapted for wind pollination. The important thing is to get the genetic information from one parent to the other.

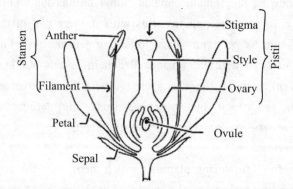

Fig. 8-4 The structures of a perfect flower
The stamen is the male organ and the pistil is the female organ.

There are over 300,000 kinds of plants that produce flowers, fruits, and seeds. The mighty oak, the delicate rose and the expensive orchid are all flowering plants. Botanists classify all angiosperms into two groups: dicots or monocots. The names dicot and monocot refer to a structure in the seeds of these plants. If the embryo has two seed leaves (cotyledons), the plant is a dicot; those with only one seed leaf are the monocots. A peanut is a dicot; lima beans and apples are also dicots; grass, lilies, and orchids are all monocots.

8.3 Uses of Plants

8.3.1 Food

Plants or their parts or components can be used as foods of humans and some animals (Fig. 8-5). For example, cereal grains such as corn, wheat, rice; potato, and legumes such as peas, beans, soybeans, and peanuts; vegetables, spices, and certain fruits, nuts, herbs, and edible flowers; beverages such as coffee, tea, wine, beer and alcohol, many other natural beverages such as fruit juices and cider. Sugar from sugar cane and sugar beet; cooking oils from maize, soybean,

Fig. 8-5 Plants or their parts or components can be used as foods of humans

rapeseed, safflower, sunflower, olive and others; food additives including gum arabic, starch and pectin. Livestock animals including cows, pigs, sheep, and goats feed on cereal plants.

8.3.2 Products

Wood is used for buildings, shelter, furniture, paper, cardboard, musical instruments and sports equipment. For example, papyrus, a grasslike plant, and some trees such as aspens and pines are used to make paper; walls in homes may be decorated with wallpaper, and many paints are derived from plant extracts. clothing is often made from cotton, fiber and synthetic fibers derived from cellulose, such as rayon and acetate. Fuels from plants include firewood, peat and many other biofuels. Green plants are the origin for the coal, oil, and gas. Medicines are derived from plants such as aspirin and vincristine, a medicine that is effectively used to fight leukemia in children. In addition, there still are other products: herbal supplements such as ginkgo and feverfew, pesticides such as nicotine and pyrethrins, drugs such as opium and cocaine, poisons such as ricin and curare, natural dyes, pigments, waxes, soaps, paints, shampoos, perfumes, cosmetics, toothpaste, rubber, lubricants, plastics, inks, chewing gum, hemp rope and so forth (Fig. 8-6). Plants are also a primary source of basic chemicals for the industrial synthesis of organic chemicals used in studies and experiments.

Fig. 8-6 A bookshelf, books, a desk and so on

8.3.3 Aesthetic Uses

Thousands of plant species are cultivated for aesthetic purposes and to provide shade and privacy, modify temperatures, reduce wind, abate noise and prevent soil erosion. People use cut flowers, dried flowers and houseplants. Lawn grasses, shade trees, ornamental trees, shrubs, vines, herbaceous perennials and bedding plants are used in outdoor gardens. Images of plants are often used in art, architecture, humor, language, photography, money, stamps, flags and coats of arms. Ornamental plants have sometimes changed the course of history, as in tulipomania. Plants are the basis of a multi-billion dollar per year tourism industry which includes travel to botanical gardens, historic gardens, national parks, tulip festivals, rainforests, forests with colorful autumn leaves and so on. Sensitive plant and resurrection plant are examples of plants sold as novelties (Fig. 8-7).

Fig. 8-7　Hong Kong sea park

8.3.4 Scientific and Cultural Uses

Basic biological research has often been done with plants, for example, the pea plants for genetics. Tree rings are an important method of dating in archeology and serve as a record of past climates. Plants are used as national and state emblems such as state trees and state flowers. Numerous world records are held by plants.

Plants are often used as memorials, gifts and to mark special occasions such as births, deaths, weddings and holidays. Plants figure prominently in mythology, religion and literature. Gardening is the most popular leisure activity in the US. Working with plants or horticulture therapy is beneficial for rehabilitating people with disabilities.

8.3.5 Negative Effects

Weeds are plants. Some of introduced plants from abroad become invasive plants, damaging existing ecosystems by displacing native species, causing billions of dollars in crop losses and increasing the cost of production and the use of chemical means. Plants may cause harm to people and animals. Many plants are poisonous, for example, toxalbumins are fatal to most mammals. Several plants cause skin irritations when touched, such as poison ivy. Certain plants contain psychotropic chemicals, including tobacco, cocaine and opium. Both illegal and legal drugs derived from plants may have negative effects on the economy, affecting worker productivity and law enforcement costs. Some plants cause allergic reactions when ingested, while other plants cause food intolerances that negatively affect health.

Vocabulary

fern /fɜːn/ *n*. 蕨类植物
mosses /ˈmɔsis/ *n*. 苔藓植物
liverwort /ˈlivəwəːt/ *n*. 苔类，地衣
hornwort /ˈhɔːnwəːt/ *n*. 金鱼藻
archaeplastida *n*. 原始色素体生物
glaucophyte *n*. 灰胞藻门
sequoia /siˈkwɔiə/ *n*. 红杉
embryophyte /ˈembriəfait/ *n*. 有胚植物
bryophyte /ˈbraiəfait/ *n*. 苔藓类植物
tracheophytes *n*. 维管植物
vascular tissues 维管束组织
gametophyte /gəˈmiːtəˌfait/ *n*. （植）配子体
sporophyte /ˈspɔːrəfait/ *n*. 孢子体

xylem /ˈzailem/ *n*. 木质部
phloem /ˈfləuem/ *n*. 韧皮部
cambium /ˈkæmbiəm/ *n*. 形成层，新生组织
gymnosperm /ˈdʒimnəuˌspəːm/ *n*. 裸子植物
angiosperm /ˈændʒiəuˌspəːm/ *n*. 被子植物
perennial /pəˈrɛniəl/ *n*. 多年生植物 *adj*. 多年生的
cone /kəun/ *n*. （松树的）球果
archegonium /ˌɑːkiˈgəuniəm/ *n*. 颈卵器
pollination /ˌpɔliˈneiʃən/ *n*. 授粉
flowering plants 显花植物
ovary /ˈəuvəri/ *n*. 子房，卵巢

Chapter 1　Reading Materials of Life Sciences

pistil /ˈpistil/, carpel /ˈkɑːpl/ *n*. 雌蕊，心皮
stamen /ˈsteimen/ *n*. 雄蕊
dicots or monocots 双子叶植物，单子叶植物
papyrus /pəˈpaiərəs/ *n*. 纸莎草
aspen /ˈæspən/ *n*. 山杨，白杨
rayon /ˈreiɔn/ *n*. 人造丝
acetate /ˈæsiˌteit/ *n*. 醋酸盐，醋酸纤维
peat /piːt/ *n*. 泥炭块，泥煤
aspirin /ˈæspərin/ *n*. 阿司匹林
vincristine /viŋˈkristiːn/ *n*. 长春新碱
ginkgo /ˈgiŋkgəu/ *n*. 银杏树
opium /ˈəupiːəm/ *n*. 鸦片
ricin /ˈraisin, ˈrisin/ *n*. 蓖麻毒素
novelty /ˈnɔvəlti/ *n*. 新奇，新颖，新鲜，小巧廉价的商品
archeology /ˌɑːkiˈɔlədʒiː/ *n*. 考古学
emblem /ˈembləm/ *n*. 象征
intolerance /inˈtɔlərəns/ *n*. （对食物、药物等）不耐性
sepal /ˈsepəl/ *n*. 萼片
carnivorous /kɑːˈnivərəs/ *a*. 肉食性的

Exercises

1. Matching Questions.

(1) dicotyledon　　　　　a. anther
(2) monocotyledon　　　 b. type of plant characterized by its two seed leaves
(3) produces sperms　　 c. ovary
(4) produces eggs　　　　d. don't possess vascular tissue
(5) vascular plants　　　 e. possess vascular tissue
(6) non-vascular plants　 f. type of plant characterized by its single seed leaf
(7) gymnosperms　　　　g. enclosed seed-bearing plants
(8) angiosperms　　　　　h. naked seed-bearing plants
(9) seed plants　　　　　i. plants that produce flowers and fruits
(10) flowering plants　　　j. seed-bearing plants

2. Fill in the blanks with the appropriate words you have just learned in this unit.

(1) Plant _____ is the study of the extermal form of the plant body.
(2) _____ tissues are made of two or more kinds of functionally related cells.
(3) Vascular tissues consist of _____, _____ and _____.
(4) _____ surround the stomates of the shoot system.
(5) The ovule and the ovary of one flowering plant develop into a _____ and a _____, respectively.
(6) Wood is _____ xylem.

(7) A _____ root system is typical of monocots.

(8) A _____ system is typical of most dicots and conifers characterized by one major root from which other roots branch.

(9) _____ are microscopic extensions from the root that participate in absorption.

(10) _____ plant organs such as roots, stems and leaves are made up of three tissue systems including _____, _____ and _____.

3. Multiple Choice Questions.

(1) Angiosperms are different from all other plants because only they have (   ).
   A. vascular system   B. flowers
   C. a life cycle that involves alteration of generations
   D. seeds   E. a sporophyte phase

(2) Which term below (   ) includes all others in the list?
   A. seed plant   B. angiosperm   C. fern
   D. gymnosperm   E. vascular plant

(3) Angiosperms and gymnosperms have the following in common except (   ).
   A. vascular tissue   B. seeds   C. pollen
   D. ovaries   E. ovules

(4) The photosynthetic symbiont of a lichen is most commonly a (an) (   ).
   A. very small vascular plant   B. moss
   C. fungus   D. alga   E. mold

(5) Which one of the following characteristics do fungi share? (   )
   A. Production of mushroom.
   B. Multicellular body plan.
   C. Heterotropic nutrition.
   D. Mutual symbiosis with plants.
   E. Alteration of generations.

(6) Non-vascular plants (bryophytes) have some common characteristics except (   ).
   A. small, short and green
   B. the gametophyte dominates the sporophyte
   C. true leaves like that of angiosperms
   D. motile sperm

(7) Pollens and seeds can be economically dispersed by some media (   ).

Chapter 1　Reading Materials of Life Sciences　　　　　　　　　　　　　　• 109 •

  A. insects　　　　　B. birds and humans　　C. wind

  D. water　　　　　E. nothing

 (8) Which of the following is common to all four major plant groups? (　　)

  A. Cuticle.　　　　　B. Pollen.　　　　　C. Seeds.

  D. Flowers.　　　　　E. Vascular tissue.

 (9) How are a flowering plant and its pollinators mutually rewarded by their relationship? (　　)

  A. The plant grows vigorously and its pollinators randomly play around it.

  B. The plant makes its pollen grains more efficiently pollinated and its pollinators obtain food from it.

  C. The plant produces eggs and its pollinators lay eggs.

  D. The plant produces eggs and its pollinators lay ova.

  E. The plant grows well, so do its pollinators.

 (10) All of plants in nature have the following characteristics (　　).

  A. cell, cell wall and nucleus　　　　　B. cell, tissue system

  C. cell wall and organ　　　　　　　　D. photosynthesis

4. Reading Comprehension.

Plant Tissue Culture

 Plant tissue culture is the culture and maintenance of plant cells or organs in sterile, nutritionally and environmentally supportive conditions. In commercial settings, tissue culture is primarily used for plant propagation, called micropropagation.

 Many early tissue culture experiments failed, at least in part, because they were not maintained in sterile conditions. Isolated fragments of a plant are extremely disadvantaged in comparison to pathogenic competitors that are complete and unhindered, in reality flourishing, in a culture environment. Bacteria, fungi, and other organisms which can be resisted to some degree by a whole plant can easily outcompete an isolated fragment of tissue from the plant in the relatively nutrient-rich environment of a culture flask. Therefore it is necessary to remove competitor organisms from the culture and isolate it in aseptic conditions. This is usually done by chemical surface sterilization of the explant with an agent such as bleach at a concentration and for a duration that will kill or remove pathogens without injuring the plant cells beyond recovery. The medium and culture flasks used must also be sterile.

 When a small portion of a plant is isolated, it is no longer able to receive nutrients or hormones from the plant, and these must be provided to allow its growth in vitro. The composition of the nutrient medium is for the most part similar, although the exact components and quantities will vary for different species and purposes of culture. Types and amounts of hormones vary greatly. In addition, the culture must be provided with the ability to excrete the waste products of cell metabolism. This is accomplished by culturing on or in a defined culture medium, which is periodically replenished.

Tissue cultures require a stable and suitable climate. Thus light and temperature must be more carefully regulated than would be the case for a whole plant. Tissue culture offers numerous significant benefits over traditional propagation methods: ① Propagation can be much more rapid than by traditional means; ② It may be possible *in vitro* to multiply plants that are very difficult to propagate by cuttings or other traditional methods; ③ Large numbers of genetically identical clones may be produced; ④ Seeds can be germinated with no risk of damping off predation; ⑤ Under certain conditions, plant material can be stored in vitro for considerable periods of time with little or no maintenance; ⑥ Tissue culture techniques are used for virus eradication, genetic manipulation, somatic hybridization and other procedures that benefit propagation, plant improvement, and basic research.

Questions for Discussion:

(1) What is Plant Tissue Culture?

(2) What conditions do plant cells need to multiply *in vitro*?

(3) Why is plant tissue culture done?

5. English Speech or Contest.

If you would like to attend an English speech or contest in your college or University, choose one any topic in biology in which you are greatly interested to make a speech within 5 – 7 minutes in class.

Unit 9　Animals and Their Uses

导语　动物是多细胞真核生物中的一大类群，归于动物界，包括鱼类、两栖类、爬行类、鸟类、哺乳类、水母、软体动物类和节肢动物类等。动物学是研究动物的的基本结构、系统分类及其生命活动规律的生物学分支学科，涉及不同动物类群的形态、结构、分类、生态、演化、保护、利用等有关动物学的基本理论、知识和技能。

本单元主要介绍动物特征、结构、组织、器官系统(尤其心血管系统和生殖系统)及其在农业、运输、食品、助人、体育运动、产品开发和科技文化等方面的应用。

9.1 Animals and Zoology

Animals are a major group of multicellular, eukaryotic organisms of the kingdom Animalia. Today there are at least 4 million known species of animals. They are not only adapted to live in just about any environment, but also vary in size from microscopic rotifers, 40 micrometers in length, to giant blue whales, 30 meters long. They show a remarkable variety of form, function, activity, sizes, colors and body shapes. They are classified into two groups such as vertebrates, including fish, amphibians, reptiles, birds and mammals, and invertebrates, composed of jellyfish, segmented worms, molluscs and arthropods based on backbones (Fig. 9-1).

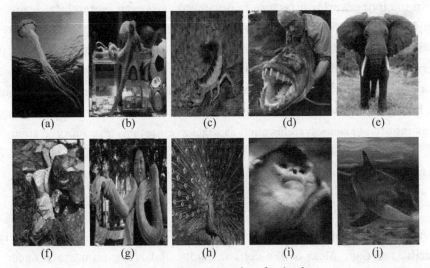

Fig. 9-1 Some examples of animals

(a) Jellyfish; (b) Paul the octopus; (c) Scorpion; (d) Megapiranha paranensis (1.5 m, 45 kg) and a man; (e) Afirica elephant (the largest land mammal); (f) Giant salamander; (g) gloden python (3 m, 15 kg) and a womam; (h) Peacock; (i) Yunnan snub-nose; (j) Blue whale (biggest mammal, also the biggest animal that ever lived on Earth)

Animals have several characteristics that set them apart from other living things: ① Animals are eukaryotic and mostly multicellular, which separates them from bacteria and most protists; ② Animals are heterotrophic, generally digesting food in an internal chamber, which separates them from plants and algae; ③ Animals lack rigid cell walls, which distinguish them from plants, algae and fungi; ④ All animals are motile, if only at certain life stages; ⑤ In most animals, embryos pass through a blastula stage; ⑥ Usually the bodies of animals are composed of groups of cells organized into tissues, organs, and organ systems.

Zoology is the branch of biology that is related to the animal kingdom, including the structure, embryology, evolution, classification, habits, and distribution of all animals. the modern areas of zoological investigation: anatomy, physiology, histology, embryology, teratology and so on.

9.2 Animal Structures

In the living world, structure is organized at several hierarchical levels. For example, the development of a fertilized egg into a newborn child requires an average of 41 rounds of mitosis, in which the cells produced by mitosis enter different pathways of differentiation. As a result, some become blood cells, some become muscle cells, and so on. More than 100 kinds of differentiated cells in the vertebrate animal are organized into tissues; the tissues into organs; groups of organs into the various systems such as digestive system, excretory system, etc. Many systems make up one whole organism body. Therefore, human structure has a hierarchy from atom level to organism level like Fig. 9-2.

9.2.1 Animal Tissues

A tissue is a cooperative unit of many very similar specilized cells that perform a specific function. Most of the cells in multicellular organism are grouped into tissues. The major types of animal tissues are as follows: ① Epithelial tissue, covering body surfaces and lining internal organs, for example, the epidermis and some epithelia in lung, kidney and intestines. ② Muscle tissue, functioning in movement, for example, skeletal muscle attached to bone by tendons, cardiac muscle forming the contractile tissue of the heart, and smooth muscle lacking striations and being in the walls of intestinal organs such as digestive tract and arteries. ③ Connective tissue, binding and supporting other tissues. They

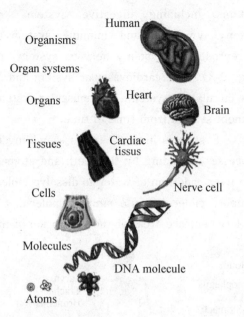

Fig. 9-2 Human hierarchy from atom level to organisms level

consists of a sparse population of cells scattered through a nonliving substance called matrix. There are several major types of connective tissue such as loose connective tissue under the skin, adipose tissue, blood, dense connective tissue composed of three types such as fibrous connective tissue, cartilage and bone. ④ Nerve tissue, forming a communication and coordination system in the body and inculding neurons and glia.

9.2.2 Animal Organs

An organ consists of several tissues adapted to perform specific functions as a group. All animals except sponges have organs. The stomach, for example, are mainly composed of three types of tissues such as epithelial tissue, connective tissue and muscle tissue. Higher animals have the following major organs: heart, lung, kidney, stomach, brain and so on.

9.2.3 Organ Systems of Animal Body

An organ system is a group of several organs that work together in a coordinated fashion to perform a vital body function. In vertebrate, there are ten major organ systems including digestive system, respiratory system, cardiovascular system, lymphatic and immune system, excretory system, endocrine system, reproductive system, nervous system, muscular system and skeletal system (Fig. 9-3). The cardiovascular system and lymphatic system are sometimes called the circulatory system. The muscular system and skeletal system are called the movement system from time to time.

(1) The Digestive System is involved in disassembling food molecules. This involves several processes: grinding by the teeth and stomach, emulsification of fats by bile from the liver, addition of water to dissolve molecules, and enzymatic action to break complex molecules into simpler molecules for absorption. The intestine provides a large surface area for the absorption of nutrients because it is

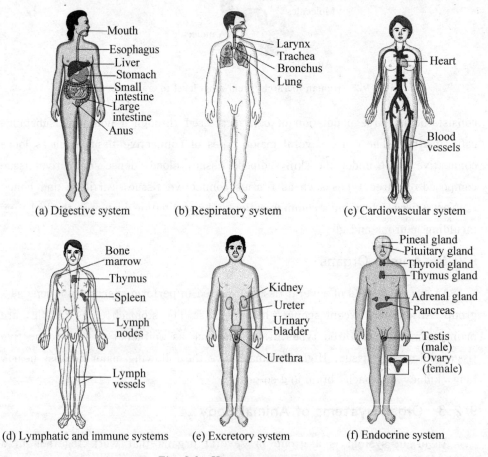

Fig. 9-3 Human organ systems

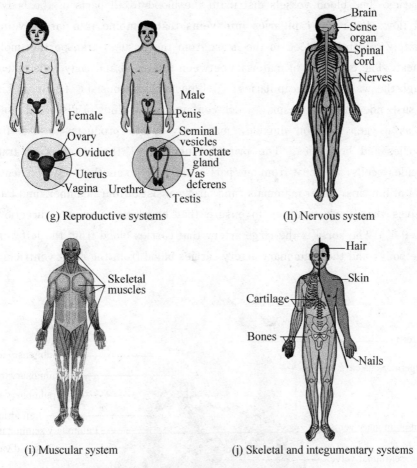

Fig. 9-3 Human organ systems (continues)

(2) The Respiratory System consists of the lungs and associated tubes that allow air to enter and leave the lungs. The diaphragm and muscles of the chest wall are important in the process of breathing. In the lungs, tiny sacs called alveoli provide a large surface area in association with capillaries, which allows for rapid exchange of oxygen and carbon dioxide.

(3) The Cardiovascular System consists of the heart and blood vessels. The heart pumps blood into arteries, which distribute blood to organs. It flows into successively smaller arteries until it reaches tiny vessels called capillaries, where materials are exchanged between the blood and tissues through the walls of the

capillaries. The blood vessels distribute the blood to all parts of the body. The blood flows from the capillaries into veins that combine into larger veins that ultimately return the blood to the heart from the tissues, transporting molecules and heat. The exchange of materials between the blood and body cells takes place through the walls of the capillaries. ① Blood. blood consists of several kinds of cells suspended in fluid plasma, which contains many kinds of dissolved molecules such as oxygen, carbon dioxide, nutrients, waste products, disease-fighting antibodies and hormones. The primary function of the blood is to transport molecules, cells, and heat from one part of the body to another. ② The heart. the hearts of humans, other mammals, and birds consist of four chambers and four sets of valves that work together to ensure that blood flows in one direction only (Fig. 9-4). The aorta is the large artery that carries blood from the left ventricle to the body, and the pulmonary artery carries blood from the right ventricle to the

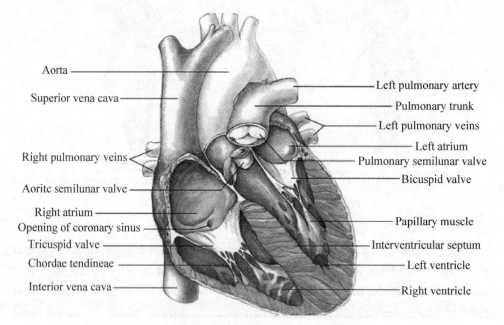

Fig. 9-4 The anatomy of the heart (Eldon, Frederick, 2004)

The heart consists of two thin-walled chambers called atria that contract to force blood into the two ventricles. When the ventricles contract, the atrioventricular valves (bicuspid and tricuspid) close, and blood is forced into the aorta and pulmonary artery. Semilunar valves in the aorta and pulmonary artery prevent the blood from flowing back into the ventricles when they relax.

lungs. The semilunar valves prevent blood from flowing back into the ventricles. If the atrioventricular or semilunar valves are damaged or function improperly, the efficiency of the heart as a pump is diminished, and the person may develop an enlarged heart or other symptoms. Malfunctioning heart valves are often diagnosed because they cause abnormal sounds as the blood passes through them. These sounds are referred to as heart murmurs. Similarly, if the muscular walls of the ventricles are weakened because of infection, damage from a heart attack, or lack of exercise, the pumping efficiency of the heart is reduced and the person develops symptoms that may include chest pain, shortness of breath, or fatigue. The pain is caused by an increase in the amount of lactic acid in the muscle because the heart muscle is not getting sufficient blood to satisfy its needs. It is important to understand that the muscle of the heart receives blood from coronary arteries that are branches of the aorta. It is not nourished by the blood that flows through its chambers. If heart muscle does not get sufficient oxygen for a period of time, the portion of the heart muscle not receiving blood dies. Shortness of breath and fatigue result because the heart is not able to pump blood efficiently to the lungs, muscles, and other parts of the body. The right side of the heart receives blood from the general body and pumps it through the pulmonary arteries to the lungs, where exchange of oxygen and carbon dioxide takes place and the blood returns from the lungs to the left atrium. This is called pulmonary circulation. The larger, more powerful left side of the heart receives blood from the lungs, delivers it through the aorta to all parts of the body, and returns it to the right atrium by way of veins. This is known as systemic circulation. Both circulatory pathways are shown in Fig. 9-5. The systemic circulation is responsible for gas, nutrient, and waste exchange in all parts of the body except the lungs. ③ Arteries and veins. arteries and veins are the tubes that transport blood from one place to another within the body. Arteries carry blood away from the heart because it is under considerable pressure from the contraction of the ventricles. The contraction of the walls of the ventricles increases the pressure in the arteries. A typical pressure recorded in a large artery while the heart is contracting is about 120 millimeters of mercury. This is known as the systolic blood pressure. The pressure recorded while the heart is relaxing is about 80 millimeters of mercury. This is known as the diastolic blood pressure. A blood pressure reading includes both numbers and is recorded as 120/80. (Originally, blood pressure was measured by how high the pressure of the blood would cause a column of mercury [Hg] to rise in a tube. Although the devices used today have dials or digital readouts and contain no mercury, they are still calibrated in mmHg. Some of the smaller arteries, called arterioles, may contract or relax to regulate the flow of blood to specific parts of the body. Veins collect blood from the capillaries and return it to the heart. The

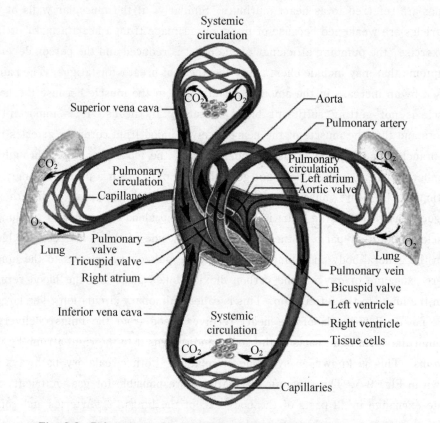

Fig. 9-5 Pulmonary and systemic circulation (Eldon, Frederick, 2004)
The right ventricle pumps oxygen-poor blood to the two lungs by way of the pulmonary arteries, where it receives oxygen and turns bright red. The blood is then returned to the left atrium by way of four pulmonary veins. This part of the circulatory system is known as pulmonary system. The left ventricle pumps oxygen-rich blood by way of the aorta to all parts of the body except the lungs. This blood returns to the right atrium, depleted of its oxygens by way of the superior vena cava from the head region and the inferior vena cava from the rest of the body. This portion of the circulatory system is known as systemic circulation. Blue indicates oxygen-poor blood. Red indicates oxygen-rich blood.

pressure in these blood vessels is very low. Because of the low pressure, veins must have valves that prevent the blood from flowing backward, away from the heart. Veins are often found at the surface of the body and are seen as blue lines.

④ Capillaries. capillaries are tiny, thin-walled tubes that receive blood from arterioles. They are so small that red blood cells must go through them in single file. They are so numerous that each cell in the body has a capillary located near it. It is estimated that there are about 1,000 square meters of surface area represented by the capillary surface in a typical human. Each capillary wall consists of a single layer of cells and therefore presents only a thin barrier to the diffusion of materials between the blood and cells.

(4) The Lymphatic System is a network of fine vessels interspersed with lymph nodes. The immune system is responsible for safeguarding the body from foreign substances and disease-causing microorganisms. Its products are white blood cells including lymphocytes and antibodies, which are transported throughout the body in blood stream and lymphatic vessels. The thymus, bone marrow and spleen also play important roles in the immune system.

(5) The Excretory System is a filtering system of the body. The kidneys consist of nephrons into which the circulatory system filters fluid. Most of this fluid is useful and is reclaimed by the cells that make up the walls of these tubules. Materials that are present in excess or those that are harmful are allowed to escape. Some molecules may also be secreted into the tubules before being eliminated from the body.

(6) The Endocrine System consists of endocrine glands, hormones and target tissues. The endocrine glands, e. g., pancreas, discharge hormones into the blood, and the blood transports the hormones into the parts of the body. Hormones regulate such activities as digestion, metabolism, growth, water balance, heart rate and reproduction.

(7) The Reproductive System is a system of organs within an organism which work together for the purpose of reproduction. Many non-living substances such as fluids, hormones, and pheromones are also important accessories to the reproductive system. For example, a human reproductive system contains the external genitalia (penis and vulva) and a number of internal organs including the gamete producing gonads (testicles and ovaries). Diseases of the human reproductive system are very common and widespread, particularly communicable

sexually transmitted diseases. Most other vertebrate animals have generally similar reproductive systems consisting of gonads, ducts, and openings.

However, there is a great diversity of physical adaptations and reproductive strategies in every group of vertebrates. Animals reproduce in different ways: ① asexual reproduction, such as budding, fission and fragmentation; ② sexual reproduction, in which there is an important step, fertilization, divided into external fertilization and internal fertilization. For example, Human reproduction takes place as internal fertilization by sexual intercourse. During this process, the erect penis of the male is inserted into the female's vagina until the male ejaculates semen, which contains sperm, into the female's vagina. The sperm then travels through the vagina and cervix into the uterus or fallopian tubes for fertilization of the ovum. Upon successful fertilization and implantation, gestation of the fetus then occurs within the female's uterus for approximately nine months, this process is known as pregnancy in humans. Gestation ends with birth, the process of birth is known as labor. Labor consists of the uterus muscle contraction, the cervix dilating, and the baby passing out the vagina. Human's babies and children are nearly helpless and require high levels of parental care for many years. One important type of parental care is the use of the mammary glands in the female breasts to nurse the baby. Humans have a high level of sexual differentiation.

In addition to differences in nearly every reproductive organ, numerous differences typically occur in secondary sexual characteristics.

① Sex determination. When a human egg or sperm cell is produced, it contains 23 chromosomes. Twenty two of these are autosomes that carry most of the genetic information used by the organism. The other chromosome is a sex-determining chromosome. There are two kinds of sex-determining chromosomes: the X chromosome and the Y chromosome. The two sex-determining chromosomes, X and Y, do not carry equivalent amounts of information, nor do they have equal functions. X chromosomes carry typical genetic information about the production of specific proteins in addition to their function in determining sex. For example, the X chromosome carries information on blood clotting, color vision, and many other characteristics. The Y chromosome, however, appears to be primarily concerned with determining male sexual differentiation and has few other genes on it. When a human sperm cell is produced, it carries 22 autosomes and a sex-determining chromosome. Unlike eggs, which always carry an X chromosome, half the sperm cells carry an X chromosome and the other half carry a Y chromosome. If an X-carrying sperm cell fertilizes an X-containing egg cell, the resultant embryo will develop into a female. A typical human female has an X chromosome from each parent. If a Y-carrying sperm cell fertilizes the egg, a male embryo develops. It is the presence or absence of the Y-chromosome that determines the sex of the developing individual.

② Male and female fetal development. Development of embryonic gonads begins very early during fetal growth. First, a group of cells begins to differentiate into primitive gonads at about week 5. By week 6 or 7 if a Y chromosome is present, a gene product from the chromosome will begin the differentiation of these gonads into testes; they will develop into ovaries beginning about week 12 if two X chromosomes are present (Y chromosome is absent). As soon as the gonad has differentiated into an embryonic testis at about week 8, it begins to produce testosterone. The presence of testosterone results in the differentiation of male sexual anatomy and the absence of testosterone results in the differentiation into female sexual anatomy.

③ Sexual maturation of young adults. Following birth, sexuality plays only a small part in physical development for several years. Culture and environment shape the responses that the individual will come to recognize as normal behavior. During puberty, normally between 12 and 14 years of age, increased production of sex hormones causes major changes as the individual reaches sexual maturity. Generally, females reach puberty six months to a year before males. After puberty, humans are sexually mature and have the capacity to produce offspring. Female children typically begin to produce quantities of sex hormones from the hypothalamus, pituitary gland, ovaries and adrenal glands at 8 or 13 years of age. During puberty, hormone production becomes regulated so that ovulation and menstruation take place on a regular monthly basis in most women, although normal cycles may vary from 21 to 45 days. As girls progress through puberty curiosity about the changing female body form new feelings leads to self-investigation. Studies have shown that sexual activity such as manipulation of the clitoris, which causes pleasurable sensations, is performed by a large percentage of young women. Self-stimulation, frequently to orgasm, is a common result. This stimulation is termed masturbation, and it should be stressed that it is considered a normal part of sexual development. Orgasm is a complex response to mental and physical stimulation that causes rhythmic contractions of the muscles of the reproductive organs and an intense frenzy of excitement. Males typically reach puberty about two years later (ages 10 to 15) than females, but puberty in males also begins with a change in hormone levels.

④ Spermatogenesis. The term spermatogenesis is used to describe gametogenesis that takes place in the testes of males. Spermatogenesis in human males takes place continuously throughout a male's reproductive life, although the number of sperm produced decreases as a man ages. Sperm counts can be taken and used to determine the probability of successful fertilization. A man must be able to release at least 100 million sperms at one insemination to be fertile. A healthy male probably releases about 300 million sperms with each ejaculation during sexual intercourse.

⑤ Oogenesis. Oogenesis refers to the production of egg cells. This process starts during prenatal development of the ovary, when diploid oogonia cease dividing by mitosis and enlarge to become primary oocytes. All of the primary oocytes that a woman will ever have are already formed prior to her birth. At this time they number approximately 2 million, but that number is reduced by cell death to between 300,000 to 400,000 cells by the time of puberty.

⑥ Fertilization and pregnancy. In most women, a secondary oocyte is released from the ovary about 14 days before the next menstrual period. The menstrual cycle is usually said to begin on the first day of menstruation. Therefore, if a woman has a regular 28-day cycle, the cell is released approximately on day 14 (Fig. 9-6). If a woman normally has a regular 21-day menstrual cycle, ovulation would occur about day 7 in the cycle. If a woman has a regular 40-day cycle, ovulation would occur about day 26 of her menstrual cycle. Some women, however, have very irregular menstrual cycles, and it is difficult to determine just when the oocyte will be released to become available for fertilization. Once the cell is released, it is swept into the oviduct and moved toward the uterus. If sperm are present, they swarm around the secondary oocyte as it passes down the oviduct, but only one sperm penetrates the outer layer to fertilize it and cause it to complete meiosis II. The other sperm contribute enzymes that digest away the protein and mucus barrier between the egg and the successful sperm. During this second meiotic division, the second polar body is pinched off and the ovum (egg) is formed. Because chromosomes from the sperm are already

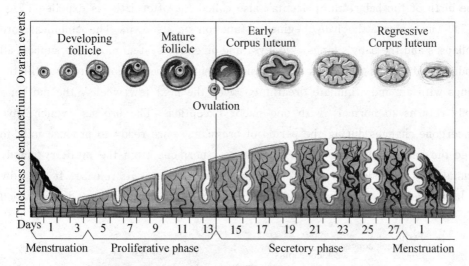

Fig. 9-6 The ovarian and uterine cycles in human females

The release of a secondary oocyte (ovulation) is timed to coincide with the thichening of thw lining of the uterus. The uterine cycles in human females involves the preparation of the uterine wall to receive the embyo if fertilization occurs. Knowing how these two cycles compare, it is possible to determine when pregnancy is most likely to happen.

inside, they simply intermingle with those of the ovum, forming a diploid zygote. Through embryonic development, human embryo forms, and the structure of the body is refined. At the end of about 9 months, hormone changes in the mother's body stimulate contractions of the muscles of the uterus during a period prior to birth called labor. These contractions are stimulated by the hormone oxytocin. The contractions normally move the baby head first through the vagina, or birth canal. Following this, the uterine contractions become stronger, and shortly thereafter the baby is born (Fig. 9-7). In some cases, the baby becomes turned in the uterus before labor. If this occurs, the feet or buttocks appear first. Such a birth is called a breech birth. This can be a dangerous situation because the baby's source of oxygen is being cut off as the placenta begins to separate from the mother's body. Occassionally, a baby may not be able to be born normally because of the position of the baby in the uterus, the location of the placenta on the uterine wall, the size of the birth canal, the number of babies in the uterus, or many other reasons. A common procedure to resolve this problem is the surgical removal of the baby through the mother's abdomen. This procedure is known as a cesarean. Following the birth of the baby, the placenta, also called the afterbirth, is expelled (Fig. 9-7). Once born, the baby begins to function on its own. The umbilical cord collapses and the baby's lungs, kidneys, and digestive system must now support all bodily needs. This change is quite a shock, but the baby's loud protests fill the lungs with air and stimulate breathing. Over the next few weeks, the mother's body returns to normal, with one major exception. The breasts, which have undergone changes during the period of pregnancy, are ready to produce milk to feed the baby. Following birth, prolactin, a hormone from the pituitary gland, stimulates the production of milk, and oxytocin stimulates its release. If the baby is breast-fed, the stimulus of the baby's sucking will prolong the time during which

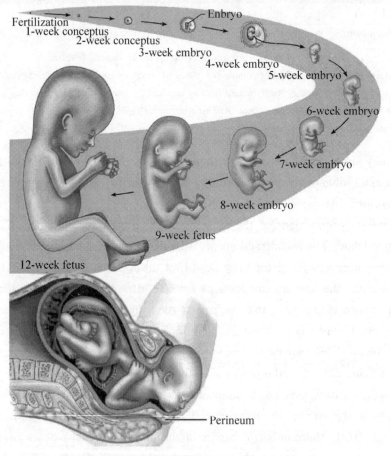

Fig. 9-7 Human pregnancy, development and birth

milk is produced. This response involves both the nervous and endocrine systems. In some cultures, breast-feeding continues for two to three days, and the continued production of milk often delays the reestablishment of the normal cycles of ovulation and menstruation. Many people believe that a woman cannot become pregnant while she is nursing a baby. However, because there is so much variation among women, relying on this as a natural conception-control method is not a good choice. Many women have been surprised to find themselves pregnant again a few months after delivery.

⑦ Types of birth control. Different contraception methods suit different people. The best choice is what feels right for you and your partner, and what will be most effective in preventing an unwanted pregnancy and sexually transmitted infections (Fig. 9-8). The oral contraceptive pill, contraceptive patch, vaginal contraceptive ring, contraceptive injection, intrauterine device (IUD) and surgical methods are all effective methods of contraception that may be a good option for women. You may want to consider non-hormonal contraceptive methods or natural methods if you think that the pill, patch, ring, IUD or injection aren't the right contraceptive choice for you. Don't forget about dual protection. Use a condom as well to protect against sexually transmitted infections (STIs).

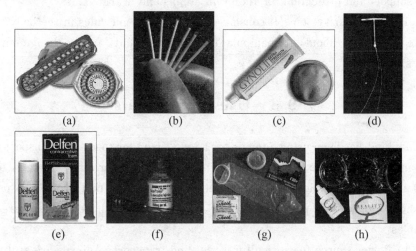

Fig. 9-8　Primary contraceptive methods used today

(a) pills for oral contraception; (b) contraceptive implants; (c) diaphragm and spermicidal jelly; (d) intrauterine device; (e) spermicidal vaginal foam; (f) depo-provera injection; (g) male condom; and (h) female condom

⑧ Sexually transmitted diseases (STDs). Sexually transmitted diseases are infections that you can get from having sex with someone who has the infection. The causes of STDs are bacteria, parasites and viruses. There are more than 20 types of STDs, including chlamydia, gonorrhea, genital herpes, HIV/AIDS, HPV, syphilis and trichomoniasis. Most STDs affect both men and women, but in many cases the health problems they cause can be more severe for women. If a pregnant woman has an STD, it can cause serious health problems for the baby. If you have an STD caused by bacteria or parasites, your health care provider can treat it with antibiotics or other medicines. If you have an STD caused by a virus, there is no cure. Sometimes medicines can keep the disease under control. Correct usage of latex condoms greatly reduces, but does not completely eliminate the risk of catching or spreading STDs.

(8) Nervous system. It is an organ system containing a network of neurons that coordinate the actions of an animal and transmit signals between different parts of its body. Human nervous system contains the brain, spinal cord, sense organ and nerves. It works together with the endocrine system to coordinate body activities.

(9) Skeletal system. It mainly consists of bones and cartilage. It can provide body support and protection for the brain, lungs and heart.

(10) Muscular system. It consists of the skeletal muscles in the body. It can enable us to move about, to manipulate our environment, and to change our facial expressions.

9.3 Uses of Animals

Mankind has been using animals for a long time, for food, for transport and as companion, to help you hunt and work, to protect things or other animals, to hear other animal, for people who can not see or are deaf, to find people, to produce medicines, to develop products and for scientific research, etc. Here are some examples:

(1) Power source for agricultural uses and transport. Animals are still widely used as a major power source in many countries. Land preparation, weed management, crop threshing and transport are all undertaken using animal power. Oxen and buffalo are the most popular animal power source for agricultural

practices although horses, donkeys, mules and camels are used in many countries for transportation.

(2) Foods from animal organs to bodies. Animals can be used for foods such as muscle (beef, chicken, pork, duck and mutton) (Fig. 9-9,(a)), fat, liver, heart, kidney, head, trotter, chick paw, intestines. or for food producers making eggs, milk, butter, cheese.

(3) Work. Police dogs, horse and cart, guide dogs for the blind (Fig. 9-9,(b)).

(4) Companion. Pets such as cats, dogs, hamsters, parrots (Fig. 9-9,(c)), etc.

(5) Sport. Jumping, greyhound races, racing pidgons and equestrian (Fig. 9-9,(d)).

Fig. 9-9 Uses of animals in human work, companion and sport
(a) Beijing roast duck; (b) guide dogs for the blind; (c) parrots; (d) horse and equestrian

(6) Products and merchandises. There are many kinds of products and merchandises made from animals (Fig. 9-10).

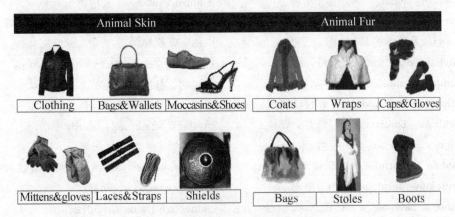

Fig. 9-10 Products and merchandises

(7) Medicines. For example, bear gall, chicken gizzards, the hairy antlers of a young stag or deerhorn, Roe Po, snake venom, scorpion venom, fish oil mainly containing EPA and DHA.

(8) Scientific and cultural uses. Some animals are used in scientific research and on national flags as symbols, for example, an eagle on a cactus, eating a snake on Mexico national flag. The proper use of animals in research is an honorable and essential contribution to the improvement of human and animal lives. For example, some animals are used to discover treatments and cures for many serious and often fatal diseases of both humans and animals. Animal studies have played an essential role in developing vaccines, medications, even surgical techniques and biological laws. For instance, rabbits are used in addictive drugs, cancer treatments, genetic models, organ transplants and whooping cough vaccine; primates are done in AIDS, Alzheimer's disease, in vitro fertilization and Polio vaccine.

Vocabulary

rotifer /ˈrɔtifə/ n. 轮虫
vertebrate /ˈvɜːtəbrit/ n. 脊椎动物 adj. 脊椎动物的
amphibian /æmˈfibiːən/ n. 两栖动物 adj. 两栖动物的
reptile /ˈreptail/ n. 爬行动物
mammal /ˈmæməl/ n. 哺乳动物
invertebrate /inˈvɜːtəbrit/ n. 无脊椎动物 adj. 无脊椎的
jellyfish /ˈdʒeliːfiʃ/ n. 水母，海蜇
mollusc /ˈmɔləsk/ n. 软体动物
arthropod /ˈɑːθrəpɔd/ n. 节肢动物
backbone /ˈbækˌbəun/ n. 脊骨，脊柱
embryo /ˈembriəu/ n. 胚胎
blastula /ˈblæstjulə/ n. 胚囊
teratology /ˌterəˈtɔlədʒi/ n. 畸形学
octopus /ˈɔktəpəs/ n. 章鱼
scorpion /ˈskɔːrpiən/ n. 蝎子

megapiranha paranensis 巨型食人鱼
salamander /ˈsæləmændə/ n. 火蜥蜴
Giant salamander 娃娃鱼，大鲵
python /ˈpaiθɔn, -θən/ n. 巨蟒
peacock n. 孔雀
snub /snʌb/ adj. 短而扁的
Yunnan snub-nose 云南滇金丝猴
hierarchical /ˌhaiəˈrɑːkikl/ adj. 分等级的，分阶梯的
excretory /eksˈkriˌtəuri/ adj. 排泄的，分泌的，有排泄功能的
epithelial /ˌepiˈθiːljəl/ adj. 上皮的
cardiac /ˈkɑːdiːˌæk, ˈkɑrdiˌæk/ adj. 心脏的
striation /straiˈeiʃən/ n. 条痕，条纹状
artery /ˈɑːtəri/ n. 动脉
connective tissue 结缔组织
adipose tissue 脂肪组织

cartilage /ˈkɑːtlidʒ/ n. 软骨 adj. 软骨的
cardiovascular system 心血管系统
lymphatic system 淋巴系统
endocrine system 内分泌系统
emulsification /iˌmʌlsifiˈkeiʃən/ n. 乳化作用
diaphragm /ˈdaiəfræm/ n. 膈膜,横膈膜
alveolus /ælˈviələs/ n. 肺泡 (pl. alveoli)
capillary /ˈkæpəleri:/ n. 毛细血管
aorta /eiˈɔːtə/ n. 大动脉
atrium /ˈɑːtriəm/, atria /ˈeitriə/ (复数) n. 心房
ventricle /ˈventrikl/ n. 心室
tricuspid /traiˈkʌspid/ adj. 有三个尖头的 n. (心脏的) 三尖瓣
pulmonary artery 肺动脉
atrioventricular valve 房室瓣
heart murmurs n. 心杂音
lactic acid /læktik æsid/ 乳酸
vein /vein/ n. 静脉
systolic blood pressure 收缩压
diastolic /ˌdaiəsˈtɔlik/ blood pressure 舒张压
arteriole /ɑːˈtiriəul/ n. 小动脉
spleen /spliːn/ n. 脾脏,坏脾气
thymus /ˈθaiməs/ n. 胸腺
nephron /ˈnefrɔn/ n. 肾单位,肾元
reclaim /riˈkleim/ n. 回收利用
genitalia /dʒeniˈteiljə/ n. 外生殖器
gonad /ˈgɔnæd/ n. 性腺,生殖腺
testis /ˈtestis/ n. 睾丸
ejaculate /iˈdʒækjəlet/ vt. 射精

fallopian tubes 输卵管
testosterone /tesˈtɔstərəun/ n. 睾丸激素,睾丸酮
hypothalamus /ˌhaipəuˈθæləməs/ n. 下丘脑
pituitary /piˈtjuːiteri/ n. 垂体
adrenal /əˈdriːnəl/ adj. 肾上腺的; n. 肾上腺
ovulation /ˌɔvjuˈleiʃən/ n. 排卵
menstruation /ˌmenstruˈeiʃən/ n. 月经
clitoris /ˈklaitəris/ n. 阴蒂
spermatogenesis /ˌspəːmətəuˈdʒenisis/ n. 精子发生
ovary /ˈəuvəri/ n. 卵巢,子房
oocyte /ˈəuəsait/ n. 卵母细胞
uterus /ˈjuːtərəs/ n. 子宫
oogenesis /ˌəuəˈdʒenisis/ n. 卵子发生
ovum /ˈəuvəm/ n. (生)卵,卵子
placenta /pləˈsentə/ n. 胎盘
cervix /ˈsəːviks/ n. 子宫颈
menopause /ˈmenəpɔːz/ n. 绝经期,更年期
contraception /ˌkɔntrəˈsepʃən/ n. 避孕,节育
chlamydia /kləˈmidiə/ n. 衣原体
genital herpes 生殖器疱疹
trichomoniasis /ˈtrikəməˈnaiəsis/ n. 滴虫病
cartilage /ˈkɑːtlidʒ/ n. 软骨
hamster /ˈhæmstə/ n. 仓鼠
chicken gizzards 鸡胗
Roe Po 獐宝
whooping cough vaccine 百日咳疫苗

Exercises

1. Matching Questions.

Write the letter of the phrase that best matches the numbered on the left. Use each only once.

(1) vertebrates
(2) primates
(3) blastula
(4) zoology
(5) epidermis
(6) stomach
(7) circulatory system
(8) uterus
(9) testis
(10) pregnancy

a. some higher animals which includes humans, monkeys and apes.
b. some animals are named for their backbone, consisting of a series of vertebrae.
c. a branch of biology, the scientific study of animals
d. a hollow sphere of cells formed during an early stage of embryonic development in animals
e. a muscular, hollow, dilated part of the alimentary canal as an important digestive organ in some animals.
f. a kind of animal and plant tissues, which the outer layer of the skin or covers plants' leaves, flowers, roots and stems.
g. a major female reproductive sex organ of most mammals including humans.
h. an organ system that distributes blood and lymph.
i. a female mammal including woman carrying one or more fetus or embryo in her womb.
j. The male reproductive gland in an external scrotum, producing sperms.

2. Fill in the blanks with the appropriate words you have just learned in this unit.

(1) _____ is a group of functionally related organs.

(2) _____ are bundles and sheets of contractile cells that shorten when stimulated, providing force for controlled movement.

(3) Movement is often accomplished as rigid skeletal elements are pulled in one direction or another by the contraction of attached _____.

(4) Some _____ may receive information concerning changes in the external environment.

(5) Hormones are released by the _____ system.

Chapter 1 Reading Materials of Life Sciences · 131 ·

(6) A barrier between an animal's body and the external environment is provided by the _____ system.

(7) Two main hallmarks of _____ are Hair and mammary glands.

(8) Positive and negative-feedback _____ similar in the response to change in the body's homeostatic set point.

(9) The _____ rid the body of waste products and maintain balanced internal concentrations of salt and water.

(10) _____ protects animals from foreign substances and invading micro-organisms.

3. Multiple Choice Questions.

(1) Which generates variability among individuals in a sexual animal population? (   )
    A. The circulatory system.   B. The immune system.
    C. The reproductive system.   D. The skeletal and muscular systems.
    E. The excretory systems.

(2) Which of the following regulates and coordinates all bodily functions? (   )
    A. The digestive and immne systems.
    B. The reproductive and endocrine systems.
    C. The reproductive and nervous systems.
    D. The endocrine and nervous systems.
    E. The integumentary and nervous systems.

(3) As the dimensions of an animal increase, its surface area (   ).
    A. increases at a greater rate than its volume
    B. increases at a less rate than its volume
    C. increases at the same rate as its volume
    D. decreases
    E. and volume remain the same

(4) When you are at rest, 90 percent of the energy you are expending goes to (   ).
    A. transmit nervous system impulses   B. power digestion
    C. maintain an elevated body temperature   D. power respiration
    E. power your muscles

(5) Reptiles are much more extensively adapted to land life than amphibians in that they (   ).

A. go through a larval stage   B. have a complete digestive system

C. have barins and legs   D. lay eggs enclosed in shells

E. are endothermic

(6) (　　) of the following answers includes all others.

A. Butterfly   B. Invertebrate   C. Insect

D. Arthropod   E. Octopus

(7) (　　) of the following animals is not included in human ancestry.

A. A primate   B. A bony fish   C. A bird

D. An amphibian   E. A reptile

(8) Vertebrates are named for (　　) of the following structures.

A. nervous system   B. mammary glands   C. backbone

D. hair   E. heart

(9) Why is it a mistake for somebody who eats pork chops to order them "rare" in a restaurant? (　　)

A. Pork chops are not delicious.

B. Pork chops are very expensive.

C. Pork chops are very precious.

D. Pork chops can easily be cooked at home.

E. Incomplete cooking does not kill nematodes and other parasites that might be present in the meat.

4. **Translate the following Chinese into English.**

动物除了海绵都具有器官，器官由几种组织组成，适应于整体执行特异功能。例如：胃主要由上皮组织、结缔组织和肌肉组织三种组织组成。高等动物具有下列主要器官：心脏、肝脏、肺、脾脏、胃、肾脏和大脑等。器官系统是由几个一起协调活动的器官形成的一个有机整体，发挥极其重要的机体功能。人类具有十大重要的器官系统，诸如消化系统、呼吸系统、心血管系统、淋巴和免疫系统、排泄系统、内分泌系统、生殖系统、神经系统、肌肉系统和骨骼系统。

Unit 10　GMF and Biosafety

导语　生物技术或者生物工程是应用生物学和工程学的原理，把生物材料、生物所特有的功能定向改造成具有特定性状的生物新品种或者生产生物产品的综合技术,包括基因工程、细胞工程、发酵工程和酶工程。现代生物技术发展到高通量组学(omics)芯片技术、基因与基因组人工设计与合成生物学等系统生物技术。其核心技术是基因工程,广泛应用在生物医学、工业、农业、环保、卫生、食品等领域。

本单元主要概述生物技术及其主要类型,基因工程技术研发转基因生物及其种类、转基因食品及其安全性。

10.1 Biotechnology and Its Main Types

Biotechnology is a field of applied biology that involves the use of living organisms and bioprocesses in engineering, technology, medicine and other fields requiring bioproducts. It can be divided into genetic engineering, cell engineering, enzyme engineering, fermentation engineering and so on. Its core is genetic engineering. Genetic engineering is the direct human manipulation of an organism's genome using modern DNA technology. It involves the introduction of foreign DNA or genes into the organism of interest, called host by different methods based on its different types. An organism that is generated through the introduction of recombinant DNA is considered to be a genetically modified organism (GMO) which contain genes from at least one unrelated organism such as a virus, plant, or other animal. The first organisms genetically engineered were bacteria in 1973 and then mice in 1974. Insulin-producing bacteria were commercialized in 1982 and genetically modified food has been sold since 1994. Genetic engineering techniques have been applied in numerous fields including medicine, research, agriculture, industry and so on. Medicines such as insulin and human growth hormone are now produced in bacteria, experimental mice such as the oncomouse and the knockout mouse are being used for research purposes, and insect resistant and herbicide tolerant crops have been commercialized. Genetically engineered plants and animals called pharming are also being developed. In 2009, the FDA approved the sale of the pharmaceutical protein antithrombin produced in the milk of genetically engineered goats. Genetically modified foods (GMF) are foods derived from GMO. GMF have distinct advantages over traditional foods and great values, but more and more attention to their biosafety has been paid by some people up to date.

10.2 Genetically Modified Organism (GMO)

10.2.1 Four Elements of Genetic Engineering

(1) Exogenous genes. They are also called foreign genes, the desired genes, the genes of interest or target genes, which are the genes to be studied or introduced to host.

(2) Vectors. They are nucleic acid molecules carrying desired genes to hosts, e.g., plasmids and viruses. Based on their functions, they can be divided into the following types: cloning vectors, expression vectors, shuttle vectors and sequencing vectors. They have some common properties such as multiple cloning sites with several single endonuclease sites, selective marker, origin of replication and so forth.

(3) Enzymes. They include endonucleases and ligases. For example, *Eco* RI, *Bam* HI, *Pst* I and so on.

(4) Hosts. Generally, they should possess the following advantages such as rapid growth in cheap medium, harmness, feasible transformation by DNA and stability.

10.2.2 Procedure for Generating GMO

The procedure for generating GMO consists of several steps (Fig. 10-1):

(1) Isolate the desired gene. Using polymerase chain reaction (PCR), restriction endonucleases, chemical synthesis, gene-tagging, genomic or cDNA pool, chromosome walking, molecular hybridization, map-based cloning, yeast two hybrid system, electric cloning and so on. For example, If the gene is short enough and its base sequence is known, it may be synthesized in the laboratory from separate nucleotides. If the gene is too long and complex, it is cut from the chromosome with restriction endonucleases, which only cut DNA at certain base sequences and work inside the DNA like molecular scissors that do not cut the DNA straight across but in a zig-zag pattern that leaves one strand slightly longer than its complement. The short nucleotide sequence that sticks out and remains unpaired is called a sticky end because it can be reattached to another complementary strand. DNA segments have been successfully cut from rats, frogs,

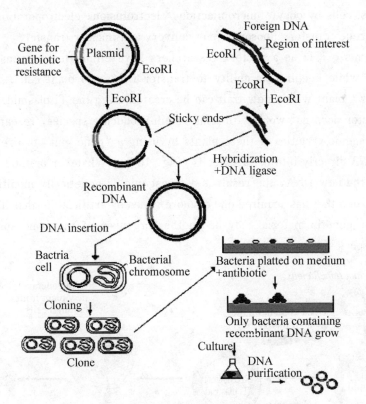

Fig. 10-1 The procedure for generating GMB

bacteria, and humans.

(2) Recombine the desired gene with a vector *in vitro*. The desired gene can be spliced into vectors to make a recombinant molecule by the different links of cohesive ends, blunt ends, homo-polymer tails and artificial linkers. For example, the desired gene with its "sticky end" is spliced into a plasmid with the same sticky end.

(3) Introduce the gene into the hosts. The recombinant molecule can be introduced into hosts by different methods. For example, it can be introduced into microbial hosts by transformation (Fig. 10-1), transduction, transfection and electroporation; and into plant host cells by vector transfer methods such as *Agrobacterium-mediated transformation* (Fig. 10-2) and virus, direct gene transfer methods, e.g., gene gun (Fig. 10-3) and PEG, and transformation via germ line system including pollen-tube-pathway and ovary microinjection; and into

animal host cells by oocyte microinjection, electrofusion, electroporation, sperm-mediated gene transfer, liposome gene delivery and nuclear transfer.

In terms of $_p$Ti as a vector, researchers have eliminated its tumor-causing properties while keeping its ability to transfer DNA into plant cells. Fig. 10-2 shows how a plant with a new trait can be created using the Ti plasmid. Although the Ti vector does not work with many grain-producing species, researchers can make transgenic varieties of these plants by using a "gene gun" to fire pieces of foreign DNA directly into cultured cells (Fig. 10-3). Whatever method is used to introduce the new DNA, the result is a transgenic or genetically modified (GM) organism, one that has acquired one or more genes by artificial means. The source of the new genetic material may be another organism of the same species or a different species.

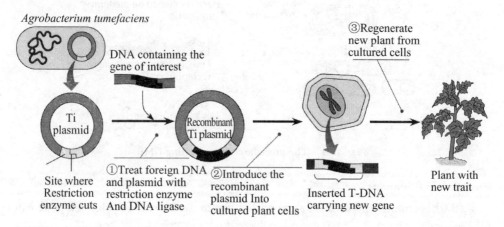

Fig. 10-2 Transgenic plant using the Ti plasmid as a vector

1. With the help of a restriction enzyme and DNA ligase, the gene for the desired trait (orange) is inserted into a segment of the Ti plasmid.
2. The recombinant plasmid is put into a plant cell, where the T-DNA carrying the new gene integrates into a plant chromosome.
3. The recombinant cell is cultured and grows into a whole plant.

In 1980, the first transgenic mouse was produced by microinjection of DNA into fertilized eggs. A recombinant viral DNA construct was successfully integrated into the mouse genome, but it was rearranged and did not express. The first visible phenotypic change in transgenic mice was described in 1982 by Richard Palmiter and Ralph Brinster. They successfully integrated and expressed the rat

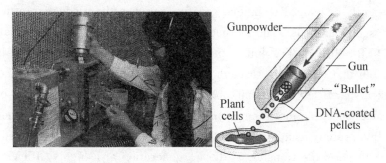

Fig. 10-3 Using a "gene gun" to insert DNA into plant cells
(Campbell, Beece, 2002)

This researcher is preparing to use a modified 22-caliber gun to shoot foreign DNA into plant cells growing in culture.

growth hormone gene coding sequence in transgenic mice. These transgenic mice called "super mice", some of which grew to be twice the size of normal siblings (Fig. 10-4). Since then, trangenics has been a rapidly growing field, with many technological advances and refinements.

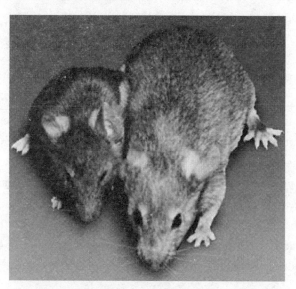

Fig. 10-4 "Super" mouse produced by microinjection
of DNA into fertilized eggs

A transgenic mouse (right) expressing the rat growth hormone gene under control of the mouse metallothionein gene promoter grew to twice the size of a normal mouse (left).

A recently developed technique greatly improves the production efficiency of large transgenic animals. The method is called linker-based sperm-mediated gene transfer (LB-SMGT). The linker protein, a monoclonal antibody (mAbC) is a basic protein that binds DNA through an ionic interaction allowing exogenous DNA to be linked specifically to sperm. mAbC is reactive to a surface antigen on sperm of all tested species, including pig, mouse, chicken, cow, goat, sheep, and human. In one study using pigs, the transgene was successfully integrated into the genome with germline transfer to the F1 generation at a highly efficient rate of 37.5%.

(4) Analyze the transformed host cells to generate the positive transformants carrying the desired gene. Once inside the host cell, the genes may be replicated, along with the rest of the DNA to clone the "foreign" gene, or they may begin to synthesize the encoded protein, which is used to generate GMO or manufacture products. The positive transformants can be identified by analyzing the stable integration and expression of the transgene by some methods such as screening by reporters, resistance to antibiotics including insertional inactivation, nucleic acid hybridization composed of Southern blot and Northern blot, immunoblotting analyses such as Westeron blot and ELISA, electrophoresis, RE cleavage, PCR, DNA sequencing, DNA microarrays and qPCR.

Example 1

If we know that our hypothetical gene V contains the sequence TAGGCT, a biochemist can use nucleotides labeled with a radioactive isotope to synthesize a short single strand of DNA with a complementary sequence (ATCCGA). This sort of labeled nucleic acid molecule is called a nucleic acid probe because it is used to find a specific gene of other nucleotide sequence within a mass of DNA (In practice, a probe molecule would be considerably longer than six nucleotides). The DNA sample to be tested is treated with heat or alkali to separate the DNA strands. When the radioactive DNA probe is added to these strands, it tags the correct molecule by hydrogen-bonding to the complementary sequence in the gene of interest.

Nucleic acid probes are powerful tools that do not require the targeted DNA to be a pure preparation. Fig. 10-5 shows how a researcher might actually use such a probe to find a bacterial clone carrying a gene of interest among the thousands of other clones produced by shotgun cloning. In the figure, a collection of bacterial clones, each consisting of millions of identical cells, appear as visible colonies growing on a solid nutrient medium. Once the researcher identifies the desired clones, the cells can be grown further and the gene of interest isolated in large amounts.

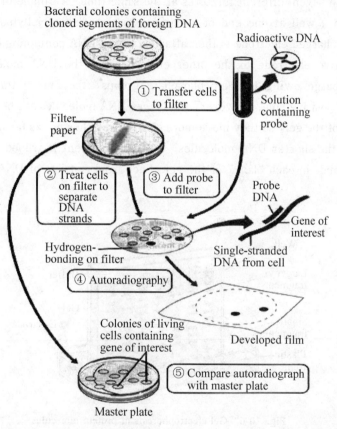

Fig. 10-5 The identification of a bacterial clone carrying a specific gene by a DNA probe (Campbell, Reece, 2002)

① A piece of filter paper is pressed against the colonies, blotting cells onto the paper.
② The paper is treated to break open the cells and separate the strands of their DNA, which stick to the paper.
③ A solution containing molecules of the probe is poured on the paper. The probe molecules bond to any complementary DNA sequences, and excess probe is rinsed off.
④ The paper is laid on photographic film, and any radioactive areas expose the film.
⑤ The developed film, an autoradiograph, is compared with the master culture plate to determine which colonies carry the desired gene.

Example 2

Gel electrophoresis is a method for sorting macromolecules—proteins or nucleic acids—primarily on the basis of their electric charge and size. Fig. 10-6 shows how we would use gel electrophoresis to separate the various protein molecules in seven different mixtures at the same time. A sample of each mixture is placed in a well at one end of a flat gel, a thin slab of jellylike material. A negatively charged electrode is then attached to the DNA containing end of the gel and a positive electrode to the other end. Because the DNA molecules have a negative charge owing to their phosphate groups, they move through the gel toward the positive pole. However, the longer DNA molecules are held back by the molecules of the gel, so they move more slowly, and thus not as far in a given time period, as the shorter DNA molecules. When the current is truned off, we see a series of bands in each "lane" of the gel. Each band consists of DNA molecules of one size.

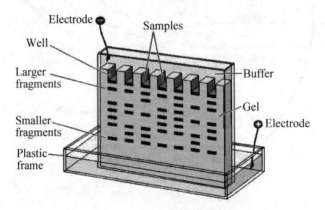

Fig. 10-6 Gel electrophoresis of protein molecules

(5) Breed for homozygotes (GMO). For eukaryotes, the positive transformants mentioned above very often are heterozygotes, so their self-fertilization is needed to get homozygotes (GMO).

10.2.3 The Achievements of Genetically Modified Organisms (GMO)

10.2.3.1 Genetically Modified Microbes (GMM)

The first organisms genetically engineered were bacteria in 1973. Genetically modified bacteria are used to produce the protein insulin to treat diabetes. Similar bacteria have been used to produce clotting factors to treat haemophilia, and human growth hormone to treat various forms of dwarfism. For example, Insulin-producing bacteria (Fig. 10-7) were commercialized in 1982 and genetically modified food has been sold since 1994.

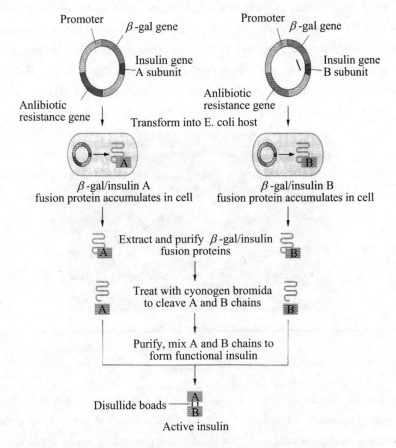

Fig. 10-7 The method used to synthesize recombinant human insulin

Synthetic oligonucleotides encoding the insulin A and B chains are inserted at the tail end of a cloned *E. coli* β-galactosidase (*β-gal*) gene. These recombinant plasmids are transferred to hosts, where the *β-gal* insulin fusion protein is synthesized and accumulates in the host cells. Fusion proteins are extracted from the host cells and purified. Insulin chains are released from the *β-gal* by treatment with cyanogen bromide, and the insulin subunits are purified and mixed to produce a functional insulin.

10.2.3.2 Genetically Modified Plants (GMP)

In most cases, the aim of GMP is to introduce a new trait to the plant which does not occur naturally in this species. Examples include resistance to certain pests, diseases or environmental conditions, or the production of a certain nutrient or pharmaceutical agent. Genetically modified plants have been developed commercially to improve shelf life, disease resistance, herbicide resistance and pest resistance. Plants engineered to tolerate abiotic stresses like drought, frost and nitrogen starvation or with increased nutritional value (e.g., Golden rice, Fig. 10-8) were developed in 2011. Future generations of GM plants are intended to be suitable for harsh environments, and produce increased amounts of nutrients

Fig. 10-8 Golden rice that produce provitamin-A (beta-carotene) as a means of alleviating vitamin A deficiencies

or even pharmaceutical agents, or are improved for the production of bioenergy and biofuels. Due to high regulatory and research costs, the majority of genetically modified crops in agriculture consist of commodity crops, such as soybean, maize, cotton and rapeseed. However, commercial growing was reported in 2009, of smaller amounts of genetically modified sugar beet, papayas, squash, sweet pepper, tomatoes, petunias, carnations, roses and poplars. Recently, some research and development has been targeted to enhancement of crops that are locally important in developing countries, such as insect-resistant cowpea for Africa and insect-resistant eggplant for India. Genetically modified plants have also been used for bioremediation of contaminated soils. Mercury, selenium and organic pollutants such as polychlorinated biphenyls (PCBs) have been removed from soils by transgenic plants containing genes for bacterial enzymes. The People's Republic of China was the first country to allow commercialized transgenic plants, introducing a virus-resistant tobacco in 1992. The first genetically modified crop approved for sale in the US in 1994 was the FlavrSavr tomato, which had a longer shelf life. In 1994, the European Union approved tobacco engineered to be resistant to the herbicide bromoxynil, making it the first commercially genetically engineered crop marketed in Europe. In 2009, 11 different transgenic crops were grown commercially on 330 million acres (134 million hectares) in 25 countries such as the USA, Brazil, Argentina, India, Canada, China, Paraguay and South Africa; transgenic maize was grown commercially in 11 countries, including the United States, Brazil, Argentina, South Africa, Canada, the Philippines and Spain; GM maize (BVLA430101) and GM rice varieties (Huahuil and BTShanyou63) were approved by Ministry of Agriculture, China to be grown commercially.

10.2.3.3 Genetically Modified Animals (GMA)

Now, there are transgenic animals such as transgenic mice, fish (Fig. 10-9), cat, rabbits, chickens, sheep, monkeys, goats, pigs, and cows. Transgenic animal can be used in breed improvement, drug production and screening, gene therapy, gene function and regulation, organ transplantation and as bioreactor. For instance, scientists might identify and clone a gene that causes the development of larger muscles in one variety of cattle and transfer it to other cattle

Fig. 10-9　GloFish, the first genetically modified animal to be sold as a pet

or even to sheep. Another type of transgenic animal is one engineered to be a pharmaceutical "factory" — a producer of a large amount of a rare biological substance for medical use. In most cases to date, a gene for a desired human protein, such as a hormone or blood-clotting factor, has been added to the genome of a farm mammal in such a way that the gene's product is secreted in the animal's milk. It can then be purified, usually more easily than from a cell culture or a transgenic plant. Human proteins produced by farm animals may or may not be structurally identical to the natural human proteins, so they have to be tested very carefully to make sure they will not cause allergic reactions or other adverse effects in patients receiving them. Also, the health and welfare of farm animals carrying genes from humans and other foreign species are important issues; problems such as low fertility or increased susceptibility to disease are not uncommon.

10.3　Genetically Modified Foods (GMF)

Genetically modified foods (GMF) are foods derived from genetically modified organisms (GMO). GM foods were first put on the market in the early 1990s. For example, Flavr Savr, a genetically modified tomato, was the first commercially grown genetically engineered food to be granted a license for human consumption (Fig. 10-10). Typically, genetically modified foods are transgenic plant products: soybean, corn, canola, and cotton seed oil. The most widely commercialized GM crops are herbicide-tolerant soybeans and insect-resistant maize and cotton. GM foods are classified into one of three generations. First-generation crops have enhanced input traits, such as herbicide tolerance, better insect resistance, and better tolerance to environmental stress. Second-generation crops include those with added-value output traits, such as nutrient enhancement for animal feed.

Third-generation crops include those that produce pharmaceuticals, improve the processing of bio-based fuels, or produce products beyond food and fiber. Animal products have also been developed, although as of July 2010 none are currently on the market.

(1) In 2006, a pig was controversially engineered to produce omega—3 fatty acids through the expression of a roundworm gene. Researchers have also developed a genetically-modified breed of pigs that are able to absorb plant phosphorus more efficiently, and as a consequence the phosphorus content of their

manure is reduced by as much as 60%.

Fig. 10-10　USDA plant physiologist with examples of bioengineered tomatoes

(2) Fish, e.g., salmon, carp (Fig. 10-11), trout and tilapia were also genetically modified. In addition, various genetically engineered micro-organisms are routinely used as sources of enzymes for the manufacture of a variety of processed foods. These include alpha-amylase from bacteria, which converts starch to simple sugars, chymosin from bacteria or fungi that clots milk protein for cheese making, and pectinesterase from fungi which improves fruit juice clarity. It has been estimated that 60% to 70% of food products in retail stores already contain genetically modified ingredients.

10.4　GMF Biosafety

Critics have objected to GM foods on several grounds, including possible safety issues (potential toxicity, allergenicity and nutritional aspects), ecological concerns (e.g., biodiversity and superweeds), and economic concerns raised by

Fig. 10-11 Transgenic carp
Up: transgenic carp expressing growth hormone gene;
Down: control carp

the fact that these organisms are subject to intellectual property law, and concerns regarding risks associated with GMF. Worldwide studies showed that consumers' concerns about GMF are rising and acceptance of GMF varies among countries. Many consumers in European countries and Japan have difficulty accepting GMF. However, the results of other studies show that the consumers are much less worried about GMF in the US and many developing countries. The findings from several recent consumer surveys in China are mixed. On one extreme, a study in Guangzhou, Shanghai, and Beijing by Greenpeace claimed that GM foods were generally not accepted by Chinese consumers. On the other extreme, other two studies showed that Chinese consumers were willing to pay a premium for GM foods (80%).

For GMF safety, on one hand, its risk assessment must be done, including direct or indirect, immediate or delayed effects, taking into account any cumulative and long-term effects on human health and the environment. A risk assessment comprises four steps: hazard identification, hazard characterisation, exposure assessment and the integrative risk characterisation. For example, the risk assessment of GM plants and products should take account of the following aspects: ① the characteristics of the donor and recipient organisms, ② the genetic modification and its functional consequences, ③ the potential environmental impact,

④ agronomic characteristics, ⑤ the potential toxicity and allergenicity of gene products, plant metabolites and the whole GM plant, ⑥ the compositional, nutritional characteristics, ⑦ the influence of processing on the properties of the food or feed, ⑧ the potential for changes in dietary intake, and ⑨ the potential for long-term nutritional impact. On the other hand, regulations on GMO authorisations and labelling have become more stringent. One type of safety measure is a set of strict laboratory procedures designed to protect researchers from infection by engineered microbes and to prevent the microbes from accidentally leaving the laboratory. In addition, strains of microorganisms to be used in recombinant DNA experiments are genetically crippled to ensure that they cannot survive outside the laboratory. Finally, certain obviously dangerous experiments have been banned. Today, most public concern about possible hazards does not centers on recombinant microbes but transgenic animals and plants. The GMO Regulations provide for human health and safety and environmental protection from genetically modified micro-organisms in contained use, and additionally the human health and safety from genetically modified plants and animals. The key requirement of the GMO Regulations is to assess the risks of all activities and to make sure that any necessary controls are put in place. The GMO Regulations provide a framework for making these judgments, and place clear legal obligations on people who work with GMOs.

In addition, there still are other kinds of questions. For example, a child is growing at a normal rate, thanks to regular injections of human growth hormone that was made by genetically engineered $E.\ coli$. Like any new drug, this GH was subjected to exhaustive laboratory tests before it was released for human use. However, because it is a powerful hormone that affects the body in a number of ways, this drug may be more likely than most ordinary drugs to produce unanticipated side effects in years to come. The increased availability of GH has also raised ethical questions by leading some parents of short but hormonally normal children to seek GH treatment. A much broader ethical question is "How do we really feel about wielding one of nature's singular powers-the ability to make new microorganisms, plants, and even animals?" Some might ask "Do we have any right to alter an organism's genes—or to add our new creations to an already beleaguered environment?". Such questions must be weighed against the apparent benefits to humans and the environment that can be brought about by transgenic technology. For example, bacteria are being engineered to clean up mining wastes and a number of industrial and domestic pollutants that threaten our soil, water, and air. These organisms may be the only feasible solutions to some of our most pressing environmental problems.

Vocabulary

genetically modified organism (GMO) 转基因生物
genetically modified foods (GMF) 转基因食品
endonuclease /ˌendəˈnjuːkliˌeis/ n. 核酸内切酶
vector /ˈvektə/ n. 载体
host n. 宿主，受体细胞
ligase /ˈliːgeis/ n. 连接酶
cohesive ends n. 粘性末端
blunt /blʌnt/ ends n. 平头末端
plasmid n. 质粒
electrophoresis /iˌlektrəfəˈriːsis/ n. 电泳
Agrobacterium-mediated transformation 农杆菌介导转化
pollen-tube-pathway 花粉管通道技术

herbicide /ˈhəːbiˌsaid/ n. 除草剂
vaccine /ˈvækˌsiːn/ n. 疫苗；adj. 疫苗的，牛痘的
probe /prəub/ n. 探针
electrofusion n. 电融合技术
electroporation n. 电击，电穿孔
liposome gene delivery 脂质体基因转移
Ti plasmid n. 肿瘤诱导质粒
microarray n. 微阵列
autoradiograph /ˌɔːtəuˈreidiəuɡrɑːf/ n. 放射自显影术
insulin /ˈinsəlin/ n. 胰岛素
haemophilia /ˌhiːməˈfiliə/ n. 血友病
chymosin /ˈkaiməsin/ n. 凝乳酶
tilapia /tiˈleipiə/ n. 罗非鱼
beleaguer /biˈliːɡə/ vt. 围攻，困扰，骚扰

Exercises

1. Matching Question.

Write the letter of the phrase that best matches the numbered term on the left. Use each only once.

(1) recombinant DNA   a. a process that use bacterial host to replicate foreign DNA molecules

(2) transgenic   b. a kind of enzymes which covalently bonds DNA fragments together.

(3) DNA probe   c. DNA formed by the insertion of foreign genes or foreign sections of DNA into the chromosomes of a host cell

(4) restriction fragment   d. sequence-specific DNA-cutting enzymes found in bacteria
(5) DNA ligase   e. an organism that possesses the genes of a different species in addition to its own
(6) DNA cloning   f. a piece of DNA created when a sample of eukaryotic DNA is treated with a restriction enzyme
(7) restriction enzyme   g. a single-strand stretch of radioactive DNA whose bases pair with that of complementary restriction fragments

2. Fill in the blanks with the appropriate words you have just learned in this unit.

(1) _____ applies the lesions of molecular biology to manufacture new medical, agricultural, and industrial products.

(2) Investigators can compare the genetic relationship among various populations of animals by studying the difference in the _____ sequence of their DNAs.

(3) Recombinant DNA molecules contain _____ sequences derived from different sources which have been joined together in the laboratory.

(4) _____ was the first usable human protein to be produced in bacterial cell.

(5) _____ plants and animals contain a gene from another species.

(6) A molecule of recombinant DNA is carried to the host cell after it has been spliced to a larger molecule of DNA called a _____.

(7) The search for specific DNA fragments in a "haystack" of different DNAs requires a _____.

3. Multiple Choice Questions.

(1) Which is an advantage of genetically engineering human blood clotting factor over harvesting it in the more taditional method? (   )
   A. The product is more easily injected.
   B. It is almost as effective in treating hemophiliacs as the clotting factor obtained from human sources.
   C. There is no risk of transmitting an infection from blood-borne viruses.
   D. It is more effective in treating hemophilicas than the clotting factor obtained from human sources.
   E. It is as cost efficient to produce as the clotting factor obtained from human source.

(2) The differences in DNA nucleotide sequences between various populations of

green sea turtles suggest (   ).

  A. they have not been reproductively isolated from each other

  B. they have no common origin

  C. they have been reproductively isolated for a few thousand years, at most

  D. they have been reproductively isolated for tens of thousands of years

  E. they have been reproductively isolated for millions of years

(3) Blood—clotting factor, human growth hormone, and tissue plasminogen activator are (   ).

  A. all products of genetically engineered cells

  B. only harvested from whole human organs

  C. only harvested from human blood

  D. only harvested from whole human organs, blood, or "nonengineered" cells grown in the laboratory

  E. currently all available in very low quantities

(4) Studies involving toxins produced by genetically engineered plants show that (   ).

  A. they are of little value in controlling insect pests

  B. they are the answer to controlling insect pests

  C. insects can develop a resistance to them

  D. insects are unable to develop a resistance to them

  E. they are more lethal than petrochemical pesticides

(5) Rat growth hormone (GH) genes were injected into fertilized mouse eggs, then the altered eggs were implanted in "surrogate" mother mice. The baby mice that these eggs produced were much larger than their litter mates because (   ).

  A. the addition of the rat GH genes meant their reproduction was not sexual

  B. the addition of the rat GH genes meant they had more chromosomes

  C. though they were born of a mouse mother and had a mouse father, they were actually rats

  D. though they were born of a mouse mother and had a mouse father, they ate like rats

  E. the rat GH genes caused relative excess quantities of growth hormone to be produced

(6) When human genes are joined to a sheep gene coding for milk protein, and the fused DNA is injected into fertilized sheep eggs, the resulting adult female sheep (   ).

  A. produce human milk

B. produce human protein in their milk

C. produce human protein in their muscle tissue

D. produce human protein in their wool

E. present symptoms of human disease

(7) Animals that possess the genes of a different species (　　).

A. successfully reproduce only "normal" offspring

B. are larger in size than their "normal" counterparts

C. can pass those genes to their offspring

D. have more chromosomes than their "normal" counterparts

E. cannot successfully reproduce

(8) A function of bacterial plasmids in recombinant DNA technology is to (　　).

A. join DNA fragments

B. clone DNA fragments

C. fragment large DNA molecules into sequence specific sections

D. carry foreign genes along with plasmid DNA into the host cell

E. carry viruses along with plasmid DNA into the host cell

(9) When host bacterial cells are used to produce human proteins, the human DNA coding for the protein must be free of introns because (　　).

A. plasmid vectors cannot carry them

B. viral vectors cannot carry them

C. otherwise the desired product will be less pure

D. otherwise the operation becomes too time-consuming, and therefore becomes no longer cost effective

E. bacterial cells haven't the machinery to remove the intervening sequences from the transcribed message

(10) In addition to its use in amplification of specific DNA fragments, the PCR is also employed in (　　).

A. gel electrophoresis

B. the DNA probe

C. mixing a large quantity of restriction fragment

D. generating large amounts of DNA from minute starting samples

E. separating a large quantity of restriction fragment

4. Reading Comprehension.

Gene Therapy in Humans

Gene therapy is the treatment of some disorders by modifying expression of genes or correcting abnormal genes. There are general classes of gene therapy: ① germ line gene replacement therapy, ② somatic gene replacement therapy, and ③ nucleotide-based therapeutics. In people with disorders traceable to a single defective gene, it should theoretically be possible to replace or supplement the defective gene with a normal allele.

Ideally, the normal allele would be put into cells that multiply throughout a person's life. Bone marrow cells are prime candidates. One type of gene therapy procedure for correcting a situation, in which bone marrow cells are failing to produce a vital protein because of a defective gene in the bone marrow cells, is as follows: ① The normal gene is cloned by recombinant DNA techniques. It is then converted into RNA and inserted into the RNA genome of a harmless retrovirus vector. ② Bone marrow cells are taken from the patient and infected with the virus. ③ The virus inserts a DNA copy of its genome, including the human gene, into the cell' DNA. ④ The engineered cells are then injected back into the patient, where they colonize the bone marrow. If the procedure succeeds, the cells will multiply throughout the patient's life and express the normal gene. The engineered cells will supply the missing protein, and the patient will be cured.

Upto date, most human gene therapy experiments have been preliminary, designed to test the safety and effectiveness of a procedure rather than to attempt a cure. Despite repeated try in the news media over the past decade, it was not until April 2000 that the first scientifically strong evidence of effective gene therapy was reported. It involved the treatment of two infants suffering from a form of severe combined immune deficiency (SCID), which prevents the development of the immune system. Unless treated with a bone marrow transplant (effective just 60% of the time), SCID patients quickly die from infections by ever-present microbes that most of us easily fend off. Working at a Paris hospital, the researchers provided the infants with functional copies of their defective gene. As of June 2000, 15 months after treatment, the children were still healthy.

Some of the other promising gene therapy trials now going on are not aimed at correcting genetic defects. Instead, researchers are engineering cells from bone marrow in attempts to enhance the ability of immune cells to fight off cancer or resist infection by HIV. This approach may lead to effective treatments for many non-hereditary diseases.

Human gene therapy raises certain technical questions. For example, how can

Chapter 1　Reading Materials of Life Sciences

researchers build in gene control mechanisms to ensure that cells with the transferred gene make appropriate amounts of the gene product at the right time and in the right parts of the body? And how can they be sure that the gene's insertion does not harm some other necessary cell function?

There are ethical questions, too. For example, who will have access to gene therapy? The procedures now being tested are expensive and require expertise and equipment found only in major medical centers. A related question is, Should gene therapy be reserved for treating serious diseases? And what about its potential use for enhancing athletic ability, physical appearance, or even intelligence?

Technically easier than modifying genes in the somatic cells of children or adults is the genetic engineering of germ cells or zygotes. But this possibility raises the most difficult ethical question of all: whether we should try to eliminate genetic defects in our children and their descendants. Should we interfere with evolution in this way? From a biological perspective, the elinination of unwanted alleles from the gene pool could backfire. Genetic variety is a necessary ingredient for the survival of a species as environmental conditions change with time. Genes that are damaging under some conditions may be advantageous under others. Are we willing to risk making genetic changes that could be detrimental to our species in the future? We may have to face this question soon.

Please answer the following questions in English!

Questions for Discussion:

(1) Why can viruses be used in gene therapy for human disorders?

(2) In which two ways is gene therapy carried out?

(3) Which two types of questions are there in gene therapy?

5. PPT Presentation and Communication.

Choose one topic in which you are greatly interested and make a 5 - 10 minute PPT courseware in advance, and then vividly introduce it to your class and teacher.

Unit 11　Biodiversity and Its Conservation

导语　生态学是研究生物与其周围环境(包括非生物环境和生物环境)相互关系的科学,分为个体生态学、种群生态学、群落生态学、生态系统生态学、景观生态学等。生物多样性是指在一定范围内多种多样活的生物有规律地结合所构成稳定的生态综合体，是衡量一个生态系统是否健康的标准。研究生物多样性如何影响生态学功能是生态学研究的重要领域之一。

本单元主要介绍生态学及其分支学科和应用，生物多样性及其主要层次、价值、危机、保护和可持续发展。

11.1 Ecology, Its Branches and Applications

All organisms on the earth interact continuously with their environments including biotic factors and abiotic factors such as sunlight, water, temperature, soil and so on. The scientific study of the interaction of organisms with their environments is called ecology, a critically important field of biology. Ecology is divided into several levels: organismal ecology, population ecology, community ecology, ecosystem ecology and so on. The most complex level in ecology is the biosphere, the global ecosystem, includes the atmosphere, the land, lakes and streams, and the ocean. Ecology is closely related to physiology, evolutionary biology, genetics and ethology. Ecology is used in conservation biology, wetland management, natural resource management, city planning (urban ecology), community health, economics, basic and applied science and human social interaction (human ecology). An understanding of how biodiversity affects ecological function is an important focus area in ecological studies.

11.2 Biodiversity

Biodiversity is the degree of variation of life forms within a given ecosystem or an entire planet. Biodiversity is one measure of the health of ecosystems. Life on Earth today consists of many millions of distinct biological species. The United Nations declared the year 2010 as the International Year of Biodiversity. Biodiversity is divided into different levels such as landscape diversity, ecosystem diversity, species diversity, genetic diversity and so on.

11.2.1 Genetic Diversity

Genetic Diversity is a term used to described genetic differences among members of a population. High genetic diversity indicates many different alleles for each characteristic, and low genetic diversity indicates that nearly all the individuals in the population have the same alleles. In general, the term gene frequency is used when discussing how common genes are within populations. However, allele frequency is more properly used when specifically discussing how common a particular form of a gene (allele) is compared to other forms. Allele frequency is commonly stated in terms of a percentage or decimal fraction (e. g., 20% or 0.2). It is a mathematical statement of how frequently a particular allele is found in a population. It is possible for two populations of the same species to have all the same alleles but with very different frequencies. As an example, all humans are of the same species and, therefore, constitute one large gene pool. There are, however, many distinct local poplations scattered across the surface of the Earth. These more localized populations (races) show many distinguishing characteristics that have been perpetuated from generation to generation. In Africa, alleles for dark skin, tightly curled hair, and a flat nose have very high frequencies. In Europe, the frequencies of alleles for light skin, straight hair, and a narrow nose are the highest. People in Asia tend to have moderately colored skin, straight hair, and broad nose. All three of these populations have alleles for dark skin and light skin, straight hair and curly hair, narrow noses and broad noses (Fig. 11-1). The three are different, however, in the frequencies of these alleles. Once a particular mixture of alleles is present in a population, that mixture tends to maintain itself unless something is operating to change the frequencies. In other words, allele frequencies are not going to change without reason. With the development of

(a) (b) (c)

Fig. 11-1 Three kinds of people in three populations with different traits such as skin, hair and nose

(a) Several African people;(b) American author Mark Twain;(c) One Asian man transportation, more people have moved from one geographic area to another, and human allele frequencies have begun to change. Ultimately, as barriers to interracial marriage are leveled, the human gene pool will show fewer and fewer racial differences. What really determines the frequency of an allele in a population is the value that the allele has to the organisms possessing it. The dark-skin alleles are valuable to people living under the bright sun in tropical Africa. These alleles are less valuable to those living in the less intense sunlight of the cooler European countries.

How does genetic diversity come about?

(1) Mutations. *Mutations* introduce new genetic information into a population by modifying genes that are already present. Sometimes a mutation is a first-time event; At other times, a mutation may have occurred before. All alleles for a particular trait originated as a result of mutations some time in the past and have been maintained within the gene pool of the species as a result of sexual reproduction. If a mutation produces a harmful allele, it will remain uncommon in the population. Many mutations are harmful and very rarely will one occur that is valuable to the organism. For example, at some time in the past, mutations occurred in the DNA of certain insect species that made some individuals tolerant to the insecticide DDT, even though the chemical had not yet been invented. These alleles remained very rare in these insect populations until DDT was used. Then, these alleles became very valuable to the insects that carried them. Because insects that lacked the alleles for tolerance died when they came in contact with DDT, more of the DDT-tolerant individuals were left to reproduce the species and, therefore, the DDT-tolerant alleles became much more common in these populations.

(2) Sexual reproduction. Although the process of *sexual reprodution* does not create new genes, it tends to generate new genetic combinations when the genes from two individuals mix during fertilization, generating a unique individual. This doesn't directly change the frequency of alleles within the gene pool, but the new member may have a unique combination of characteristics so superior to those of other members of the population that the new member will be much more successful in producing offspring. In a corn population, there may be alleles for resistance to corn blight (a fungal disease) and resistance to attack by insects. Corn plants that possess both of these characteristics are going to be more

successful than corn plants that have only one of these qualities. They will probably produce more offspring (corn seeds) than the others because they will survive fungal and insect attacks; Moreover, they will tend to pass on this same genetic combination to their offspring.

(3) Migration. The *migration* of individuals from one genetically distinct population to another is also an important way for alleles to be added to or subtracted from a local population. Whenever an organism leaves one population and enters another, it subtracts its genetic information from the population it left and adds it to the population it joins. If it contains rare alleles, it may significantly affect the allele frequency of both population. The extent of migration need not be great. As long as alleles are entering or leaving a population, the gene pool will change.

(4) Population size. The *size of the population* has a lot to do with how effective any of these mechanisms are at generating variety in a gene pool. The smaller the population, the less genetic variety it can contain. Therefore, migrations, mutations, and accidental death can have great effects on the genetic makeup of a small population. For example, if a town has a population of 20 people and only two have brown eyes and the rest have blue eyes, what happens to those two brown-eyed people is more critical than if the town has 20,000 people and 2,000 have brown eyes. Although the ratio of brown eyes to blue eyes is the same in both cases, even a small change in a population of 20 could significantly change the frequency of the brown-eye allele.

11.2.2 Species Diversity

Species diversity is the variety of life forms found on Earth (Fig. 11-2), a measure of the diversity of species within an ecological community that incorporates both species richness and evenness.

(1) A combination of the number of species and their relative abundance defines species diversity. Ecologists define it on the basis of two factors: ① the number of species in the community, which they are usually called species richness, and ② the relative abundance of species, or species evenness (Fig. 11-3). The influence of species richness on community diversity is clear. A community with 20 species is obviously less diverse than one with 80 species. The effects of species evenness on diversity are more subtle but easily illustrated.

Fig. 11-2 Species diversity

Fig. 11-3 contrasts two hypothetical forest communities. Both contain five species, so they have equal levels of species richness. However, community b is more diverse than community a because its species evenness is higher.

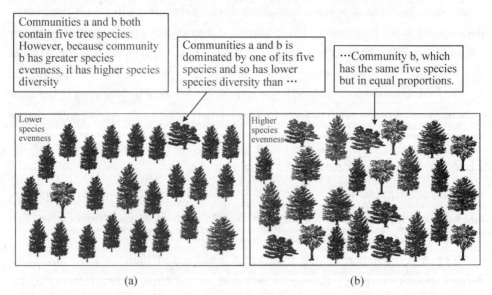

Communities a and b both contain five tree species. However, because community b has greater species evenness, it has higher species diversity

Communities a and b is dominated by one of its five species and so has lower species diversity than …

…Community b, which has the same five species but in equal proportions.

Fig. 11-3 Species richness and species evenness (Molles M C, 2007)

Community a and b both contain five tree species. However, because community b has greater species Evenness, it has higher species diversity. Community a is dominated by one of its five species, while Community b has the same five species but in equal proportions.

(2) Species diversity is higher in complex environments. In general, species diversity increases with environmental complexity. However, one aspect of environmental structure important for one group of organisms may not have a positive influence on another group.

(3) Intermediate levels of disturbance promote higher diversity. What constitutes disturbance varies from one organism to another and from one environment to another. A disturbance for one organism may have little or no impact on another, and the nature of disturbance may be quite different in different environments. Therefore, it is very difficult to define disturbance. How can intermediate levels of disturbance promote higher diversity? Joseph Connell suggested that at intermediate levels of disturbance there is sufficient time between disturbances for a wide variety of species to colonize but not enough time to allow competitive exclusion.

11.2.3 Ecosystem Diversity

It refers to the diversity of a place at the level of ecosystems (Fig. 11-4), can also refer to the variety of ecosystems present in a biosphere, the variety of species and ecological processes that occur in different physical settings.

Fig. 11-4 Forest ecosystem diversity

11.2.4　Landscape Diversity

It is the diversity of the structure, function and time of a landscape. A landscape is a heterogeneous area composed of several ecosystems (Fig. 11-5). The ecosystems making up a landscape generally form a mosaic of visually distinctive patches, called landscape elements. The elements of a mountain landscape may include forests, meadows, bogs, and streams, while those in urban landscape include parks, industrial districts, and residential areas. Landscape ecologists define a patch as a relatively homogeneous area that differs from its surroundings, for example, an area of forest surrounded by agricultural fields. Landscape ecology is the study of landscape structure and processes.

(1) Landscape structure includes the size, shape, composition, number, and position of patches in a landscape.

(2) Landscape structure influences processes such as the flow of energy, materials, and species across a landscape.

(3) Landscape structure changes in response to geological processes, climate, activities of organisms, and fire.

Fig. 11-5　Much of the landscape of southwestern Finland consists of patchwork of pastures, medowa and woods (Molles M C, 2007)

11.3 Human Benefits from Biodiversity

11.3.1 Food and Products

Human beings depend on many other species for food (Fig. 11-6, (a)), nutrition, shelter, clothing and other products. Although about 80 percent of humans' food supply comes from just 20 kinds of plants, humans use at least 40,000 species. Many people depend on these species for food, shelter, and clothing. Surviving biodiversity on Earth provides resources for increasing the range of food and other products suitable for human use.

(a)　　　　　　　　(b)　　　　　　　　(c)

Fig. 11-6　Plants used as food, traditional and modern medicine
(a) peanut intercropping with cotton and watermelon; (b) Rehmannia glutinosa (Gaertn.) Libosch ① plant ② tuber; (c) primrose

11.3.2 Medicines and Health

Biodiversity provides critical support for drug discovery and the availability of medicinal resources. A significant proportion of drugs are derived from biological sources. More than 70,000 plant species, for example, are used in traditional and modern medicine (Fig. 11-6, (b) - (c)). Among the 120 active compounds currently isolated from the higher plants and widely used in modern medicine, 80 percent show a positive correlation between their modern therapeutic use and the traditional use of the plants from which they are derived. Biodiversity influences some of the health issues suah as dietary health and nutrition security, infectious disease, medical science and medicinal resources, social and psychological health. Biodiversity is also known to have an important role in reducing disaster risk, and in post-disaster relief and recovery efforts. In addition, increased diversity of genes within species, e. g., as represented by livestock breeds or strains of plants, reduces risk from diseases and increases potential to adapt to changing climates.

11.3.3 Business and Industry

Many industrial materials derive directly from biological sources, which include building materials, fibers, dyes, rubber and oil. Biodiversity is also important to the security of resources such as water, timber, paper, fiber, and food.

11.3.4 Ecological Services

Biodiversity supports ecosystem services including air quality, climate, water purification, pollination, and prevention of erosion. The value of global ecosystem services is estimated at $16 - $64 trillion. Biodiversity also helps people to adapt to climate change through providing the ecosystem services which reduce their vulnerability and enhance their adaptive capacity to change.

11.3.5 Leisure, Cultural, Educational and Aesthetic Value

Biodiversity have spiritual and aesthetic values, knowledge systems and the value of education. For instance, biodiversity enriches leisure activities such as hiking, birdwatching or natural history study; biodiversity inspires musicians, painters, sculptors, writers and other artists; many cultures view themselves as an integral part of the natural world which requires them to respect other living organisms; popular activities such as gardening, fishkeeping and specimen collecting strongly depend on biodiversity; Philosophically it could be argued that biodiversity has intrinsic aesthetic and spiritual value to mankind; Many organism, such as fruit flies, peas and yeasts, are used in the scientific research and education.

11.4 Biodiversity Crisis

Biodiversity crisis is a precipitous decline in the great variety of life on Earth. It is part of the larger environmental crisis. The escalating extinction crisis shows that the diversity of nature cannot support the current pressure that humanity is placing on the planet. The loss of biodiversity limits the potential for new discoveries and reflects large-scale changes in the biosphere that could have catastrophic consequences. Biodiversity crisis (Fig. 11-7) is caused by the following main causes:

Fig. 11-7 Several main causes of the biodiversity crisis
(a) habitat destruction: rubbish pollution; (b) water hyacinth (*Eichhornia crassipes*) in Dianchi, Yunnan, China; (c) brown tree snake; (d) bearbile extraction; (e) killed Zang chiru; (f) Chinese yew trees cut down

(1) Habitat destruction. Human alteration of habitats for agriculture expansion, urban development, mining, pollution (Fig. 11-9, (a)) and so on, poses the single greatest threat to biodiversity. Habitat loss and degradation affects 86% of all threatened birds, 86% of the threatened mammals assessed and 88% of the threatened amphibians.

(2) Introduced and invasive species that establish and spread outside their

normal distribution. Some of the most threatening invasive species include cats and rats, green crabs, zebra mussels, *Eichhornia crassipes* and the brown tree snake (Fig. 11-9, (b)-(c)).

(3) Over-exploitation of natural resources. Resource extraction, hunting, and fishing for food, pets, and medicine (Fig. 11-9, (d)-(f)).

(4) Diseases. For example, excessive fertilizer use leads to excessive levels of nutrients in soil and water.

(5) Human-induced climate change.

For example, climate change is altering migratory species patterns, and increasing coral bleaching. Biodiversity loss has negative effects on our health, material wealth and it largely limits our freedom of choice. Furthermore, biodiversity loss also strongly influences our social relations.

11.5 Biodiversity Conservation and Sustainable Development

Conservation is the protection, preservation, management, or restoration of wildlife and natural resources such as forests and water. Biodiversity conservation provides substantial benefits to meet immediate human needs, such as those for clean, consistent water flow, protection from floods and storms, and a stable climate. There are two methods of biodiversity conservation, *in situ* and *ex situ*. The former envisages conservation within the natural ecosystem such as protected areas (wildlife sanctuaries, national parks, biosphere reserves, heritage sites, etc.), for example, Sichuan Wolong Giant Panda Nature Reserve (Fig. 11-8), and the latter is a method of conservation outside natural habitats (botanical and zoological gardens, gene banks, seed banks, etc) (Fig. 11-9). In case of domesticated or cultivated species, conservation means conservation in the surroundings where they have developed their distinctive properties. Through the conservation of biodiversity, the survival of many species and habitats which are threatened due to human activities can be ensured. Other reasons for conserving biodiversity include securing valuable natural resources for future generations and protecting the well being of ecosystem functions.

The areas to conserve are:

(1) Biodiversity hot spots. A biodiversity hot spot is a relatively small area

Fig. 11-8 Sichuan Wolong giant panda nature reserve

Established in 1963, the reserve covers an area of about 200,000 hectares. Wolong Nature Reserve houses more than 150 highly endangered giant pandas.

with an exceptional concentration of species, in which many of the organisms are endemic species. For example, about 30% of all bird species are confined to nearly 2% of the land area on Earth. And 20% of all known plant species inhabit 18 hot spots making up only about 0.5% of the global land surface.

(2) Threatened species. An endangered species is one in danger of extinction through all or a significant portion of its range, while a threatened species is one likely to become endangered in the foreseeable future through all or a significant portion of their geographic range.

(3) Threatened habitats. Habitat destruction comes in many forms from clear felling of forests to simple changes in farming practices that change the overall surrounding habitat. If a habitat is degraded or disappears, a species may also become threatened.

(4) Flagship and keystone species. Conservation efforts are often focused on a single species. This is usually for two reasons: ① Some species are key to the functioning of a habitat and their loss would lead to greater than average change in other species populations or ecosystem processes. These are known as keystone species. ② Humans will find the idea of conserving one species more appealing

Fig. 11-9 Shenzhen Xianhu lake botanical garden

Established in 1963, it covers an area of about 586.7 hectares housing more than 4,000 plants.

than conserving others. Using a flagship species such as a tiger will attract more resources for conservation which can be used to conserve areas of habitat.

(5) Complementarity. It is a method used to select areas for conservation. These methods are used to find areas that in sum total have the highest representation of diversity. In addition, conservation can not be conducted in isolation from humans and for conservation to be successful and sustainable, there needs to be local community involvement.

Sustainable development is the development that meets the needs of the present without compromising the ability of future generations to meet their own needs. Three types of capital in sustainable development are economic capital, social capital and natural capital, which may be non-substitutable and whose consumption might be irreversible. Green development is generally differentiated from sustainable development in that Green development prioritizes what its proponents consider to be environmental sustainability over economic and cultural considerations. Environmental sustainability is the process of making sure current processes of interaction with the environment are pursued with the idea of keeping the environment as pristine as naturally possible based on ideal-seeking behavior. Economic sustainability is the term used to identify various strategies that make it possible to utilize available resources to best advantage. The idea is to promote efficient and responsible usage of those resources, and likely to provide long-tem benefits.

Vocabulary

biodiversity /ˌbaiəudai'və:səti/ n. 生物多样性
ecology /i'kɔlədʒi/ n. 生态学
abiotic /ˌeibai'ɔtik/ adj. 无生命的，非生物的
ecosystem /'ekəuˌsistəm, 'i:kəʊ-/ n. 生态系统
ethology /i'θɔlədʒi/ n. 动物行为学
biosphere /'baiəˌsfiə/ n. 生物圈
disturbance /dis'tə:bəns/ n. 干涉
genetic diversity 遗传多样性
allele frequency 等位基因频率
blight /blait/ n. 植物枯萎病 v. 枯萎
migration /mai'greiʃən/ n. 迁移

vulnerability /ˌvʌlnərə'biləti/ n. 易感性
birdwatching n. （在大自然中）观察研究野鸟
precipitous /pri'sipətəs/ adj. 非常大的
zebra mussels 斑马贻贝（河蚌）
Eichhornia crassipes 凤眼莲
chiru /'tʃiru:/ n. 羚羊
Chinese yew trees n. 红豆杉树
coral bleaching 珊瑚白化
envisage /in'vizidʒ/ vt. 设想
sanctuary /'sæŋktʃuˌeri:/ n. 保护区
flagship and keystone species 旗舰物种和关键物种

Exercises

1. Matching Questions.

Write the letter of the phrase that best matches the numbered on the left. Use each only once.

(1) ecology　　　　　　　　a. the study of populations in terms of population size, growth, density, and structure.

(2) organismal ecology　　　b. a system formed by the interaction of a community of organisms with their environment.

(3) population ecology　　　c. the scientific study of the interaction of organisms with their environments.

(4) community　　　　　　　d. study of individuals within a species and how they adapt to their environment.

(5) ecosystem   e. all the populations in a specific area.
(6) bioshere   f. the global ecosystem including the atmosphere, land, lakes, streams and ocean.
(7) biodiversity   g. the science of studying and improving relationships between urban development and ecological processes in the environment and particular ecosystems.
(8) landscape ecology   h. the protection, preservation, management, or restoration of wildlife and natural resources.
(9) biodiversity conservation   i. a development which aims to meet human needs while preserving the environment so that these needs can be met not only in the present, but also for generations to come.
(10) sustainable development   j. the variety of all forms of life, from genes to species to the broad scale of ecosystems

2. Fill in the blanks with the appropriate words you have just learned in this unit.

(1) _____ is the study of populations and their interactions in a specific geographic area including interspecific relationships such as competition, predation and symbiosis, and food chains and food webs.

(2) _____ consists of the same species located in the same location at the same time.

(3) _____ is the study of communities and how they interact with the abiotic factors.

(4) _____ includes organismal ecology, population ecology, community ecology and ecosystem ecology.

(5) The six abiotic factors affecting the environment are soil and rocks, _____, _____, _____, wind, and periodic disturbances.

(6) Solar energy is such an important abiotic factor because _____ provides most of the organic fuel and building material for the organisms of most ecosystems.

(7) The three major aspects studied in organismal ecology are anatomical response, _____ and behavioral response.

(8) The genetic diversity can be changed by _____, sexual reproduction, migration and population size.

Chapter 1   Reading Materials of Life Sciences   · 169 ·

(9) Human benefits from biodiversity includes _____, medicines and health, ecological srevices, leisure, cultural, educational and aesthetic value and so on.

(10) Biodiversity crisis has been caused by habitat destruction, introduced species, _____ of natural resources, etc.

3. Multiple Choice Questions.

(1) An exotic or introduced species is a species that (   ).

    A. humans have transferred from its native location to another one

    B. comes from anywhere beyond Earth

    C. comes from a species beyond Earth

    D. scientists select a variety from a natural organism population

(2) A bat locates insect prey in the dark by bouncing high-pitched sounds off them. One species of moth escapes predation by diving to the ground when it hears "sonar" of particular bat species. This illustrates (   ) between them.

    A. interspecific competition   B. competition exclusion

    C. mutualism   D. coevolution

(3) The disturbances that are most likely to enhance species diversity in a community are those that are (   ).

    A. caused by invasive species   B. sever and rare

    C. caused by humans   D. moderate in severity and frequency

(4) Local conditions, including heavy rainfall, the removal of plants and so forth, may limit the amount of nitrogen, phosphorus, or calcium available to a particular ecosystem, but the amount of carbon available to it is seldom a problem. Why? (   )

    A. Many nutritions come from the soil, but carbon does from the air.

    B. Plants can make their own carbon from water and sunlight.

    C. Symbiotic bacteria help plants capture carbon.

    D. Organisms do not need very much carbon.

    E. Plants are much better at absorbing carbon from the soil.

(5) The increase in atmospheric CO_2 concentration is mainly a result of an increase in (   ).

    A. the biomass of biosphere

    B. cellular respiration by the exploding human population

    C. primary productivity   D. the burning of fossil fuels and wood

(6) Which one of the following answers most comprehensively shows what conservation biologists mean by biodiversity crisis? (   )

A. The rate of patent applications for pharmaceuticals developed from organisms is currently declining.
B. Harvests of some sea fish are declining.
C. Some introduced species have rapidly expanded their ranges.
D. Worldwide extinction rates are currently 50 times than at any time during the past 100,000 years.

(7) The No. 1 cause of biodiversity loss is currently (   ).
A. biological magnifications   B. habitat destruction
C. introduced species   D. excessive hunting of wildlife

(8) "Balance in nature" is used to describe an ecosystem in which (   ).
A. the biotic factors and abiotic ones interact in such as a way that neither type of factor changes appreciably over time
B. the biotic factors do not change appreciably through time, but the abiotic ones do
C. individual plants and animals can obtain the nutritions and energy
D. the abiotic factors interact in such as a way that they do not change appreciably over time

Unit 12　Technologies and Applications of Aquaculture

　　导语　水产养殖学是研究水生经济动、植物养殖原理和技术的学科。水产养殖是人为控制下繁殖、培育和收获水生动植物(如鱼类、虾蟹、龟鳖、牡蛎和藻类)的生产活动,分为淡水养殖和海水养殖,具有巨大的发展潜力和广阔的发展前景。它一般包括在人工饲养管理下从苗种养成水产品的全过程。水产养殖有粗养、精养和高密度精养等方式。它能够为人类生产丰富的鱼、虾、海带和紫菜等水产品,也会对环境产生影响。

　　本单元主要介绍水产养殖概况、鱼类养殖、虾类养殖、龟鳖养殖、牡蛎养殖和藻类养殖的技术与应用。

12.1　Aquaculture

　　Aquaculture is a rapidly growing industry and farming practice, which can directly interact with and depend upon the surrounding environment. Therefore, the effects of all types of aquaculture on living natural resources and ecosystems are of significant and increasing national and international interest. Aquaculture is the farming of aquatic organisms such as fish, crustaceans (shrimp and crab), molluscs (oyster and abalone), reptiles (turtles), echinoderms (sea cucumbers and sea urchins) and aquatic plants (seaweed and kelp). Aquaculture involves cultivating freshwater and saltwater populations under controlled conditions, and can be contrasted with commercial fishing, which is the harvesting of wild fish. In current aquaculture practice, products from several pounds of wild fish are used to produce one pound of a piscivorous fish like salmon. Particular kinds of aquaculture include fish farming, shrimp farming, oyster farming, algaculture (such as seaweed farming) and so on. The reported output from global aquaculture operations would supply one half of the fish and shellfish that is directly consumed by humans. Aquaculture can be more environmentally damaging than exploiting wild fisheries on a local area basis but has considerably less impact on the global environment on a per kg of production basis. Local concerns include waste handling, side-effects of antibiotics, competition between farmed and wild animals, and using other fish to feed more marketable carnivorous fish. Fish waste is organic and composed of nutrients necessary in all components of aquatic food webs. In ocean aquaculture often produces much higher than normal fish waste concentrations. The waste collects on the ocean bottom, damaging or eliminating bottom-dwelling life. Waste can also decrease dissolved oxygen levels in the water column, putting further pressure on wild animals.

12.2　Fish Aquaculture

Fish aquaculture is the principal form of aquaculture. It includes ① extensive aquaculture based on local photosynthetical production and ② intensive aquaculture, in which the fish are fed with external food supply. Within intensive and extensive aquaculture methods, there are numerous specific types of fish farms, each has benefits and applications unique to its design. For example, integrated recycling systems, irrigation ditch or pond systems, composite fish culture, cage system and so on. Global demand for fish is rising even as many ocean stocks are declining, and aquaculture techniques and technology continue to improve. In addition, small-scale aquaculture offers farmers a ready source of both subsistence food and cash, and these benefits are likely to promote expansion beyond its traditional stronghold in Asia. However, there are also serious constraints on aquaculture's future growth. For instance, fish farming requires both land and water resources already in short supply in many areas. The most common fish species raised by fish farms are salmon, carp, tilapia, bigeye tuna, catfish and cod (Fig. 12-1).

Fig. 12-1 Several most common fish species raised by fish farms
(a) red salmon; (b) tilapia; (c) common carp

The four major carp species—silver carp, grass carp, black carp, and bighead carp (Fig. 12-2), account for more than one third of world aquaculture production —nearly all of it in China, which are raised primarily as a supplementary activity to regular crop agriculture on Chinese farms in relatively low-tech inland ponds for local consumption. Carp are herbivores and can survive on low-cost, readily available feed material, and make a direct, significant contribution to the protein needs of less affluent rural Chinese.

For example, common carp (Cyprinus carpio) farming. Common carp is the main aquaculture species in many European and Asian countries, including China. This fish has several advantages that made it so popular for commercial culture: ① very fast growth rate, ② high tolerance and easiness to handle, ③ ability to be raised in high density and to give high production per square unit, ④ ability to utilize prepared diet with relatively low content of protein, and ⑤ occurrence of highly productive strains and breeds reared during a long-term process of selection and domestication. Most carp is sold on the market as live fish or as whole carcass. However, because some consumers do not like to eat fish meat with small bones

Fig. 12-2 the four famous Chinese carps
(a) black carp; (b) grass carp; (c) silver carp; (d) bighead carp

and prefer boneless fish, the main obstacle for acceptance of carp as edible fish in the world is the presence of many intramuscular bones in the muscles. Possibly, a change in consumers' attitudes to carp may be achieved by applifying new types of carp meat processing. There are a variety of common carp farming such as pond farming, cage or enclosure farming, flowing water farming, rice farming and so on (Fig. 12-3).

In addition, there are still crucian carp farming, goldfish farming, catfish farming, eel farming, loach farming and so on.

12.3 Shrimp Farming

Shrimp are small animals, invertebrates that have a thin, smooth, hard, and almost transparent, tough exoskeleton. They live on the floor of oceans, lakes, river and ponds and vary widely in color (pink, gray, brown or yellow). Once cooked, Shrimp flesh becomes opaque and cream or pinkish in color. Shrimp is found throughout almost the entire world. There are over 2,000 different species of shrimp worldwide, of which over 300 different species are harvested worldwide, in which thousands of varieties are available. While many countries raise shrimp, much of the world's supply comes from the United States, South and Central America, Japan, Thailand and Taiwan. In China, there are also some important

Fig. 12-3　Common carp farming ways
(a) pond farming; (b) cage farming

types of shrimp, for example, prawn, lobster, white shrimp and so on (Fig. 12-4). we are able to enjoy fresh and frozen shrimp throughout the year. In addition, shrimp are also eaten by many other animals, including many fish, many birds, octopi, squid, and cuttlefish. Our food ranking system qualified shrimp as an excellent source of selenium and unusually low-fat and low-calorie protein. Shrimp also emerged as a very good source of vitamin D and vitamin B12.

　　Shrimp farming is the purposeful raising of shrimp for human consumption and use or an activity to produce large volumes of shrimp which are then sold for profit. Shrimp farming creates a controlled population of shrimp for use as food. Shrimp aquaculture as a small business is centuries old, but in the late 20th and early 21st century it has grown to be a booming enterprise around the globe. There are two kinds of shrimp aquaculture, saltwater and freshwater shrimp culture. These shrimp can be grown in many different culture media, including hatcheries, ponds, reservoirs, concrete raceways, and even on lakes and ocean when

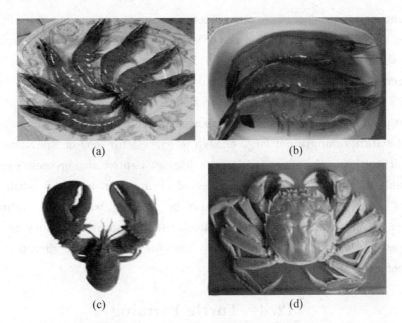

Fig. 12-4 Several important types of shrimp and Chinese river crab

(a) prawm; (b) white shrimp; (c) a lobster (Palinuridae); (d) Chinese river crab

conditions are proper with different methods (Fig. 12-5). Shrimp aquaculture typically works in three stages: hatchery, nursery, and growout. Companies may specialize in one stage or may comprehensively cover all three stages. A shrimp hatchery handles the spawning and larval stages of the process, providing nutrients and proper water density to feed and sustain the spawning shrimp and larvae. A

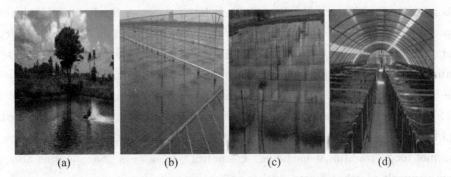

Fig. 12-5 different methods for shrimp farming

(a) the pond farming; (b) big canopy farming; (c) stereo faming; (d) the factory system of shrimp farming

single shrimp can produce up to one million eggs in one spawn, but mortality rates between spawning and maturation maybe extremely high. Nursery businesses tend to take shrimp in the post-larval stage but before they are at the adult stage. These have decreased in popularity, as the multiple changes in tanks seem to increase mortality rates due to disease and poor adaptability in many shrimp species. A growout pond is the final stage of shrimp aquaculture and handles shrimp that have reached maturity but are not large enough to harvest for food or sale. One of the major difficulties in shrimp aquaculture is disease. Captive shrimp seem extremely susceptible to viruses, and a single infected shrimp can destroy a whole pond. Farmers often attempt to reduce disease by treating water with antibiotics. Additionally, algae and other microorganisms used for shrimp food may be treated with a pesticide, which, like antibiotics, finds its way into the shrimp and thus into whomever consumes the shrimp.

12.4 Turtle Farming

Turtles are reptiles, characterised by a special bony or cartilaginous shell developed from their ribs that acts as a shield. Some turtles live in the sea, some live in fresh water. Those that live on the land are called tortoises. Most turtles eat plants and meat. Their bodies are protected by a shell on top and underneath. Their backbone, breastbone and ribs have become part of the shell, so they cannot remove their shells. Like all other reptiles, turtles are cold-blooded. Most hibernate during winter. Turtles pull their legs, tails and heads into the shell for protection. Some turtles pull their necks into their shells in an "s" shaped curve, and others pull the neck sideways into their shell. Female turtles lay eggs after mating with a male. A female digs a hole on land and lays many eggs, then covers the hole and leaves the eggs. When the eggs hatch, the tiny hatchlings dig to the surface and fend for themselves. Turtle farming is the practice of raising turtles and tortoises of various species commercially. Farmed turtles are sold for use as gourmet food, traditional medicine, cosmetics, or as pets. Some farms also sell young animals to other farms, either as breeding stock, or more commonly to be raised there to a larger size for further resale. Twenty-six varieties of turtles are farmed. The most common turtle used is the Red-eared slider turtle (Fig. 12-6, (b)). Over 15 million turtles are harvested yearly. Turtle farmers worldwide raise primarily freshwater turtles (primarily, Chinese soft-shelled turtles (Fig. 12-6, (a)) as a food source and sliders (Fig. 12-6, (b)) and cooter turtles (Fig. 12-6, (c)) for the pet trade. Therefore, turtle farming is usually classified as aquaculture. Japan is said to be the pioneer of soft-shelled turtle (*Pelodiscus sinensis*) farming, with the first farm near Tokyo in 1866. Now, turtle farming exists in many counties such as Thailand, Vietnam, the United States, China and so on. The majority of world's turtle farms are probably located in China. The most common species raised by Chinese turtle farmers is the Chinese soft-shelled turtle (*Pelodiscus sinensis*), accounting for over 97% of all reported sales.

(a) (b) (c)

Fig. 12-6 Three common turtles

(a) Chinese soft-shelled turtles; (b) one red eared slider turtle with very high diet therapy, medical and ornamental value from; (c) Florida red-bellied turtle (*Chrysemys nelsoni*), also called Cooter

12.5 Oyster Farming

Oyster is a common name for a number of distinct groups of bivalve molluscs which live in marine or brackish habitats. Some kinds of oyster are commonly consumed, cooked or raw, by humans (Fig. 12-7, (a)). There are the over 50 different kinds that are in the oceans today, out of which several different types of oysters are edible. Oysters are an excellent source of zinc, iron, calcium, selenium as well as Vitamin A and Vitamin B12. Oysters are low in food energy. One dozen raw oysters contain approximately 110 kilocalories (460 kJ). Oysters are considered the healthiest when eaten raw on the half shell. Traditionally, oysters were considered to be an aphrodisiac, because they were rich in amino acids that trigger increased levels of sex hormones, and their high zinc content aids the production of testosterone. Other kinds of oyster, such as pearl oysters, are not used as food by humans. Both cultured pearls and natural pearls can be obtained from pearl oysters (Fig. 12-7,(b)). The largest pearl-bearing oyster is the marine *Pinctada maxima*, which is roughly the size of a dinner plate. Not all individual oysters produce pearls naturally. In fact, in a harvest of three tons of oysters, only three to four oysters produce perfect pearls. In nature, pearl oysters produce natural pearls by covering a minute invading parasite with nacre, not by ingesting a grain of sand. Over the years, the irritating object is covered with enough layers of nacre to become a pearl. There are many different types, colours and shapes of pearl; these qualities depend on the natural pigment of the nacre, and the shape of the original irritant. Pearl farmers can culture a pearl by placing a nucleus, usually a piece of polished mussel shell, inside the oyster. In three to six years, the oyster can produce a perfect pearl. These pearls are not as valuable as natural pearls, but look exactly the same. In fact, since the beginning of the 20th century, when several researchers discovered how to produce artificial pearls, the cultured pearl market has far outgrown the natural pearl market. Oyster predators include starfish, oyster drill snails, oyster flatworms, stingrays, crabs, birds and humans. Oyster crabs may live in an endosymbiotic commensal relationship within a host oyster. Since oyster crabs are considered a food delicacy, they may not be removed from young farmed oysters, as they can themselves be harvested for sale. Oysters are subject to various diseases, such as Dermo (*Perkinsus marinus*) and MSX (*Multinucleated Sphere X*) caused by a protozoan parasite and the protozoan *Haplosporidium nelsoni*, respectively, which can reduce harvests and severely deplete local populations. Disease control focuses on containing infections and breeding resistant strains.

  Oyster farming is an aquaculture (or mariculture) practice in which oysters are raised for human consumption. Oyster farming is most likely developed in tandem with pearl farming, in which oysters are farmed for the purpose of developing pearls. Commonly farmed food oysters include the Eastern oyster *Crassostrea virginica*, the Pacific oyster *Crassostrea gigas* and so on. When oysters are farmed, the temperature and salinity of the water are controlled to induce spawning and fertilization and to speed the rate of maturation, which can take several years. Three methods of cultivation are commonly used (Fig. 12-7, (c)). In each case oysters are cultivated to the size of "spat".

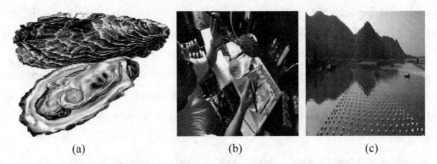

(a)　　　　　　　　　　(b)　　　　　　　　　　(c)

Fig. 12-7　Oyster uses and farming

(a) oyster samples; (b) pearls taken out of one pearl oyster from; (c) fried oyster with egg and flour; (d) one oyster farm in Wuqin town, Lufeng city, Guangdong province, China

(1) The spat or seed oysters are distributed over existing oyster beds and left to mature naturally. Such oysters will then be collected using the methods for fishing wild oysters, such as dredging.

(2) The spat or seed may be put in racks, bags, or cages which are held above the bottom. Oysters may be harvested by lifting the bags or racks to the surface and removing mature oysters, or simply retrieving the larger oysters when the enclosure is exposed at low tide. The latter method may avoid losses to some predators, but it is more expensive.

(3) The spat or seed are placed in a culch within an artificial maturation tank, which may be fed with water that has been especially prepared for the purpose of accelerating the growth rate of the oysters. In particular, the temperature and salinity of the water may be altered somewhat from nearby ocean water. Oyster farming is relatively benign or even restorative environmentally, and holds promise for relieving pressure on land-based protein sources.

12.6　Algaculture

Aquatic plants are plants that have adapted to living in aquatic environments. They require special adaptations for living submerged in water or at the water's surface. Many aquatic plants are used by humans as a food source. Most algae, all seaweed, lotus and water lily and kelp are some important examples of aquatic plants (Fig. 12-8).

Algaculture is a type of aquaculture in which algae and seaweed are cultivated. Although it is possible to grow seaweed (Fig. 12-8,(d)), nearly all algaculture farms grow microalgae. Microalgae are considered one of the most promising feedstocks for biofuels. The procedure for algaculture is the following.

(1) Isolate the desired algae strain. Algaculture farms typically grow just one type of algae. Water samples are taken from the wild and sent to a lab, where serial dilution is used to isolate the water sample with the greatest content of desirable algae.

(a)　　　　　　(b)　　　　　　(c)　　　　　　(d)

Fig. 12-8　Several aquatic plants

(a) one piece of seaweed and its slices; (b) a laver or nori and egg soup; (c) lotus and pork spareribs soup; (d) seaweed farming

(2) Build an environment for the algae to grow. Once a desirable algae strain has been isolated, it is cultivated in either an open pond or a photobioreactor, basically a sealed clear container. Open ponds can be used if the environment is managed in such a way that the desired algae strain has a growth advantage, pushing out other organisms. A photobioreactor prevents invasion from other species of algae, but it also requires the addition of fertilizer and air or carbon dioxide.

(3) Maintain algae growth. Air or carbon dioxide will be pumped into the bioreactor to fuel the cells. Nutrients will be added to the water, including potassium and phosphorus. Algae can grow so thick that it prevents sunlight from penetrating the water, yet UV rays from direct sunlight can be fatal to them. Tanks and ponds must be stirred using either air bubbles or paddle wheels to ensure that the algae is neither cut off from sunlight nor overexposed (Fig. 12-9, (a)).

(4) Harvest. The algae will be separated from the water using filters, centrifuges, or chemicals. In bioreactors the air supply can be cut off, killing the cells and forcing them out of suspension.

The most familiar use for farmed seaweed is nori. Agar also comes from microalgae. The algae strain *Spirulina* is used as a dietary supplement and can be found in some shampoos. Algae may soon be an important source of fuel. On a per-acre basis algaculture can produce ten times as much oil as an oil palm plantation and one hundred times as much as a soybean farm. Once extracted, this oil can be mixed with methanol to create methyl esters, commonly called "biodiesel". Algaculture is also being looked at as a way to sequester carbon emissions from coal power plants. The algae can use photosynthesis to convert the sun's energy to sugar to fuel the cell in a way that produces oxygen as a byproduct into the atmosphere. However, some types of microalgae, for example, microcystis, forms a harmful algal bloom (Fig. 12-9,(b)-(c)), a rapid increase or accumulation in the population of algae in an aquatic system. Algal blooms may occur in freshwater and marine environments. They can cause negative impacts to other organisms via production of natural toxins, mechanical damage to other organisms, or by other means. Examples of their common harmful effects include: ① the production of neurotoxins which cause mass mortalities in fish, seabirds, sea turtles, and marine mammals. ② human illness or death via consumption of seafood contaminated by toxic algae. ③ mechanical damage to other organisms, such as disruption of epithelial gill tissues in fish, resulting in asphyxiation. ④ oxygen depletion of the water column from cellular respiration and bacterial degradation.

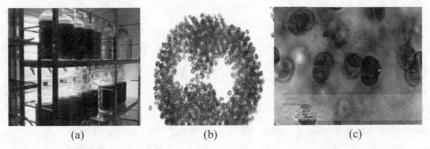

Fig. 12-9 large-scale culture of microalgae and microcynstis and huge algal bloom
(a) large-scale culture of microalgae; (b) *Microcystis aeruginosa*, a kind of microcynstis;
(c) huge algal blooms can present problems for ecosystems and human society

Vocabulary

aquaculture /ˈækwəˌkʌltʃə/ n. 水产养殖，养鱼

molluscs n. 软体动物

carp /kɑ:p/ n. 鲤鱼

crustacean /krʌˈsteiʃən/ n. 甲壳动物

oyster /ˈɔistə/ n. 牡蛎

abalone /ˌæbəˈləuni/ n. 鲍鱼

echinoderm /iˈkainədə:m/ n. 棘皮动物

kelp /kelp/ n. 大型褐藻

piscivorous /piˈsivərəs/ adj. 食鱼的

salmon /ˈsæmən/ n. 鲑鱼，大马哈鱼

aquaponics n. 水培

Mariculture /ˌmæriˈkʌltʃə/ n. 海洋生物养殖

carnivorous /kɑːˈnivərəs/ adj. 食肉的

asphyxiation /æsˌfiksiˈeiʃən/ n. 窒息

silver carp 白鲢

grass carp 草鱼

common carp 鲤鱼

bighead carp 鳙鱼

bigeye tuna 大眼金枪鱼

tilapia n. 罗非鱼

catfish /ˈkætˌfiʃ/ n. 鲶鱼

black carp n. 青鱼

crucian /ˈkruʃən/ n. 鲫鱼

finless eel 黄鳝

loach /ləutʃ/ n. 泥鳅

carcass /ˈkɑːkəs/ n. 尸体

intramuscular /ˌintrəmʌskjulə/ adj. 肌肉内的

shrimp /ʃrimp/ n. 虾，矮小人

exoskeleton /ˌeksəuˈskelitən/ n. 外骨骼

opaque /əuˈpeik/ adj. 不透明的，难理解的

prawn /prɔːn/ n. 对虾，明虾，大虾

lobster /ˌlɔbstə/ n. 龙虾

octopi /ˈɔktəpai/ n. pl. 章鱼

squid /skwid/ n. 乌贼，墨鱼，鱿鱼

cuttlefish /ˈkʌtlˌfiʃ/ n. 乌贼，墨鱼

selenium /səˈliːniəm/ n. 硒

hatchery /ˈhætʃəri/ n. 孵化，孵化场

raceway /ˈreswei/ n. 水沟，跑道，风口循环区

growout n. 成虾养殖（阶段）

big canopy /ˈkænəpi:/ n. 大棚

cartilaginous /ˌkɑːtəˈlædʒənəs/ adj. 软骨的

tortoise /ˈtɔːrtis/ n. 乌龟

hibernate /ˈhaibəˌneit/ vi. 冬眠

hatchling /ˈhætʃliŋ/ n. 孵化的鱼苗，小鸟或小龟

gourmet /ˈguəˌmei/ n. 美食

Florida red-bellied Turtle (Chrysemys nelsoni) 纳氏彩龟，佛罗里达红腹龟

brackish /ˈbrækiʃ/ adj. 微咸的，味道不好的

aphrodisiac /ˌæfrəˈdiziæk/ adj. 催欲的，激发性欲的； n. 壮阳药，春药，催欲药

nacre /ˈneikə/ n. 珍珠母，珍珠层，珍珠贝

oyster drill snails 海蜗牛

oyster flatworms 牡蛎扁虫

stingray /ˈstiŋrei/ n. 黄貂鱼

endosymbiotic /ˈendəuˌsimbaiˈɔtik/ adj. 内共生的

Chapter 1　Reading Materials of Life Sciences

commensal /kɔˈmensəl/ *adj.* 共生的，共餐的；*n.* 共餐者，共生动植物

protozoan /ˌprəutəuˈzəuən/ *n.* 原生动物；*adj.* 原生动物的

spawn /spɔːn/ *vt.&vi.* 产卵，大量生产；*n.* 卵

spat /spæt/ *n.* 特蛎卵，幼牡蛎；*v.* spit 的过去式和过去分词

dredging /ˈdredʒiŋ/ *n.* 挖泥

culch /kʌltʃ/ *n.* 贝壳屑，废物，垃圾，沙砾

benign /biˈnain/ *adj.* 仁慈的，亲切的；良性的；有利的，吉利的

restorative /risˈtɔːrətiv/ *adj.* 恢复健康的

water lily 睡莲，荷花

algaculture /ˈælɡəkʌltʃə/ *n.* 藻类养殖

feedstock /ˈfiːdstɔk/ *n.* 原料

sequester /siˈkwestə/ *vt.* 隔离，隔绝

Exercises

1. Matching Questions.

Write the letter of the phrase that best matches the numbered on the left. Use each only once.

(1) intensive aquaculture　　a. a system of fish aquaculture based on the natural productivity of wetlands.

(2) extensive aquaculture　　c. a system of fish aquaculture with external food supply

(3) the four famous Chinese carps　　c. a facility where eggs are hatched under artificial conditions, especially those of fish, shrimp or poultry.

(4) hatchery　　d. black carp, grass carp, silver carp and bighead carp.

(5) hibernation　　e. an oyster in the larval stage, especially when it settles to the bottom and begins to develop a shell.

(6) spat　　f. a state of inactivity and metabolic depression in animals, characterized by lower body temperature, slower breathing, and lower metabolic rate.

2. Fill in the blanks with the appropriate words you have just learned in this unit.

(1) The procedure for algaculture includes: isolate desired algae strain, build its culture environment, _____ and harvest cultured algae.

(2) Algal bloom is a rapid accumulation in the population of _____ in an aquatic system, which can cause _____ impacts to other organisms.

(3) _____ is a type of aquaculture in which algae and seaweed are cultivated.

(4) Oysters are used as food and to produce _____ and so on by humans.

(5) Farmed turtles are sold for use as _____, _____, cosmetics and pets.

(6) Shrimp aquaculture typically works in three stages: hatchery, nursery, and _____.

3. Multiple Choice Questions.

(1) (　　) are an excellent source of selenium.
　　A. Microalgae　　　B. Oysters　　　C. Carp
　　D. Shrimp　　　　　E. Aquatic plants

(2) Which of the following answers are common carp's advantages? (　　).
　　A. Fast swimming　　B. Very fast growth rate　　C. Giant size
　　D. High production per square unit　　　E. High tolerance

(3) Which are used in somecommonly used fish farms (　　)?
　　A. integrated recycling systems　　　B. missile system
　　C. pond systems　　D. tissue system　　E. cage system

(4) Particular kinds of aquaculture include (　　) crap farming and turtle farming.
　　A. pig　　　　　　　B. fish farming　　　C. oyster farming
　　D. shrimp farming　　E. algaculture

4. Reading Comprehension.

Directions: This passage is followed by six questions. You carefully read it first and then answer them one by one.

Tilapia Farming

Today, Tilapia has emerged to become the second biggest aquatic species group after the carp group, with a worldwide harvest of over 2 million metric tons, about 5% of global finfish aquaculture. Because of their large size, rapid growth and palatability, they are at the focus of major aquaculture efforts. Like other large fish, they are a good source of protein and a popular target for artisanal and commercial fisheries.

Of the 70 species of tilapia, nine are used in farming and, of these, the Nile tilapia (*Oreochromis niloticus*) is the main cultured species and responsible for the significant increase in global tilapia aquaculture production. The major tilapia-producing countries are China, Egypt, Indonesia, Philippines, Mexico, Thailand, Taiwan and Brazil.

Growout strategies for tilapia range from the simple to the very complex. Simple strategies are characterized by little control over water quality and food supply and by low fish yield. As greater control over water quality and fish nutrition are imposed, the production cost and fish yield per unit area increases. In traditioanal pond culture of tilapia, proper environmental conditions are maintained by balancing the inputs of feed with the natural assimilative capacity of the pond. The pond's natural biological productivity (algae, higher plants, zooplankton and bacteria) converts the wastes through natural biological processes. Increasing stocking densities places increasing demands on the production system. Additional energy inputs in the form of labor, water exchange, aeration and feeds are all required to sustain the intensive system. As pond production intensifies and feed rates increase, supplemental aeration and some water exchange are required to maintain good water quality. There is a point where the incremental returns are not worthy of the additional inputs and risks. Increasing the intensity of the system does not necessarily reflect an increase in profitability. All tilapia production systems must provide a suitable environment to promote the growth of the aquatic crop. Critical environmental parameters include the concentrations of dissolved oxygen, unionized ammonia nitrogen, nitrite nitrogen, and carbon dioxide in the water. Other important parameters include nitrate concentration, pH, and alkalinity levels within the system. To produce tilapia in a cost effective manner, production systems must be capable of maintaining proper levels of these water quality variables during periods of rapid fish growth. To provide for such growth, tilapia are fed high protein pelleted diets at rates ranging from 1.0% to 30% of their body weight per day depending upon their size and species.

Ponds, tanks, raceways, hapas and cages, for holding broodfish, fry, fingerlings, juveniles, subadult and adult tilapias are available to the prospective farmer. Tanks and raceways involve considerably greater expense to construct but offer greater control. They are usually used in intensive and superintensive culture of tilapias. Ponds are much cheaper to construct and allow management to stimulate natural productivity more readily. The major drawback of pond culture of tilapias is the greater risk of uncontrolled reproduction, which will occur if certain measures are not taken to minimize this possibility. Ponds are used in extensive, semiintensive and intensive tilapia production. Pond culture is by far the most common method because it is the cheapest method and also is one of the best. Ponds are the traditional and inexpensive way to hold spawning populations of broodfish. In some parts of the world, the pond system has been made more efficient through the use of cages or net enclosures (hapas). Basically, the hapas are fine mesh net enclosures that are about 40 square meters in size and arranged into units within a larger pond. This segregates the pond into more easily managed units. On a per unit area basis, tanks are the most efficient method of collecting and raising tilapia, followed by hapas and simple ponds. From the different pathogens found, *Streptococcus* is the most common, widespread and pathogenic, while rickettsia-like organism is an emerging pathogen. *Flavobacterium columnare* infection is a common pathogen in early stages. Iridovirus is the only documented viral disease in tilapia. Commercially grown tilapia are almost exclusively male. Being prolific breeders, female tilapia in the ponds or tanks will result in large populations of small fish. Whole tilapia can be processed into skinless, boneless fillets: the yield is from 30% to 37%, depending on fillet size and final trim.

Questions for Discussion:

(1) Which fish group is the first biggest aquatic species group based on this passage? ( )

    A. Tilapia.   B. Carp group.   C. Giant salamander.   D. Whale.

(2) How many tilapia species isresponsible for the significant increase in global tilapia aquaculture production? ( )

    A. Seventy.   B. Nine.   C. Three.   D. One.

(3) By what are simple growout strategies for tilapia characterized? ( )

    A. Little control over water quality and food supply and low fish yield.

    B. Fish anatomy.   C. Stocking density.   D. Labor.

(4) How many importantenvironmental parameters are included in tilapia farming? ( )

    A. Four.   B. Seven.   C. One.   D. Ten.

(5) What isthe most common and cheapest method for tilapia culture? ( )

    A. Tank culture.   B. Cage culture.

    C. Hapas culture.   D. Pond culture.

(6) What determines yield of skinless and boneless fillets, when whole tilapia can be processed into them?

5. Invite one foreign biologist to give English academic lectures to students or let students watch English movies on biology.

Unit 13　Bioinformatics and Genomics

导语　生物信息学是一个新兴的综合学科,是当今生命科学和自然科学的重大前沿领域之一。它基于网上大量DNA和氨基酸及其相关资料,综合使用生物学、物理学、化学计算机科学、信息技术和数学等学科的技术与工具进行生物信息的获取、处理、储存、分配、分析和注释等各方面研究工作。其研究重点主要体现在基因组学(Genomics)和蛋白质组学(Proteomics)两方面。

　　本单元主要介绍生物信息学、基因组学、结构基因组学、转录组学、蛋白质组学、代谢组学和比较基因组学的技术、原理和应用。

13.1　Bioinformatics

Bioinformatics is a scientific discipline that encompasses all aspects of biological information acquisition, processing, storage, distribution, analysis and interpretation and combines the tools and techniques of biology, physics, chemistry, computer science, information technology and mathematics based on the enormous volume of data (DNA and animo acid sequences and related information) available on the internet. It is a rapidly growing and changing field. Its main contents include ① its computer base such as databases, computer knowledge and internet. For example, there are more than four hundred key databases, including International Nucleotide and Protein Sequence Databases such as the National Center for Biotechnoloy Information (NCBI), the European Molecular Biology Laboratory (EMBL) and DNA Data Bank of Japan (DDBJ), HIV Databases (http://www.hiv.lanl.gov/content/index), Human Protein Reference Database(HPRD)(http://www.hprd.org/). ② bioinformatic resources and tools. For example, BLAST (Basic Local Alignment Search Tool), which is the most commonly used genome tool, MATLAB (matrix laboratory), which allows matrix manipulations, plotting of functions and data, implementation of algorithms, creation of user interfaces, and interfacing with programs written in other languages, including C, C++, Java, and Fortran. ③ DNA sequencing, ④ molecular phylogenetic analysis, ⑤ genomic analyses including functional genomics, comparative genomics and so on.

Bioinformatics has been widely used in the discovery and identification of human diseases and functional genes, the study of gene expression and protein functions, drug design and development, education and so forth. For instance, BLAST programs find the regions of similarity between different protein-coding genes. A BLAST search often involves searching a genome or the genomes of many different organisms for all of the predicted sequences which are related to the sequence of interest, called query sequence. Statistical methods are used by BLAST programs to determine the likelihood that the "hits", which are the genes or encoded proteins identified by the query sequence, have a similar function. Fig. 13-1 indicates that the genes encoding regulatory proteins containing a specislized form of the zinc finger DNA-binding motif when a similar motif from the thyroid hormone receptor is used as a query. A particular gene may be found to make a protein involved in regulating blood pressure. From this understanding, we can determine if certain individuals who are predisposed to abnormal blood pressure have a mutation in that gene that causes its protein product to malfunction. We can also ascertain whether it would be worthwhile to develop a drug that affects the activity of the protein as a way to treat high blood pressure (i.e., if the product of the gene is a good drug target). Recently, there has also been tremendous interest in determining the genetic basis of the different responses of patients to the same drugs. This knowledge will allow pharmaceutical companies to determine if particular drugs are applicable to all patients, or only a subset, which will in turn allow them to develop more effective clinical trials.

>☐ gi|55932|emb|CAA31237.1| **G** c-erb-A thyroid hormone receptor [Rattus norvegicus]
　　　　Length = 398

　　Score = 73.6 bits (179),　Expect = 2e-12
　　Identities = 30/30 (100%),　Positives = 30/30 (100%),　Gaps = 0/30 (0%)

　　Query　 1　　CVVCGDKATGYHYRCITCEGCKGFFRRTIQ　　30
　　　　　　　　 CVVCGDKATGYHYRCITCEGCKGFFRRTIQ
　　Sbjct　41　　CVVCGDKATGYHYRCITCEGCKGFFRRTIQ　　70

>☐ gi|47216914|emb|CAG02086.1| unnamed protein product [Tetraodon nigroviridis]
　　　　Length = 385

　　Score = 73.6 bits (179),　Expect = 2e-12
　　Identities = 30/30 (100%),　Positives = 30/30 (100%),　Gaps = 0/30 (0%)

　　Query　 1　　CVVCGDKATGYHYRCITCEGCKGFFRRTIQ　　30
　　　　　　　　 CVVCGDKATGYHYRCITCEGCKGFFRRTIQ
　　Sbjct　28　　CVVCGDKATGYHYRCITCEGCKGFFRRTIQ　　57

>☐ gi|209662|gb|AAA42393.1| polyprotein gag-p75-erbA [Avian erythroblastosis virus]
　　　　Length = 455

　　Score = 71.2 bits (173),　Expect = 9e-12
　　Identities = 29/30 (96%),　Positives = 29/30 (96%),　Gaps = 0/30 (0%)

　　Query　 1　　CVVCGDKATGYHYRCITCEGCKGFFRRTIQ　　30
　　　　　　　　 CVVCGDKATGYHYRCITCEGCK FFRRTIQ
　　Sbjct　94　　CVVCGDKATGYHYRCITCEGCKSFFRRTIQ　　123

>☐ gi|22087251|gb|AAM90896.1| **G** farnesoid X receptor [Gallus gallus]
　gi|45383880|ref|NP_989444.1| **G** nuclear receptor subfamily 1, group H, member 4
　　　　Length = 473

　　Score = 62.4 bits (150),　Expect = 4e-09
　　Identities = 24/29 (82%),　Positives = 27/29 (93%),　Gaps = 0/29 (0%)

　　Query　　1　　CVVCGDKATGYHYRCITCEGCKGFFRRTI　　29
　　　　　　　　　CVVCGDKA+GYHY +TCEGCKGFFRR+I
　　Sbjct　128　　CVVCGDKASGYHYNALTCEGCKGFFRRSI　　156

Fig. 13-1 The genes encoding regulatory proteins containing a specislized form of the zinc finger DNA-binding motif are identified by a BLAST search when a similar motif from the thyroid hormone receptor is used as a query (Allison L A, 2008)

A sequence of amino acid residues from the specislized zinc finger DNA-binding domain of thyroid hormone receptor α, which is a ligand-activated transcription factor, from the brown Norway rat was used to query the protein sequence database via the publicly available BLAST website. The results of a search are usually available within less than a minute. The first one of the hits with the highest scores shown is the rat thyroid hormone receptor α itself. The second is an unnamed protein product from the pufferfish. A score of 179 is assigned to the match between the rat thyroid hormone receptor α and the pufferfish protein. A total of 30 out of 30 amino acid residues are identical between the two (100% identity), suggesting the pufferfish protein may also function as a ligand-activated nuclear factor. A score of 173 was obtained for the polyprotein v-ErbA. In this case, there are 29 out of 30 exact matches (96% identity). The third hit shown is for the farnesoid X receptor from chicken. A score of 150 was assigned to the match. A total of 24 out of 29 amino acid residues are identical between the two (82% identity), 27 of the residues are either identical or similar. The farnesoid X receptor has recently identified as a bile acid-activated nuclear receptor that controls synthesis, conjunction, transport and lipid metabolism.

13.2 Genomics and Its Main Branches

13.2.1 Genomics

The genome is the entirety of an organism's hereditary information. It is encoded either in DNA or, for many types of virus, in RNA. The genome includes both the genes and the non-coding sequences of the DNA/RNA. Genomics is a branch of molecular biology studying the structure, function and products (proteins and RNAs) of whole sets of genes (genomes). Genomics is based on automated, high-throughput methods of generating experimental data, such as DNA microarrays and single nucleotide polymorphisms (SNPs). Genomics has the potential of offering new therapeutic methods for the treatment of some diseases, as well as new diagnostic methods. Other applications are in the food and agriculture sectors. The major tools and methods related to genomics are bioinformatics, genetic analysis, measurement of gene expression, and determination of gene function. Genomics can now be broadly divided into three different branches: structural genomics, functional genomics and comparative genomics. Post-genomics is a discipline mainly studying genes' functions, interactions and controlling mechanisms. Its core is functional genomics, which is a field of molecular biology that attempts to make use of the vast wealth of data produced by genomic projects to describe gene and protein functions and interactions. Functional genomics uses high throughput techniques like transcriptomics, proteomics, metabolomics and mutation analysis to describe the function and interactions of genes, and helps to co-relate the structure and sequence of the genome to its function. Because of the large quantity of data and the desire to be able to find patterns and predict gene functions and interactions, bioinformatics is crucial to this type of analysis.

13.2.2 Structural Genomics

Structural genomics involves the construction of high-resolution genetic, physical, or transcript maps of the organism usually during the initial phase of genome analysis which results in the ultimate physical map of an organism with its complete genome sequencing. In recent years, due to the completion of the various genome-sequencing projects, Structural genomics now also includes the high throughput determination of three-dimensional structures of all proteins. Hence the structural genomics establishes the relationship between the sequence and structure of a genome. For example, 4 maps such as genetic maps, physical maps, sequences and transcriptional maps had been constructed, when human complete genome sequencing was finished.

In practice, the generation of sufficient sequence data is one of the more routine aspects of a genome project. The first real problem that arises is the need to assemble the thousands or perhaps millions of individual sequences into a contiguous genome sequence. Two different strategies have been developed for sequence assembly: ① The shotgun approach, by which the genome is randomly broken into short fragments. The resulting sequences are examined for overlaps and used to build up the contiguous genome sequence. ② The clone contig approach, which involves a presequencing phase during which a series of overlapping clones is identified. Each piece of cloned DNA is then sequenced and placed at its appropriate position on the contig map in order to gradually build up the overlapping genome sequence.

Once a genome sequence has been completed, the next step is to locate all the genes and determine their functions.

(1) Gene location.

Locating a gene is easy if the amino acid sequence of the protein product is known, allowing the nucleotide sequence of the gene to be predicted, or if the corresponding cDNA or EST has been previously sequenced. But for many genes there is no prior information that enables the correct DNA sequence to be recognized. Under these circumstances, gene location might be difficult even if a map is available. Most maps have only a limited accuracy and can only delineate the approximate position of a gene, possibly leaving several tens or even hundreds of kilobases to search in order to find it. And many genes do not appear on maps because their existence is unsuspected. How can these genes be located in a genome sequence? The DNA sequence of a gene is an open reading frame (ORF), a series of nucleotide triplets beginning with an initiation codon (usually but not always AUG) and ending in a termination codon (TAA, TAG or TGA in most genomes). Searching a genome sequence for ORFs, by eye or more usually by computer, is therefore the first step in gene location. It is important to search all six reading frames because genes can run in either direction along the DNA double helix (Fig. 13-2). With a bacterial genome the typical result of this search is identification of long ORFs that are almost certainly genes, with many shorter ORFs partly or completely contained within the genes but lying in different reading frames (Fig. 13-2). These short sequences are almost certainly combinations of nucleotides that by chance form an ORF but are not genes. If one of these short ORFs lies entirely between two genes, there is a possibility that it might mistakenly be identified as a real gene, but in most bacterial genomes there is very little space between the genes so the problem arises only infrequently.

Gene location in eukaryotes is much more difficult. Eukaryotic genomes are not as densely packed as bacterial ones and there are much longer spaces between genes. This means that inspection of the sequence reveals many short ORFs that cannot be discounted because they do not overlap with real genes. Analysis of the yeast genome, for example, identified over 400 short ORFs that were placed in this "questionable" category. Possibly some of these are real genes but probably most of them are not. In humans and other higher eukaryotes, the search for genes is made even more complicated by the fact that many are split into exons and introns. Particular nucleotide sequences always occur at exon-intron boundaries but these sequences are also found within exons and within introns. Working out which of these sequences mark true exon-intron boundaries can be very difficult.

Some genomes provide helpful signposts that indicate the presence of a gene. The human and other vertebrate genomes are particularly helpful to the molecular biologist, because 50 – 60% of the genes are accompanied by a CpG

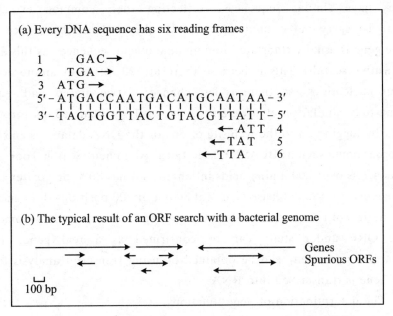

Fig. 13-2 Searching for open reading frames (Brown, 2002)
(a) Every DNA sequence has six open reading frames, any one of which could contain a gene. (b) The typical result of a search for ORFs in a bacterial genome. The arrows indicate the directions in which the genes and spurious ORFs run.

island, a distinctive GC-rich sequence whose position indicates the approximate start point for gene. But features such as these are the exception rather than the rule and more general methods for identifying genes are needed. With many genomes, codon bias provides a useful means of assigning a degree of certainty to a possible gene identification. All amino acids except methionine and tryptophan are specified by two or more codons. Displaying a distinct bias for certain codons; for example, within the alanine codon family, humans use GCC four times more frequently than GCG. If an ORF contains a high frequency of rare codons then it probably is not a gene. By taking account of the codon bias displayed by an ORF, an informed guess can therefore be made as to whether the sequence is or is not a gene. Tentative identification of a gene is usually followed by a homology search, in which the sequence of the gene is compared with all the gene sequences present in the international DNA databases, not just known genes of the organism under study but also genes from all other species. The rationale is that two genes from different organisms that have similar functions have similar sequences, reflecting their common evolutionary histories. To carry out a homology search, the nucleotide sequence of the tentative gene is usually translated into an amino acid sequence, as this allows a more sensitive search. This is because there are 20 different amino acids but only four nucleotides, so there is less chance of two amino acid sequences appearing to be similar purely by chance. The analysis is carried out through the internet, by logging on to the web site of one of the DNA databases and using a search programme such as BLAST (Basic Local Alignment Search Tool). If the test sequence is over 200 amino acids in length and has 30% or greater identity with a sequence in the database (i.e., at 30 out of 100 positions the same amino acid occurs in both sequences), then the two are almost certainly homologous and the ORF under study can be confirmed as a real gene. Further confirmation, if needed, can be obtained by using transcript analysis to show that the gene is transcribed into RNA.

(2) The determination of gene functions.

Homology search is also used to give an indication of the function of the gene, presuming that the function of the homologous gene is known. Almost 2,000 of the genes in the yeast genome were assigned functions in this way. Frequently, however, the matches found by homology search are to other genes whose functions have yet to be determined. These unassigned genes are called orphans and working out their function as one of the major challenges of post-genomics research. In future years it will be possible to use bioinformatics to gain at least an insight into the function of an orphan gene. It is already possible to use the nucleotide sequence of a gene to predict the positions of α-helices and β-sheets in the encoded protein with limited accuracy, and the resulting structural information can sometimes be used to make inferences about the function of the protein. Proteins that attach to membranes can often be identified because they possess α-helical arrangements that span the membrane, and DNA binding motifs such as zinc fingers can be recognized. A greater scope and accuracy to this aspect of bioinformatics will be possible when more information is obtained about the relationship between the stucture of a protein and its function.

13.2.3 Transcriptomics

The sum of all RNAs, including mRNA, rRNA, tRNA, and other non-coding RNA produced by an organism is its transcriptome. Transcriptomics is the branch of molecular biology that study the transcripts in a transcriptome. However, generally, transcriptomics is the study of the mRNAs in a transcriptome.

There are three types of techniques for studying the transcriptome: ① hybridization-based methods, such as microarrays and DNA chips; ② sequencing-based methods, including cDNA library, EST library and SAGE; and ③ clustering gene expression data. For example, microarrays (Fig. 13-3) are now being used to monitor changes in the transcriptomes of many organisms. To prepare the DNA microarray or chip, individual gene sequences (partial cDNA or oligonucleotides) are applied to glass microscope side by a robotic device and amplified by PCR. A microarray for all the human genes could be carried by just 10 glass slides of 18 mm by 18 mm, but preparing clones of every one of the 30,000 – 40,000 human genes would be a massive task. Fortunately this is not necessary. For example, to study changes in the transcriptome, a microarray could be

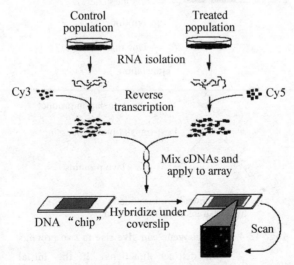

Fig. 13-3 Microarray analysis

The microarray shown here has been hybridized to two different cDNA preparations, each labeled with a fluorescent dye (Cy3 or Cy5). The clones which hybridize with the cDNAs are identified by confocal microscopy

prepared with a cDNA library from control population. Hybridization with labelled cDNA from treated population would then reveal how genes are expressed.

13.2.4 Proteomics

The proteome is the entire collection of proteins in a cell. The word "proteome" is a blend of "protein" and "genome", and was coined by Marc Wilkins in 1994. Proteomics is the large-scale study of proteins, particularly their structures and functions, which was first coined in 1997 to make an analogy with genomics.

Proteome studies provide additional information that is not obtainable simply by examining the transcriptome, because a single mRNA (and hence gene) can give rise to more than one protein, because of post-translational processing (Fig. 13-4). In eukaryotes, most of the polypeptides are further processed by addition of chemical groups after translation. The particular additions determine the precise function of the protein. Phosphorylation, for example, is an important modification used to activate some proteins.

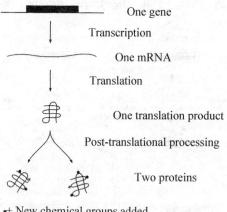

+ New chemical groups added by post-translational processing

Fig. 13-4 A single gene can give rise to two proteins with distinct functions, if the initial translation product can be modified in two different ways by post-translational processing (Brown, 2002)

To study the proteome, the entire protein content of a cell or tissue is first separated by two-dimensional electrophoresis. In this technique, the proteins are loaded into a well on one side of a square of polyacrylamide gel and separated according to their molecular weights. The square is then rotated by 90° and a second electrophoresis performed, this time separating the proteins on the basis of their charges. The result is two-dimensional pattern of spots, of different sizes, shapes and intensities, each representing a different protein or related group of proteins. Differences between two proteomes are apparent from differences in the pattern of spots when the two gels are compared. To identify the protein in a particular spot, a sample is purified from the gel and treated with a protease that cuts the polypeptide at a specific amino acid sequence. The resulting peptides are then examined by mass spectrometry. The mass spectrometer determines the amino acid composition of each peptide. This information is usually sufficient to enable the gene coding for the protein to be identified from the genome sequence. In addition, protein arrays formats allow rapid analysis of protein activity on a proteomic scale.

13.2.5 Metabolomics

Metabolome refers to the complete set of small-molecule metabolites (such as metabolic intermediates, hormones, other signaling molecules, and secondary metabolites) to be found within a biological sample, such as a single organism. Within the context of metabolomics, a metabolite is usually defined as any molecule less than 1 kDa in size. Metabolomics is the scientific study of chemical processes involving metabolites. Specifically, it is the study of their small-molecule metabolite profiles. Separation methods of metabolomics are mainly gas chromatography, high performance liquid chromatography (HPLC) and capillary electrophoresis (CE). Detection methods of metabolomics are mainly mass spectrometry (MS), nuclear magnetic resonance (NMR) spectroscopy and so on. Metabolomics is used in toxicity assessment, the determination of the phenotype caused by a genetic manipulation, such as gene deletion or insertion, nutrigenomics (a generalised term which links genomics, transcriptomics, proteomics and metabolomics to human nutrition) and the environmental sciences (called environmental metabolomics, the application of metabolomics to characterise the interactions of organisms with their environment). One of the challenges of systems biology and functional genomics is to integrate proteomic, transcriptomic, and metabolomic information to give a more complete picture of living organisms.

13.2.6 Comparative Genomics

Comparative genomics is the analysis and comparison of genomes from different species. The purpose is to gain a better understanding of how species have evolved and to determine the function of genes and noncoding regions of the genome. Comparative genomics involves the use of computer programs that can line up multiple genomes and look for regions of similarity among them. For example, evolutionary relationship between humans, pufferfish and other vertebrates (Fig. 13-5).

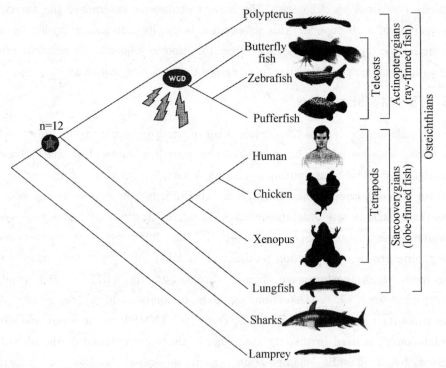

Fig. 13-5 Evolutionary relationship between humans, pufferfish and other vertebrates (Allison L A, 2008)

By comparing the genome sequence of the spotted green pufferfish, *Tetraodon nigroviridis*, with that of humans, researchers have deduced that the extinct ancestor of actinopterygians (ray-finned fish including pufferfish) and sarcopterygians (lobe-finned fish, the lineage that gave rise to humans) have twelve pairs of chromosomes. In contrast, the modern pufferfish has twenty-one pairs of chromosomes. In addition, a whole-genome duplication (WGD) occurred during the evolution of ray-finned fish.

Vocabulary

bioinformatics /baiəuinfə'mætiks/ n. 生物信息学
disseminate /di'semineit/ vt. 传播
database /'deitəbeis/ n. 数据库
genomics /dʒə'nəumiks/ n. 基因组学
algorithm /'ælgəriðəm/ n. 运算法则，算法，计算程序，演示
phylogenetic /ˌfailəudʒi'netik/ adj. 系统发生的
promoter /prə'məutə/ n. 启动子
overlap /ˌəuvə'læp/ vt. 重叠
query sequence 查询序列
malfunction /mæl'fʌŋkʃən/ vi. 功能异常，故障，障碍
high-throughput 高通量的
motif /məu'ti:f/ n. 基序
microarray /'maikrəurei/ n. 微阵列
Post-genomics n. 后基因组学
transcriptomics n. 转录组学
Proteome n. 蛋白质组
metabolomics n. 代谢组学
shotgun approach 鸟枪法
contiguous /kən'tigju:əs/ adj. 重叠的，相接的
clone contig approach 克隆重叠群法
delineate /di'linieit/ vt. 描绘，描写
wafer /'weifə/ n. 薄脆饼，圣饼

signpost /'sainˌpəust/ n. 路标
lamprey /'læmpri/ n. 七鳃鳗；八目鳗
transcriptome n. 转录组
SAGE (Serial analysis of gene expression) n. 基因表达系列分析
oligonucleotide n. 寡聚核苷酸
denovo /di:'nəuvəu/ n. 重新，更始
Proteomics n. 蛋白质组学
mass spectrometry /mæs spekˌtrɒmitri/ n. 质谱
chromatography /ˌkrəumə'tɒgrəfi/ n. 色谱分析法
nuclear magnetic resonance (NMR) spectroscopy 核磁共振波谱
Tetraodon nigroviridis 绿河豚，又叫潜水艇、金娃娃、狗头、鸡泡鱼或斑点-绿色-河豚(spotted green pufferfish)
actinopterygians 辐鳍鱼类
ray-finned fish 条鳍鱼
sarcopterygians 肉鳍鱼类：拥有肉质叶状鳍，偶鳍为原鳍型的硬骨鱼类
lobe-finned fish 总鳍鱼
osteichthyans n. 硬骨鱼
tetrapods n. 四足动物
teleosts n. 真骨鱼类
polypterus n. 多鳍鱼
xenopus n. 非洲爪蟾

Exercises

1. Matching Questions.

Write the letter of the phrase that best matches the numbered on the left. Use each only once.

(1) bioinformatics
(2) a database
(3) bioinformatic tools
(4) DNA-binding domain
(5) consensus sequences
(6) genomics
(7) single nucleotide polymorphisms (SNPs)
(8) post-genomics
(9) open reading frame (ORF)
(10) functional genomics

a. a library housing DNA and amino acid sequences and related information in bioinformatics.
b. computer and some softwares used in bioinformatics.
c. an independently folded protein domain that contains at least one motif that recognizes DNA.
d. a DNA sequence variation occurring when a single nucleotide in the genome or other shared sequence differs between members of a biological species in an individual.
e. the study of the genes' functions, interactions and controlling mechanisms at the genome level.
f. a series of nucleotide triplets beginning with an initiation codon and ending in a termination codon.
g. a discipline describing gene and protein functions and interactions with bioinformation data and high-throughput techniques.
h. a discipline in genetics concerning the study of the genomes of organisms.
i. the most common nucleotide or amino acid at a particular position after multiple sequences are aligned in bioinformatics.
j. a discipline studying biological information with mathemetical, statistical, computer scientific, and information technological methods, and the enormous volume of data available on the internet.

Chapter 1 Reading Materials of Life Sciences

2. Fill in the blanks with the appropriate words you have just learned in this unit.

(1) _____ is the branch of molecular biology that study the transcripts in a transcriptome.

(2) DNA microarrays can measure the differential _____ of many genes by means of molecular hybridization.

(3) Techniques for studying the transcriptome can be divided into 3 types, such as hybridization-based methods, sequcencing-based methods and _____.

(4) According to the text, the techniques widely used in proteomics are two-dimensional _____, mass spectrometer and _____.

(5) _____ is a disciplince which deals with all metabolites of an organism.

(6) Detection methods of metabolomics are mainly _____ and nuclear magnetic resonance (NMR) spectroscopy.

(7) Comparative genomics is the analysis and comparison of _____ from different species.

(8) Only about _____ of the human genome differs from one person to another.

3. Please answer the sequence alignment question: HbB vs. Hbs using the internet.

Chapter 2 Translation Techniques of English for Science and Technology (EST)

Unit 1 Writing Rules of English Articles for Science and Technology and Examples

导语 科技英语(English for Science and Technology,EST)在词汇构成、语法结构、语篇等方面都具有鲜明的特点和规律。

本单元主要介绍科技术语的构词,科技英语在词汇、句法和语篇等方面的特点及其实例。

1.1 Characteristics of EST Words

There are many special technical words and terms in biology, so we have difficulties in memorizing all of them one by one. However, we can know them by means of word formation methods. Generally speaking, there are three main kinds of word formation methods: conversion, compounding and derivation.

1.1.1 Conversion (转化)

由一类词转化为另一类词。例如:
water (noun) → water (verb, 浇水)。

1.1.2 Compounding (合成)

由两个以上的词组合成一个词。例如:
wood(木) + cut(刻)→woodcut(木刻), blood(血) + test(测验)→blood test (验血)。

1.1.3 Derivation(派生)

在词根（base）前或后加前缀或后缀构成新的词。
Derivation words are composed of bases and prefixes or/and suffixes.

1.1.3.1 How to Add a Prefix

(1) To add a prefix with a hyphen
Take "semi-" for example:
① semi-continuous replication（半连续复制）
② semi-aerobic（半好氧的）
③ semi-professional（半专业的）
④ semi-monthly（半月刊）
The prefix "semi-" means half, partial or incomplete and twice per a period.
(2) To add a prefix without a hyphen
① disulfide（二硫化物，其中 di-为前缀）
② divalent chromosome（二价染色体，其中 di-为前缀）
③ isotope（同位元素，其中 iso-为前缀）

1.1.3.2 How to Add a Suffix

To add a suffix without a hyphen, for example:
Lysosome（溶酶体，其中-some 为后缀，意思是"……体"）

1.1.4 Some Common Prefixes and Suffixes and Term Examples

1.1.4.1 Some Prefixes and Terms

① cell, cyto, cellular: of cell 细胞的
    e.g., cell differentiation 细胞分化　　cytology　　　　细胞学
         cytoplasm　　　　　细胞质　　cellular immunity　细胞免疫
         cellular substance　细胞间质

② nucle(o), nucleic, nuclear: of nucleus 核的
    e.g., nucleolus　　　核仁　　　nucleoside　　　　核苷
         nucleotide　　核苷酸　　nucloprotein　　　核蛋白
         nuclic acid　　核酸　　　nuclear membrane　核膜

③ de: remove 脱

E.g., deoxyribonucleotide   脱氧核糖核苷酸
       dehydratase   脱氢酶

④ ribo：of ribose 核糖的

E.g., ribosome   核糖体   ribonuclease   核糖核酸酶
       riboflavin   核黄素

⑤ bio：biological 生物的

E.g., biotin   生物素   biotechnology   生物技术
       bioengineering   生物工程

⑥ root，rhizo：of root 根的

E.g., root-inducing plasmin   致根质粒
       rhizobium   根瘤菌

⑦ trans, reverse, anti and retro：backward, resistant 转（移），反，抗，逆

E.g., transformation   转化   transduction   转导
       translation   翻译   transcription   转录
       transfection   转染   transplantation   移栽
       transposon   转座子   transaminase   转氨酶
       anticodon   反密码子   antibody   抗体
       retrotransposon   逆转座子
       reverse polymerase chain reaction   逆转录 PCR

⑧ gene, geno, genetic：of gene 基因的，遗传的

E.g., genetics   遗传学   genome   基因组

⑨ hypo：below 下的

E.g., hypocotyle   下胚轴

⑩ hyper：above, super 上的，过的

E.g., hypercotyle   上胚轴   hyperoxidase   过氧化物酶

⑪ pro, proto：promitive 自始的

E.g., protoplasm   原生质   protoplast   原生质体
       prokaryote   原核生物

⑫ euo：true 真的

E.g., euokaryote   真核生物

⑬ mal：not good 不良的

E.g., malformation   畸形   maladjustment   失调
       malnutrition   营养不良   malady   歪风
       a social malady   社会歪风

⑭ self：personal 自己的，个人的
　　E.g., self-pollination　　自花授粉　　self-evaluation　　自我评价
⑮ ultra：super, exo 超的
　　E.g., ultraviolet　　紫外线
⑯ thermo：warm 热的
　　E.g., thermogenesis　　生热作用　　thermometer　　温度计
　　　　　thermocycler　　PCR 仪
⑰ endo, intro：inside 内的
　　E.g., endonuclease　　核酸内切酶　　endotoxin　　内毒素
　　　　　endoplasmic reticulum 内质网　　intron　　内含子
⑱ exo：outside 外的
　　E.g., exonuclease　　核酸外切酶　　exon　　外显子
　　　　　exogenous　　外源的
⑲ chromo(a)：colorful 有色的
　　E.g., chromosome　　染色体　　chromatin　　染色质
⑳ physio：of physiology 生理的
　　E.g., physiotherapy　　生理疗法
㉑ zoo：of animal 动物的
　　E.g., zoology　　动物学
㉒ micro：tiny, mini, small 微小的
　　E.g., microorganism　　微生物　　microscope　　显微镜
　　　　　microinjection　　显微注射
㉓ macro：big, large 宏大的
　　E.g., macromolecule　　大分子　　macrospore　　大孢子
㉔ homo, iso：same, pure 同的，纯的
　　E.g., homozygote　　纯合子　　homosexual love　　同性恋
　　　　　isogenous　　同源的
　　　　　isotope labelled method　　同位素标记法
㉕ hetero：different, mixed 不同的，混合的
　　E.g., heterozygote　　杂合子　　heterosis　　杂种优势
　　　　　hctcrosex　　异性
㉖ ga：half 半
　　E.g., galactose　　半乳糖

1.1.4.2 Some Suffixes and Terms

① -ose: of sugar 糖的
E.g., glucose 葡萄糖　　　sucrose 蔗糖
　　　lactose 乳糖　　　fructose (fruit sugar) 果糖

② -ology: what a branch of science studies 学科
E.g., ecology 生态学　　　embryology 胚胎学
　　　freshwater planktology 淡水浮游生物学
　　　ichthyology 鱼类学

但是，不是所有的学科名字都具有-ology 后缀。例如：
　　　botany 植物学　　　anatomy 解剖学
　　　genetics 遗传学

③ -ase: of enzyme 酶
E.g., protease 蛋白酶　　　ribonuclease 核糖核酸酶
　　　dehydrogenase 脱氢酶

④ -mycin: a component of moulds 霉素
E.g., kanamycin 卡那霉素　　　streptomycin 链霉素

⑤ -in: of elements 素
E.g., Penicillin 青霉素　　　Ampicillin 氨苄青霉素
　　　Biotin 生物素

In addition, sometimes, several other prefixes or suffixes are added to a base. For example:

① radioautography　　　放射自显影
② deoxynucleotidyl transferase　　　脱氧核苷酸转移酶

Certainly, there are many biological words and terms for you to study in the near future.

1.2　Characteristics of EST Sentences

科技英语着重于描述客观事物或者逻辑推理，在词汇、句法和语篇等方面具有与公共英语不同的独特特点及其自身鲜明的文体风格。

1.2.1 Characteristics of EST Vocabulary

科技工作者为了科学、准确地用科技英语阐述科技领域内的新理论和新发现，

在遣词方面独具匠心。因此,其词汇独具以下特点:

(1) 多来源于拉丁语和希腊语,字形比较长。例如:

1. The word "biology" (生物学) comes from the Greek bios, which means life, and logos, which means "word" or "thought".

2. The word "eukaryote" (真核生物) comes from the Greek for "true nucleus".

(2) 同义词语的词义多专业化

同一个英语单词可以被多个领域使用,在不同领域中的词义差异很大。例如:"cell"一词在细胞生物学领域、物理学领域和通讯技术领域的意思分别是"细胞"、"电池"和"小区"。

(3) 常常使用缩略语

在科技英语中缩略语的构成有以下三种形式:

① 首字母连在一起构成缩略词,有两种读法:或首字母依次读出,或当做一个词读出。例如:ATP (adenosine-triphosphate,腺嘌呤核苷三磷酸), RNA (Ribonucleic Acid,核糖核酸), AIDS (Acquired Immune Deficiency Syndrome,获得性免疫功能丧失综合症,即艾滋病), WTO (World Trade Organization,世界贸易组织)。

② 两个或多个单词中抽出部分构成新词,例如:bioinformatics (生物信息学)。

③ 抽出一个词的一部分构成一个新词,例如:influenza — flu (流感), refrigerator — refrige (冰箱), parachute — chute (降落伞)。

(4) 大量使用名词和名词词组

① 把动词转化为名词使用,例如:"实用润滑剂能够提高离心机性能"应译为"an improvement (名词) of the centrifuge performance can be achieved by the use (名词) of lubricants",而不宜译作"You can improve the centrifuge performance by using lubricants"。

② 广泛使用名词词组,简短而明确地表达概念或其他,例如:plant tissue culture, human genome project, polymerase chain reaction。

1.2.2 Characteristics of EST Syntax

科技英语文章句法具有无人称句多、专业名词和术语多、非谓语动词多、被动语态多和长句子多、习惯使用后置定语等特点。

① 无(非)人称句多 (More Impersonal Pronouns)

因为专业英语文章的主要目的在于说明科学事实、发现、实验结果和证据等,而不在于介绍其发明人,所以,专业英语文章的语句往往是无人称的,无人称句多是专业英语文章的一个显著特点。无人称性主要指避免直接提及说话者或受话者,例如避免使用人称代词。但是,有时因为写作的需要,也会使用少量的人称句。仔细研读 Example 1 - 4,你会发现,其中没有一个人称句子。

② 专业名词和术语多(More Special Nouns and Terms)

科技英语文章涉及特定的专业领域,专业性非常强,文体正式,使用的专业名词和专业术语很多,而且其中相当大一部分是缩略词或者拉丁文。仔细研读 Example1 和 Example 2,你会发现其中能够体现此特点的专业名词和专业术语有:transgenic hairy roots(转基因发状根), *Aralia elata*(楤木), *A. rhizogenes*(发根农杆菌), hairy root induction(发状根诱导), somatic embryogenesis(体细胞胚胎发生), RT-PCR(逆转录多聚酶链式反应), IAA(吲哚乙酸)和 single nucleotide polymorphisms(SNPs,单核苷酸多态性),等等。

Example 1

Transgenic hairy roots were induced from petiole and root segments of *in vitro plant Aralia elata*, a medicinal woody shrub, after co-cultivation with *A. rhizogenes* 15834. The percentage of putative hairy root induction from root segments was higher (26.7%) than petiole explants (10.0%).

Hairy roots showed active production of lateral roots with vigorous elongation. Transgenic plants were regenerated from hairy roots via somatic embryogenesis. These plants had wrinkled leaves, short petioles and numerous lateral hairy roots. The RT-PCR analysis showed the expression of several genes differed between the transgenic lines. Endogenous IAA level was higher in transgenic than non-transgenic plants. Conclusively, transgenic hairy roots were developed for first time in *A. elata* and the transgenic hairy root lines showed distinct morphological growth pattern and gene expression.

③ 非谓语动词多(More Non-finite Verbs)

非谓语动词(the Non-finite Verbs)是指在句子中不作谓语的动词,主要包括不定式、动名词和分词(现在分词和过去分词),即动词的非谓语形式。非谓语动词除了不能独立作谓语外,可以承担句子的任何成分。科技英语中大量使用非谓语动词简洁明了地描述现象与表达意思。在 Example 2 中使用了五个非谓语动词,诸如:leading to(导致)、to be useful(使用)、referred to(称作)、to detect(检测)、to cut DNA(酶切 DNA)。其中有动名词、动词不定式和过去分词。

Example 2

All organisms are subject to mutations as a result of their interactions with the environment, leading to genetic variation. For this variation to be useful to geneticists, it must be (1) heritable and (2) discernable to the researcher, whether as a recognizable phenotypic variation or as a genetic mutation distinguishable through molecular techniques. At the DNA level, types of genetic variation include: base substitutions, commonly referred to as single nucleotide polymorphisms (SNPs), insertions or deletions of nucleotide sequences (indels) within a locus, Inversions and rearrangements that involve restriction sites can be easy to detect because they disrupt the ability of a restriction enzyme to cut DNA at a given site and thus can produce relatively large changes in DNA fragment sizes.

④ 被动语态多 (Extensive Use of the Passive Voice)

英语中有两种语态：主动语态和被动语态。被动语态 (the Passive Voice) 是在不知道或不必要说出动作执行者或强调动作承受者时使用的一种语态。科技英语以客观陈述为主，表述科学事实、科学发现、图表说明和报告等，所以大量使用被动语态。例如：Example 1 中的 induced, regenerated, developed 和 Example 3 中的 proposed, isolated 与 examined 所在的句子都使用了被动语态。

Example 3

Expansin proteins are proposed to mediate the cell wall loosening that leads to cell expansion. Nine expansin cDNAs were isolated from potato (*Solanum tuberosum*), and their expression was examined in developing tubers and in rapidly growing etiolated stems.

⑤ 长句子多 (More Long and Complicated Sentences)

英语长句子是指各种复合句，其中可能包含多个从句，而且从句和从句之间的关系可能是平行的、并列的、镶套的和包孕的。从功能上看，复杂句可以分为3种：名词性从句，如主语从句、宾语从句、同位语从句和表语从句；状语从句和定语从句，又称形容词性从句。在科技英语中用于解释科技术语内涵和说明事物内在关系的长句很多。其中除了上述公共英语中常见的三种复合句以外，还有形容词短语、介词短语、分词短语和副词短语等作为后置定语等情况。

Example 4

Amino acid is the individual subunit of which proteins are made, composed of a central carbon atom to which are bonded an amino group (-NH2), a carboxyl group (-COOH), a hydrogen atom, and a variable group of atoms denoted by the letter "R".

在此氨基酸定义中,有两个 which 引导出的从句和两个过去分词短语作定语。

⑥ 习惯使用后置定语(The Post-position of the Attributive)

在汉语和公共英语(少数特例除外)中,定语常常被置于其所修饰的名词前,但是在科技英语中,习惯使用后置定语。如上述 Example 4 中 4 个划线部分均体现出科技英语中使用后置定语这一特点。

1.3 Characteristics of EST Discourses

语篇是指实际使用的语言单位,是一次交际过程中的一系列连续的话段或句子所构成的语言整体。它可以是对话,也可以是独白,它包括书面语,也包括口语。语篇由一组相互连贯的句子组成。语篇特点体现在衔接手段和语篇结构两方面。连接手段包括词汇连接、逻辑连接、指称(用人称代词或物主代词)、替代或省略(用 do/such/so)。

① 词汇衔接

词汇衔接指语篇中通过重复、泛指词、同义词、反义词、上下文关系和搭配等手段达到语义的贯通。词汇衔接手段的运用与语篇构建的质量有直接的关系。

Example 1

Many stories about the spread of AIDS are false. You can not get AIDS working and attending with someone who has AIDS. You can not get it by touching drinking glasses or other objects used by such persons.

由例 1 可知,关键词 AIDS 的重复出现使语篇具有连贯性,使读者意识到有关 AIDS 的错误认识,从而使作者达到准确传递有关 AIDS 信息的目的。

② 逻辑连接

逻辑连接即语法衔接,指用连词、副词或相当于连词或副词的短语将句子和段落联系起来的手法。

逻辑连接充分体现了科技英语的逻辑推理性和严密性。

Example 2

The present study showed that domestic cats may not only reduce their feed intake, but also become sedentary and spend more of their time engaged in negative encounters, as a result of lengthy periods of group housing in a shelter. The development of behavioural traits suggestive of compromised welfare may reduce the chance of an animal being adopted because they could be perceived as unattractive by the visitors, <u>ultimately</u> leading to long term confinement. It is <u>also</u> worthwhile to keep in mind that the longer animals stay in the shelter, the higher the risk for disease and death, <u>therefore</u>, highlighting the need for early adoptions and improvement of their quality of life. A clearer understanding of the effect of group composition on the behaviour and welfare of cats in confinement will contribute to improve their well being <u>while</u> they are kept in shelter environments.

本例中有下划线的连词或者副词将句子有机地联系起来,形成具有逻辑推理性和严密性的一个段落。

③ 语篇结构

科技英语文章的语篇结构一般由导言、正文、结果或者结束语三部分组成。不过,其语篇结构可以因其陈述的内容、时间、场合和对象的不同而不同。

Unit 2 General Idioms and Examples

导语 科技英语中拥有大量的习惯表达法,即惯用语。惯用语是指一些具有特殊含义的词,词组甚至是句子。其结构固定、含义晦涩,是一个独立的语义单位。惯用语的组成部分、词序及其含义应当作一个整体来理解,不得改动。

本单元主要介绍用作惯用语的词、词组和句型和实例。

2.1 Words as Idioms

用作惯用语的词很多,例如有关人体部位的习语(Idioms involving Parts of Body):arm 手臂,back 背部,belly 肚子和 body 人体等;有关颜色词的习语(Idioms Involving Colours):black 黑色的,blue 蓝色的,brown 棕色的和 pink 粉红色的 等;有关鸟、兽、虫、鱼等类词的习语(Idioms Involving Birds, Animals, Insects, Fish):bird 鸟,sheep 绵羊,goldfish 金鱼和 butterfly 蝴蝶等。生物分类惯用词:kingdom 界,Phylum 门,class 纲,family 科,genus 属和 species 种。

2.2 Phrases as Idioms

在科技英语中用作惯用语的词组也很多。

Example 1

In vivo and in vitro（活体与离体）

In vivo is an experimentation using a whole, living <u>organism</u> as opposed to a <u>partial</u> or dead organism, or an <u>in vitro</u> ("within the glass", i. e., in a test tube or petri dish) controlled environment. An important objective of pharmaceutical product development is to gain better understanding of the in vitro and invivo drug performances.

Example 2

not only ... but also ...

This study showed specific contamination patterns in city and VAC (Vegetable, Aquaculture and Caged animal) environments and concluded that ARB (antibiotic-resistant bacteria) occurred <u>not only</u> within contaminated sites <u>but also</u> those less contaminated.

Example 3

On the other hand

On the other hand, a variety of antibiotics have been detected in the aquatic environments.

Example 4

In the present study

In the present study, we first characterized the pattern of contamination by antibiotics and antibiotic-resistant bacteria in the rainy and dry seasons in the Red River delta area.

有些英语惯用语表达的真正含义是其喻义或引申义，假如只将其字面意义直译出来，就可能产生误译。

This is a dangerous and violent city. In some parts of it, the only law is the law of the jungle.

误译：这是一个危险的充满暴力的城市。在有些地方，唯一的原则就是森林法则。

应译为：这是一个危险的充满暴力的城市。在有些地方，唯一的原则就是弱肉强食。

这里"the law of the jungle"引申为"principle for surviving in a violent and dangerous situation, no rules at all"，如译为"森林法则"，则含义不明。"弱肉强食"才是准确、明了地传达了原文所要表达的意义。

2.3　Sentence Patterns as Idioms

在科技英语中,用作惯用语的句子(句型)也很多。

Example 1

It was thus hypothesized that(人们推测)the net contribution of the AM fungal symbiosis to plant element uptake would be higher for SUT1 sense and lower for SUT1 antisense transformants, compared with the WT.

Example 2

It can be assumed that(人们假设), under High P fertilization levels, P uptake via the AM fungal pathway was small in relation to P uptake directly via the root surface in all plant genotypes.

Example 3

If it is believed that(人们相信)the dust deposits only on the clean patches preferably, then shortly after regeneration the clean patches should have disappeared and fractal dimension of the cake patches boundary must have reduced to one.

Example 4

It is considered that(人们认为,据估计)the production of these substances is controlled by feedback inhibition due to their accumulation.

Example 5

In humans, it has been found that(人们发现)the exons of a single gene may be spliced together in three different ways resulting in the production of three different mature messenger RNAs.

更多惯用语的句子(句型)的汉英对照如下:

① 有人认为　　　　　It's thought that-clause
② 也许,可能　　　　 It is possible that-clause
③ 有人指出　　　　　It's been shown that-clause
④ 有人感到　　　　　It was felt that-clause
⑤ 已准备,已商定　　 It is arranged that-clause
⑥ 有人以为　　　　　It's taken that-clause
⑦ 人们通常认为　　　It's generally accepted that-clause

⑧	人们注意到	It's noted that-clause
⑨	人们猜测（推测，假定）	It's supposed that-clause
⑩	有人主张	It's asserted that-clause
⑪	人们强调说	It's stressed (emphasized) that-clause
⑫	据报道	It's reported that-clause
⑬	前面曾经指出	It's noted above that-clause
⑭	可见，可以看出	It can be seen that-clause
⑮	必须承认，老实说	It must be admitted that-clause
⑯	可以有把握的说	It may be safely said that-clause
⑰	很清楚	It is understood that-clause
⑱	据证实	It is demonstrated that-clause
⑲	概括了	It is outlined that-clause
⑳	讨论了，检查了	It's been reviewed that-clause
㉑	据称，据说	It's alleged that-clause
㉒	无可否认	It can't be denied that-clause
㉓	最好	It's preferred (advisable) that-clause
㉔	一目了然	It's at once apparent (obvious, evident) that-clause
㉕	足以	It is enough that-clause
㉖	可能	It is likely that-clause
㉗	成问题的	It is questionable that-clause

Unit 3　The Translation Rules and Examples of English Articles for Science and Technology

导语　科技英语具有专业性强、被动句多、词义多、非谓语动词多、长句多、词性转换多等特点,因此,科技英语的翻译有别于非科技英语文体的翻译。要做好科技英语的英汉互译工作,科技工作者必须精通英汉两种语言,掌握必要的翻译理论、方法技巧,不断提高自己的语言文字水平、专业技术与专业知识水平,并进行大量的翻译实践。

本单元主要介绍专业英语翻译的特点和技巧。

3.1 Translate English into Chinese

The theories and skills of special English translation are divided into two parts: Translate Chinese into English and translate English into Chinese. First, we study how to translate English into Chinese.

* For example: A rotor, rotating at 1,000 RPM, may be so well-balanced that the motion, except for sound, is only just perceptible.

* Analysis: ① 专业词汇:rotor, RPM (rotation per minute);
② 句型:so ...that ...
③ 转变词性:motion ($n.$)→move ($v.$), perceptible ($adj.$)→ perceive ($v.$);
④ 词组:only just, expect for;
⑤ 省译

* Translation:一个每分钟一千转的转头可以平衡的很好,以至于除了声音以外,可勉强觉察到它在运转。

由此可见,要做好翻译,仅凭英文词典和汉英语规则逐字逐句的翻译是行不通的,需要灵活掌握和运用两条:① 理解专业术语、句型和词组的确切涵义;② 理解增译,转译和省译等技巧。

在专业英语英译汉中要有较高的语言文字水平、文化专业知识,必须掌握一些常见的翻译方法。翻译方法分为:直译法和意译法、合译和分译、增译和省译、顺译和倒译四类或者直译法和转换法两类。在此按照直译法和转换法2类简介之。

(1) 直译法:主要针对专业技术术语的译法,包括下列三种:
① 意译法:Co-suppression 共抑制。
② 音译法:Vitamin 维他命(维生素), penicillin 盘尼西林(青霉素),很多外国人名的翻译如:Mendel's genetic laws 孟德尔基因定律。
③ 形译法:x-ray x-射线, θ-replication θ-复制, D-loop D-环(mtDNA)

(2) 转换法:包括词类、句子成分和修饰词等的转换以及从句间转化和否定成分转换等。
① 词类转换法:包括名词变为动词和形容词、形容词变为名词以及动词变为名词等多种形式。

Example 1

One of our ways to get food is planting crops and vegetable. (动名词→动词)

译:种植庄稼和蔬菜是我们获取食物的方法之一。

Example 2

That student has made a careful study of the properties of these proteins (careful→carefully; study(n.)→study(v.))

译:那个学生仔细研究了这些蛋白质的特性。

② 句子成分转换法:主语→定语和宾语等。

Example

In case of shortage of water and fertilizer, wheat would undergo extreme difficulties in their growth and development. 主语 subject→定语 attributive

译:要是缺水缺肥,小麦的生长发育将经历极端的困难。(将会遇到很大的难题)

③ 词序转换法:转换词序可使意思表达清楚。包括主谓转换、宾语、同位语和状语等转换。英文中有两个宾语时,英译汉时经常把一个宾语放在谓语前面,而且加译"把","给"等助词。

Example

X-ray will show the doctor clearly how the lung suffers.

译:X 光会把肺部损害的程度显示给医生。

④ 词的省译:因为表达方式不同,在英语中经常使用的一些词,如介词、冠词和代词等在汉语中不易译出,译出后会显得累赘,甚至不通顺,但翻译时不能篡改英语原文。

Example 1

Any living thing has life whether it is a plant, an animal, or a germ.

译:任何生物,不论是动物,植物,还是微生物,都有生命(省冠词 a, an)。

Example 2

We can't see any virus around us. 译:我们周围的病毒是看不见的(省代词 any)。

Example 3

The students, being in laboratory, are all familiar with the operation of microscopes.

译:曾在实验室做过实验的学生都熟练显微镜的操作方法(省介词 with)。

⑤ 词的增译:译文时,增加一些原文中无其形而有其义的词,使译文意义完整通顺,更符合汉语的表达习惯。常用的包括复数名词,动作意义名词(现象、效应、方法、加工和变化等)、解说性词和语气连词等的增译。

Example 1

After a series of experiments important phenomena have been ascertained.

译:一系列实验后,确定了(许多)重要现象。

Example 2

Oxidation will make carbohydrate decompose.

译:氧化(作用)将使碳水化合物分解。

⑥ 复合句译法:包括定语从句,状语从句和长句的译法。在此仅讲长句译法。长句翻译要抓住中心内容,摸清各部分关系、前后关系和上下属关系,按汉语特点和表达方式正确译出,不要过分拘泥于原文形式。

具体长句译法有3种:a. 顺序译法(与叙述层次相同);b. 变序译法(与叙述层次相反);c. 分句译法(各成分在意义上相同)。

Example 1

A student of biology must become familiar with all the signs and symbols commonly used in biology and bear them in mind firmly, and be well-versed in the technical terms, in order that he may be able to build up the foundation of the biological subject and master it well for pursuing advanced study.

变序译法:为了打好生物学基础,掌握好生物学知识,以便学习深造,生物学专业的学生必须熟悉和牢记生物学中常用的记号和符号,精通其专业术语。

Example 2

Untold numbers of organisms in the past were buried beneath silt and sand and in the absence of oxygen, were transformed by heat, pressure, and time into the deposits of fossil-fuels — coal, petroleum and natural gas—that now yield their bound energies to man.

分句译法:无数的生物被埋在淤泥和沙粒下。在缺氧环境条件下,由于长期温度和压力的影响而转化为矿物燃料——煤,石油和天然气。这些燃料现在为人类产生多种多样的结合能。

3.2 Translate Chinese into English

根据英语惯用表达法,把汉语原文的含义确切、完整地转换为英语。科技文献中要注意单词选用、搭配和常用句型等。

3.2.1 汉语单词和词组的译法

(1) 词类转换译法:$v.\rightarrow n.$,$n.\rightarrow v.$,$v.\rightarrow adj.$,$n.\rightarrow adj.$。

例 学生完全不知道糖和蛋白质都是天然有机物质。

译:Students are entirely ignorant of carbohydrates and proteins to be natural organic materials.

(2) 词义引申法(近似法,上下文体会法,利用英语中的惯用语)

例1 在微生物实验中,他非常仔细,因为一有疏忽,往往功败垂成。

逐词译法:In course of microbiological experiments, he was very careful, because through negligence there would be the failure on the verge of success.

引伸译法(惯用语):There would be many a slip between the cup and the lip in the course of microbiological experiments.

例2 李老师的解释使同学们懂得了什么是分子生物学。

逐词译法:Teacher Li's explanation makes his students understand what molecular biology is.

上下文体会法:What teacher Li has explained leads his students to understand what molecular biology is.

(3) 加译法;翻译时,加上某些英语词或词组,以免"中国腔"。

例1 棉花有根,茎,叶,花和果实。

译:Cotton plants are comprised of several parts such as roots, stems, leaves, flowers and fruits. (增加了"are comprised of 包括"、"several parts such as 诸如……几部分")

例2 没关系。

译:It doesn't matter.

(4) 减译法:翻译时减去某些汉语词或词组,或减去不能译出的词。

例1 由于分子运动而引起的力势必会使分子保持分离状态。

译:The force due to the motion of molecules tends to keep them apart. (减去了"引起,状态")。

3.2.2 汉语句型译法

(1) 只要(有)……才会(能)……

Only can (will, is it possible) ... Only when … can (will, is it possible)

(2) 要……,必须……

It is imperative to do ... It is necessary to do ... It is essential to do ...

例　每个人都必须改造世界观。

译：It is imperative for everyone of us to remould his world outlook.

(3) 一面(边)……，一面(边)……。在……同时

主句 + while or while + 主句

例　他一面做实验，一面看英语书。

译：While doing experiments, he referred to English books.

(4) ……谈到这里，下面开始(讨论)……

So much for ... go on to discuss or discussing that

例　生命现象谈到这里，下面开始讨论新陈代谢。

译：So much for the phenomena of life, now go on to discuss metabolism.

(5) ……一下……就能对……得到一个概念

By doing ... can get an idea of ...

例　观察一下新药给病人的效应，你就能对药的疗效得到一个概念。

译：By observing the effect of the new drug upon the patients, you can get an idea of its efficiency of cure.

(6) 不……便不能……

It is (was) impossible to do ... without ...

例　如果水稻没有充分的水肥，我们便不能使其很好地生长发育。

译：It is impossible for us to make rice plants grow very well without a sufficient supply of water and fertilizer for them.

(7) 为了……，非……不可。

To have to do ...

例　为了解决酶的作用机理，我们非学习折叠蛋白的表面结构不可。

译：To solve the problem of enzyme action, we have to study the surface structure of the folded protein.

(8) 就……而言，这……已经达到标准。

So (as) far as ... is (was) concerned ... is (was) up to the standard.

例　就速度而言，这台离心机已达到制备 DNA 的标准。

译：As far as speed is concerned, the centrifuge is up to the standard of preparing DNA.

(9) 要不是……

Only that-clause

例　要不是忙于做英语作业，我就去踢足球了。

译：I would go to play football only that I am busy doing English homework.

3.2.3　句子成分换译法

使英文译文规范化，包括状语与主语互换，主语和宾语互换，表语和主语互换等。

例　自然界很多化合物都含有氢。

译：Hydrogen is found in many compounds in nature（主语→宾语）。

3.2.4　复合句的译法

确定复合句中各组成部分后，按照英语句法结构把汉语译成规范英语。

例　近年来，生物学家已经看到，能用激光对细胞内部进行手术（宾语从句）。

译：In recent years, biologists have seen the possibility of performing operations with laser light within the cells.

Exercises

1. Translate Chinese into English.

(1) 蛋白质分析原理就谈到这里，下面开始测定几种蛋白质的结构。

(2) 很清楚，生物化学是我们所知道的科学上发展最快的学科之一。

2. The translation of Some selected English passages in some units of Chapter 1 into Chinese.

(1) The Passage from Unit 4

In 2009, the Food Safety Commission of Japan concluded that "foods derived from somatic cell nuclear transfer, cloned cattle and pigs and their offspring, would have equivalent safety as those derived from cattle and pigs produced by the conventional technologies. However, cloning remains a very controversial topic. Genetic improvements allow producers to potentially lower prices, increase the quality of meat and milk products, and possibly increase resistance to diseases. Nevertheless, many have expressed concern over the technology and outrage over the use of meat and milk from cloned animal and their offspring. These consumers and animal welfare organizations oppose the technology due to moral and ethical objections and concerns about food safety and potential harm to the cloned animal and their surrogate mothers.

(2) The Passage from Unit 7

A microorganism or microbe is an organism that is unicellular or non-cellular. Microorganisms are very diverse, including bacteria, fungi, archaea, and protists, green algae (plant), animals such as plankton and the planarian, viruses and so on. They are called microorganisms or microbes because the majority of them are small and cannot be seen without some type of magnification. Members of the bacteria, protista, and fungi share several characteristics that set them apart from plants and animals.

(3) The Passage from Unit 8

The term "plant" implies an association with certain traits, such as being multicellular, possessing cellulose, and having the ability to carry out photosynthesis. In 2010, it is estimated that there are 300 – 315 thousand species of plants on Earth, of which some 260 – 290 thousand are seed plants. Plants are mainly divided into several groups such as land plants (e. g., liverworts, hornworts, mosses, vascular plants, and fossil plants similar to these surviving groups), green plants (land plants plus green algae) and Archaeplastida (green plants plus red algae, cyanobacteria and glaucophyte algae). Green plants obtain most of their energy from sunlight via photosynthesis using chlorophyll contained in chloroplasts, which gives them their green color.

(4) The Passage from Unit 10

If the gene is too long and complex, it is cut from the chromosome with restriction endonucleases, which only cut DNA at certain base sequences and work inside the DNA like molecular scissors that do not cut the DNA straight across, but in a zigzag pattern that leaves one strand slightly longer than its complement. The short nucleotide sequence that sticks out and remains unpaired is called a sticky end because it can be reattached to another complementary strand.

(5) The Passage from Unit 11

① Among the 120 active compounds currently isolated from the higher plants and widely used in modern medicine today, 80 percent show a positive correlation between their modern therapeutic use and the traditional use of the plants from which they are derived.

② In case of domesticated or cultivated species, conservation means conservation in the surroundings where they have developed their distinctive properties. Through the conservation of biodiversity, the survival of many species and habitats which are threatened due to human activities can be ensured. Other reasons for conserving biodiversity include securing valuable natural resources for future generations and protecting the well being of ecosystem functions.

(6) The Passage from Unit 12

Pearl farmers can culture a pearl by placing a nucleus, usually a piece of polished mussel shell, inside the oyster. In three to six years, the oyster can produce a perfect pearl. These pearls are not as valuable as natural pearls, but look exactly the same. In fact, since the beginning of the 20th century, when several researchers discovered how to produce artificial pearls, the cultured pearl market has far outgrown the natural pearl market.

(7) The Passage from Unit 13

With a bacterial genome, the typical result of this search is identification of long ORFs that are almost certainly genes, with many shorter ORFs partly or completely contained within the genes but lying in different reading frames. These short sequences are almost certainly combinations of nucleotides that by chance form an ORF but are not genes. If one of these short ORFs lies entirely between two genes, there is a possibility that it might mistakenly be identified as a real gene, but in most bacterial genomes there is very little space between the genes so the problem arises only infrequently.

Chapter 3 Writing Techniques of English Articles for Science and Technology

Unit 1 English Articles for Science and Technology and Their Types

导语　科技论文是科技工作者对其创造性研究成果进行理论分析和科学总结,并且要通过答辩或者公开发表的科技写作文体。科技论文因其作者写作目的和议论方式的不同可以分为多种类型。

本单元主要介绍科技论文的内涵和主要类型。

1.1 English Articles for Science and Technology

科技论文是科学研究成果的总结,是介绍、推广成果和进行学术交流的手段,它可以反映一个国家、一个单位或一个科技工作者的科学水平。因此,科技论文的写作是科学研究必不可少的一个重要环节,也是衡量科技工作者成绩和能力的一个重要指标。例如,河南师范大学生命科学学院 2005 级生物科学专业邵恒熠同学自 2005 年 10 月被选拔进入河南省-科技部共建细胞分化调控国家重点实验室"大学生创新团队"肝再生基因组学研究组以来,利用课余时间进行系统生物学学习和研究工作,在副校长徐存拴教授的指导下,用生物信息学方法分析了大鼠肝再生相关基因的表达变化和作用关系,为进一步阐明肝再生中生理生化活动分子机制以及寻找肝病治疗基因靶点提供了理论基础,将研究成果撰写成数篇论文,分别发表在《World Journal of Gastroenterology》、《Scandinavian Journal of Gastroenterology》、《分子细胞生物学报》和《自然科学进展》等国内外重要学术期刊上,并荣获第五届中国青少年科技创新奖,被免试推荐为中国科学技术大学的研究生。

1.2 The Types of English Articles for Science and Technology

科技论文因其作者写作目的和议论方式的不同可以分为多种类型。广义上分为两大类:(1) 学位论文或毕业论文。它们是大学本科生、研究生为毕业和获得学位而写的科技论文,包括学士论文、硕士论文和博士论文。这类论文的篇幅比较长,学士论文、硕士论文和博士论文一般要求达到一万字、五万字和五至十万字。例如:同学们大学毕业后所要写的毕业论文,我校要求三万字。基于学科分类,学位论文分为自然科学学位论文和技术科学学位论文。(2) 学术论文。科技工作者的最新科技成果大部分是以议论文形式发表于期刊杂志上,因此,学术论文也叫杂志论文。一般学术论文分为立论文和驳论文两类。前一类论文侧重于提出作者的观点、见解和理论或假说,而后一类则旨在批驳某些错误的观点、见解和理论。例如:Jieun Junga 等在其文章"Expression of multiple expansin genes is associated with cell expansion in potato organs"前言末尾写到"Expansin gene families have been described in full for several species, notably Arabidopsis, rice and poplar, but so far α-expansins have not been reported from potato. We present the first steps towards characterizing the expansin gene family of potato, and report the expression and regulation of a number of these genes in expanding cells of potato tuber and stem."[译文:迄今,几个物种,尤其是拟南芥、水稻和白杨,的膨大素基因家族已经有详细报道,但是,西红柿α膨大素(基因家族)尚未见报道。我们介绍西红柿膨大素基因家族鉴定的开始几步,报道其中的几个基因在土豆块茎及其植株茎膨大细胞内的表达和调控。]这是一篇典型的立论文。其作者以自己的实验结果为依据,实事求是地阐述自己的观点,接受读者的评判与检验。

另外,某网站上一位编辑从目前期刊所刊登的科技论文总结出五种类型:(1) 论证型——对基础性科学命题的论述与证明,或对提出的新的设想原理、模型、材料、工艺等进行理论分析、补充或修正,使其完善。(2) 科技报告型——描述一项科学技术研究的结果或进展,或一项技术研究试验和评价的结果,或论述某项科学技术问题的现状和发展的文件。记述型文章是它的一种特例。(3) 发现、发明型——记述被发现事物或事件的背景、现象、本质、特性及其运动变化规律和人类使用这种发现前景的文章。(4) 设计、计算型——为解决某些工程问题、技术问题和管理问题而进行的计算机程序设计,某些系统、工程方案、产品的计算机辅助设计和优化设计以及某些过程的计算机模拟,某些产品或材料的设计或调制和配制等。(5) 综述型——在综合分析和评价已有资料的基础上,提出在特定时期内有关专业课题的发展演变规律和趋势的文章。综述型文章通常有两类写法：一是以汇集文献资料为主，辅以注释，客观而少评述。二是着重评述，通过回顾、观察和展望，提出合乎逻辑的、具有启迪性的看法和建议。例如：P. Manimaran et al 在其综述文章"Suitability of non-lethal marker and marker-free systems for development of transgenic crop plants: Present status and future prospects"（译文：适用于开发转基因作物的非致死标记系统和无标记系统：现状与未来展望）的摘要中，在综合分析和评价已有资料基础上，写到"we examine the availability, and the suitability of wide range of non-lethal selection markers and elimination of SMG methods to develop marker-free transgenics for achieving global food security. As the strategies for marker-free plants are still in proof-of-concept stage, adaptation of new genomics tools for identification of novel non-lethal marker systems and its application for developing marker-free transgenics would further strengthen the crop improvement program."[译文：为了实现全球食品安全，开发无标记转基因作物，我们评价了非致死标记和去除选择标记基因方法的可行性和适应性。因为（适于开发）无标记（转基因）植物的策略仍然处于概念证实阶段，所以采用新的基因组学工具鉴定新的非标记系统，应用基因组学开发无标记转基因作物，将进一步加强作物改良项目（研究实施）]。

除了上述各种各样的类型之外，本人认为科技工作者和各级各类大专院校的大学生、研究生的科技读书报告、实验报告、开题报告和项目申请书等也应该属于科技论文的特殊类型。

Unit 2　The Characteristics of English Articles for Science and Technology

导语　科技论文的种类很多，其写作目的和表达方式各不相同，但是它们具有学术性、创造性、科学性、准确性、通俗性和规范性、客观性，经常使用图表、公式和代号等共同特点。

本单元主要介绍科技论文的特点。

2.1　Technicality

科学性是科技论文的最基本条件。科技论文侧重于基础性及其延伸理论的探究与讨论，得出相应的结论与判定，在于理论水平的提升。因此，科技论文是按照科技工作者思维的认识规律抽象地反映客观事物的发生、发展与变化的规律性。例如:2009 年，Victoria C. Lapitan 等在其题为"Molecular characterization and agronomic performance of DH lines from the F1 of *indica* and *japonica* cultivars of rice (*Oryza sativa* L.)"的文章摘要中写到"SSR analysis of the DH population showed an expected 1∶1 ratio of *indica* and *japonica* alleles. It revealed homozygosity for 99.84% of the total marker loci in the 141 lines evaluated suggesting that the AC-derived plants originated from the F1 pollen. Heterozygosity was observed in only 10 DH lines for one or three marker loci out of 107 polymorphic SSR markers.〔译文:简单重复序列标记技术对水稻双单倍体群体的分析结果表明，印度亚种和日本亚种的等位基因的预期比率是 1∶1；揭示了在评价的 141 个双单倍体品系中，总标记位点的纯合度为 99.84%，建议这些花药培养植株来源于杂交第一代的花粉；只在 10 个双单倍体品系中观察到杂合现象，杂合度占 107 个多态性简单重复序列标记(位点)的 1 或 3。〕

2.2　Creativity

创造性是衡量科技论文价值的根本标准。科技论文是为国内外交流学术新成就、发表新理论、新方法、新假说、新定律而写的，其创造性越大，学术价值越高，参考价值越大，对科技的贡献越大。如果某项科技成果填补了国内外某一项空白，那它就是一项国际重大科技成果。例如:Sindhu 等在其题为"Chemoprevention by essential oil of turmeric leaves (*Curcuma longa* L.) on the growth of *Aspergillus flavus* and aflatoxin production"的文章前言中写到"Little work is done to manage fungal deterioration of stored products by the use of plant derived bioactive compounds despite their good pharmacological actions ... The objective of the present study is to evaluate the chemopreventive effect of the essential oil from turmeric leaves on the aflatoxin production of *Aspergillus sp.* in vitro."〔译文:尽管植物提取的生物活性化合物具有良好的药用活性，但是使用它们防控真菌引起的储藏产品变质研究工作还非常少……本研究旨在评价姜黄叶油

对离体黄曲霉菌产生黄曲霉毒素的化学防控作用。]

2.3 Scientificness

科技论文的科学性是其所写的科技内容及其表达形式符合科技理论可以揭示的客观规律，体现科技发展的最新水平。从科技论文内容上衡量其科学性，要求真实、成熟、先进和可行；从科技论文表述上衡量其科学性，要求准确、明白和全面。反科学和伪科学的科技论文不会给人们带来好处，只会带来混乱、危害和损失。例如：Guangyu Gu and Arthur R. Brothman 在其题为"Cytogenomic aberrations associated with prostate cancer"的文章中写到"Genetic changes associated with prostate cancer have finally begun to elucidate some of the mechanisms involved in the etiology of this complex and common disease. We highlight consistent and relatively frequent abnormalities seen by various methodologies. Specifically, the results of conventional and molecular cytogenetic studies, genome-wide association studies with single nucleotide polymorphisms, recurrent gene fusions, and epigenetic analyses are discussed."[译文：前列腺癌相关的遗传变异终于开始阐明一些涉及这种复杂而常见疾病的病原学的机制。我们强调采用各种各样的方法观察连续和相对频繁发生的变异。具体讨论了经典和分子细胞遗传学研究、用单核苷酸多态性进行的全基因组关联研究、反复发生的基因融合和表观遗传学分析的结果。]其科学性在于前列腺癌是客观存在的复杂而常见疾病；讨论范围是病原学领域的前沿；使用的研究方法是科学的；揭示了遗传变异是前列腺癌发病机制；建立了研究其遗传变异的综合技术体系。

2.4 Accuracy

准确性体现在科技论文的用词上。用词要准确，不能含糊不清或者一词多义。科技词汇来源于英语中原有词汇（例如：probability 在英语中意为可能性，而在遗传学中意为概率）、拉丁语和希腊语的词汇（例如：parasite 寄生，pneumonia 肺炎）以及新造词汇（例如：bioinformatics 生物信息学，proteomics 蛋白质组学）。

2.5 Popularity and Normalization

这两个特性表现在科技论文的表达和篇章结构方面。要求表达通俗易懂、清楚明了，结构严谨，层次分明（详见下文中（5）正文），没有倒叙和插叙等情况。例如：Brian D. Nordmann 在其文中写的"Governments are slowly beginning to understand and embrace the concept of 'One World, One Health'. Of the 1,461 diseases now recongnised in humans, it is estimated that a full 60% are caused by multihost pathogens that affect several species. The seemingly obvious fact that everything on earth is related, and that which affects one affects all—humans, animals, plants —has not yet been fully accepted, but is slowly being understood. As the One Health Commission has pointed out, the convergence of people, animals, and our environment has created a new dynamic in which the health of each group is inextricably interconnected. The challenges associated with this dynamic are demanding, profound, and unprecedented."[译文：政府慢慢开始理解和接受"同一个世界，同一个健康"的概念。在迄今确诊的1,461中人类疾病中，估计60%是由影响几个物种的多宿主病原体（侵染）所致。地球上的所有生物都是相关的，影响一个生物的生物就能够影响所有的生物——人、动物和植物，这样看似明显的事实没有完全被人们接受，但是正在慢慢被了解。正像一个健康委员会指出的那样，人类、动物和环境的共存创造了一种新的动态范围，其中（生活的）每一组生物的健康都是相互联系的。与这种动态范围相连的挑战都是需要的、有深远意义的和前所未有的。]这一段话，体现了上述特点。但是，有些专业性特别强的科技论文由于专业词汇和专业知识等原因使非专业人员乃至专业人员难以理解。

2.6　Objectivity

　　科技论文客观陈述事实与结果，不带主观感情色彩，所使用的词汇一般具有陈述事实的性质。客观性体现在文章语法方面具有高频使用被动语态、句子结构完整、常用定语从句下定义和解释等特点。例如：Thusith S. Samarakone and Harold W. Gonyou 的一篇论文中的 2.2.2. Behaviour observations 一节 "Immediately after pigs were regrouped into the four different treatment combinations, the behaviours of focal pigs were observed by direct observations for 2 h at 1 min scan sampling. In total, there were four observers for behaviour observations. The first observer began observing the focal pigs that were mixed into different groups starting at 0 min and the second observer followed the first observer starting at 1 min. Once all four observers completed their observations at 1 min intervals for a period of 4 min, the first observer restarted observing the focal pigs, once again, at the 4th min following regrouping. The focal pigs were observed long enough to determine the behaviour at the instant of each observation point. This procedure was carried out over a period of 2 h. Aggressive behaviours as described in Table 1 were recorded. From the behaviour observations, the percentage of time spent in aggressive behaviour during the 2 h was calculated for each individual focal pig."体现了上述客观性的特点。

2.7　Figures and Tables, Formulae and Signs

在生物学科研论文中,作者经常使用图表、公式和代号代替繁琐的文字表达,显得一目了然、清楚易懂。例如:

(1) Bengt Zöller 等在其题为"Risk of coronary heart disease in patients with cancer: A nationwide follow-up study from Sweden"的论文中使用了如下 6 个表、2 个缩写代号(CHD 和 SIR)和 1 个公式:

Table 1—Basic characteristics of patients diagnosed with CHD(冠状动脉心脏病) between 1987 and 2008.

Table 2—SIRs(标准化发病率) for subsequent CHD in cancer patients by follow-up interval.

Table 3—SIRs for subsequent CHD between 2002 and 2008 in cancer patients with and without metastasis.

Table 4—SIR for subsequent CHD in cancer patients by period of diagnosis.

Table 5—SIR for subsequent myocardial infarction in cancer patients.

Table 6—SIR for subsequent coronary heart disease in cancer patients by risk factors.

$$SIR = \frac{\sum_{j=1}^{k} O_j}{\sum_{j=1}^{k} n_j \lambda_j^*} = \frac{O}{E^*}$$

(2) Zhou et al. 在其题为"Hairy Root Induction and Plant Regeneration of *Rehmannia glutinosa* Libosch. *f. hueichingensis* Hsiao via *Agrobacterium rhizogenes*-Mediated Transformation"的论文中使用了 12 张图片(Fig. 1 ~ Fig. 12)。

Unit 3 Basic Formats of English Articles for Science and Technology

导语 科技论文可以分为不同的类型,各类科技论文的格式没有统一的、一成不变的规定,但是,它们也有常用的基本格式,例如标题、作者及其单位、摘要、关键词、引言、正文、结论,致谢和参考文献等。

本单元主要介绍学位论文和学术论文的基本格式,并举例说明。

3.1 Basic Formats of English Alticles for Bachelor

例如河南师范大学本科毕业生的理科中文学士论文的基本格式:(1) 论文封面包含河南师范大学本科毕业论文、学号、题目、学院、专业、年级班级、姓名、指导老师和时间;(2) 中文摘要,附加几个关键词;(3) 英文摘要,附加几个关键词;(4) 论文主体部分包括前言、实验部分和实验结果;(5) 参考文献;(6) 致谢;(7) 附录。

3.2 Basic Formats of Research Paper

科技论文结构三个层次:整篇论文的结构安排、论文各个部分内部的结构安排和每一个句子的结构。保证一篇论文正确的结构,使各个部分保持相对的匀称,非常重要。科技论文的基本格式主要指整篇结构,包括 Title with the names of authors and company (work unit), Abstract with Key words (5-8 special terms); Introduction, Materials and methods, Results, Discussion, Conclusions, Acknowledgements and References。其整篇结构是按以上 9 个部分的先后顺序依次进行组织。其信息分类和整理(这是形成论文纲要关键性的一步)按两个步骤进行:① 按照论文中信息的重要性进行等级划分,最重要的信息为主要标题,次重要的信息为副标题;② 把等级划分的信息进行排序。这样使论文各部分呈现明确的逻辑关系。

3.2.1 Title

科技论文的题目是一篇文章内容的高度浓缩和集中,就好像一个人的姓名,对其他要找他的人来说非常重要。读者查阅一篇科技论文,首先查看其题目,再决定阅读其内容、节选其内容、参考其方法。一般科技论文的题目要达到准确得体、简短精炼、观点明确和概念统一的要求。例如:一篇论文的题目"Molecular breeding in developing countries: challenges and perspectives"(译文:发展中国家的分子育种:挑战与展望)就达到了准确得体、简短精炼和观点明确的要求。

3.2.2 Authors and Companies

科技论文题目下要署名作者及其单位。这既表明其成果有他们所做、报道、负责和赢得荣誉,也便于读者与其联系、交流、请教和索要论文。其科技论文所报道的成果可能是一个人所为,也可能是多个人所为,这个人或这些人可能属于一个单位,也可能属于两个或者两个以上的单位。不同人和不同单位对其成果的贡献和责任等方面也不尽相同。因此,作者和单位的署名的先后顺序不同。在正常情况下,按照贡献大小依次排列。另外,多单位多作者的情况下,常常在单位的左侧编号,也在作者姓名的右上方标明单位编号。其中一位是整个课题的负责人,称作通讯作者,可以排在所有作者中任何位置,而且通常在其姓名右上角还要用特殊符号标明,或者在论文第一页左下角注明通讯作者及其联系方式。Challabathula Dinakar et al. 发表的一篇论文所署作者和单位情况如下所示:

  题目:Photosynthesis in desiccation tolerant plants: Energy metabolism and antioxidative stress defense

  作者:Challabathula Dinakar[a], Dimitar Djilianov[b], Dorothea Bartels[a]

  单位:**a** Institute of Molecular Physiology and Biotechnology of Plants, University of Bonn, Kirschallee 1, 53115 Bonn, Germany

  b Abiotic Stress Group, Biotech Info Center, AgroBioInstitute, 1164 Sofia, 8 Dragan Tzankov Blvd, Bulgaria

  通讯作者:Dorothea Bartels[a]

3.2.3 Abstract

摘要是客观地、简明扼要地、确切地概括论文重要内容的短文,是论文的一个重要组成部分,具有让读者尽快了解全文的主要成果、以补充题名的不足、吸引读者阅读全文、便于检索、引用和转载等作用。按照性质或者内容的不同,摘要被分为指示性摘要(indicative abstract)、报道性摘要(informative abstract)、资料性摘要或者报道-指示性摘要(informative-indicative abstract)(http://baike.baidu.

com/view/123897.htm)。另外一种摘要叫做结构式摘要(structured abstract),实质上是报道性摘要的结构化表达,强调摘要应该有比较多的信息量,便于读者了解论文内容。

一般作者向学术性期刊投稿,选用报道性摘要,但是当论文创新内容较少时,也可以选用指示性摘要。不同期刊杂志对其形式、内容与长短的要求不尽相同,但是,一般要求其简短,200~500字,精准概括研究目的、方法、结果、结论和意义,成为结构严谨和逻辑性强的完整独立短文,忠实介绍内容。例如:

In order to learn the role of protein synthesis in early development of the sea urchin, newly fertilized embryos were pulse-labeled with tritiated leucine, to provide a time course of changes in synthetic rate, as measured by total counts per minute (cpm)."[译文:为了了解蛋白质合成在海胆(胚胎)发育早期的作用,用氚标记的亮氨酸脉冲标记刚刚受精的海胆胚胎,通过测定其每分钟脉冲总点数,描绘其蛋白质合成速率变化的时间过程。]

Analyses:

① This sentence provides the overall question, methods, and type of analysis, all in one sentence. The writer can now go directly to summarizing the results.

② Summarize the study, including the following elements in any abstract. Try to keep the first two items to no more than one sentence each.

③ Purpose of the study—hypothesis, overall question, objective.

④ Model organism or system and brief description of the experiment.

⑤ Results, including specific data—if the results are quantitative in nature, report quantitative data; results of any statistical analysis should be reported.

⑥ Important conclusions or questions that follow from the experiment(s).

学位论文的摘要可以类似于上述学术论文的摘要,也可以是写得比较长、比较详细的摘要,2 500~3 000字,主演包括目的和重要性、内容和过程、结论和创新点及其意义。另外,在摘要下面,经常有几个关键词。

3.2.4 Introduction

在文章正文之前有一部分内容,是文章的引子,叫作前言,对文章非常重要。其内容主要包括研究材料及其价值、前人的研究进展及其空白、理由与目的、预期结果及其意义。其中,引用前人的研究结果要标明参考文献。另外,如果引言中出现了前人未使用过的概念,作者要对其加以定义与说明。例如作者周延清一篇文章的前言:

There are seven species in the genus Rehmnnia of the *Scrophulariaceae* family. However, only three species are used for medicinal purposes: *R. glutinosa* Libosch in Korea, *R. glutinosa* var. purpurea Makino in Japan, and *R. glutinosa var. hueichingensis* (Chao and Schih) Hsiao in China (Chung et al., 2006). Moreover, they are far more frequently prescribed in China than in other countries (Zhang et al., 2007). Rehmnnia glutinosa (Dihuang), a comprehensive traditional Chinese medicinal herb, is distributed in the provinces of Henan, Shandong, Shaanxi, Shanxi, Hebei, Liaoning, Inner Mongolia, Jiangsu, Zhejiang, Hunan, Hubei, Sichuan in China; Rehmannia glutinosa produced in Wen County, Meng County, Boai County, Qinyan County in Henan Province is called R. glutinosa f. hueichingensis or HuaiDihuang, the genuine medicinal herb, one of world-famous "Four famous Huai herbs", which has better quality and curative effects than that in other provinces. In terms of the processing method, there are three types of rehmannia referring to the root of *R. glutinosa* used as medicinal materials: fresh rehman-nia root (Xian Dihuang), dried rehmannia rhizome (Sheng Dihuang) and prepared rehmannia root (Shu Dihuang) (Zhang et al., 2008). Each is known to have different effects (Chung et al., 2006; Yu et al., 2006). More than seventy compounds including iridoids, saccharides, amino acid, catalpol, aucubin, rehmannin, rehmannioside (A, B, C, and D), stachyose, verbascose, leonuride, monomelittoside, vitamin A, inorganic ions, as well as other trace elements have been found in the herb (Chung et al., 2006; Liu et al., 2006; Oh et al., 2003; Dirk et al., 2007; Zhang et al., 2008), of which catalpol is the main medical ingredient, performing pharmacological action in rehmannia, as standard preparation when rehmannia is identified (Liu et al., 2006). Rehmannia is commonly used to replenish vitality, strengthen the liver, kidney, and heart, and for treatment of a variety of ailments like diabetes, anemia, urinary tract problems, anti-tumor and anti-senescence (Zhang et al., 2007, 2008). In addition, the root of the wild *R. glutinosa* is slight and often used as fresh rehmannia root, while that of cultural *R. glutinosa* is massive, often used as three types of rehmannia (Zhang et al., 2008). Now there are more than fifty cultivars of cultural *R. glutinosa* in China. Yield of fresh rehmannia root of one good-quality and high-yield cultivar is about $(3.8-4.5) \times 10^4$ kg/ha, equaling 1,200 US \$/ha. Year demand of fresh rehmannia root is 2×10^7 kg, a part of which is exported into Southeast, Korea and Japan. Therefore, good-quality and high-yield Rehmannia cultivars are very important for the rehmannia industry, local economy, income of rehmannia farmers and marketing demands. The taxonomy and phylogeny of rehmannia are very complicated, controversial and confusing, mainly due to its high heterozygosity, self-incompatibility, mad segregation from hybrid offsprings, continuous vegetative propagation and the long history of cultivation and wide dispersion as well as cultivar complexity. Moreover, breeding and selection of Rehmannia cultivars with improved characteristics currently suffer from the fact that traditional cultivars have not been adequately characterized, and considerable linguistic variation exists in the nomenclature of Rehmannia cultivars, with each locality having its own unique series of names for different cultivars. These factors mentioned above cause good Rehmannia cultivars to be mixed with bad ones, and lead to genetic variation among *Rehmannia* cultivars. In the previous studies, rehmannia taxonomy and germplasm identification were mainly based on morphological and biological data (Li et al., 2007a, b; Yan et al., 2007), cytological studies (Yan et al., 2007) and allozyme (Li et al., 2007a, b). Only a few of studies have been reported on DNA markers such as ITS region, trnL-F region and rps16 intron (Dirk et al., 2007), AFLP (Yuan and Hong, 2003), RAPD (Choi, 1997; Hatano, 1997; Chen et al., 2002; Zhou et al., 2007), ISSR (Zhou et al., 2007). Nevertheless, because each of them has its disadvantages, it is necessary to utilize more advanced DNA markers to identify rehmannia germplasm. Sequence-related amplified polymorphism (SRAP), a PCR-based marker system utilizing amplification of open reading frames as described by Li and Quiros (2001) has successfully been adapted for a variety of purposes in different crops, including map construction, gene tagging, genomic and cDNA fingerprinting, map-based cloning (Uzun et al., 2009) and QTL analysis (Yuan et al., 2008). It has several advantages over other DNA molecular marker systems. For example, it is simple, has reasonable throughput rate, discloses numerous co-dominant markers, targets open reading frames (ORFs), and allows easy isolation of bands for sequencing (Uzun et al., 2009). Recently, it has been used to determine genetic diversity and cultivar identifications in Dendrobium officinale (Ding et al., 2008), Chinese Hedychium (Gao et al., 2008), maize (Jiang et al., 2007), pea (Espósito et al., 2007), Porphyra (Qiao et al., 2007), tree peony (Han et al., 2008), radish (Liu et al., 2008), citrus and related genera (Uzun et al., 2009). However, up to now, there is no report of measuring genetic diversity of R. glutinosa by SRAP markers. In this work, we investigated SRAP markers to better identify genetic diversity and relationship among *R. glutinosa* cultivars.

该前言首先叙述地黄材料的种类、分布、药用价值、有效成分、治疗疾病和经济价值。其次,介绍造成地黄品种混杂和变异的原因。然后,说明前人鉴定和分类地黄的研究方法和成果,但是其技术不够先进有效。最后,描述相关序列扩增多态性技术的先进性、特点和应用及其没有用于地黄品种遗传多样性分析的事实,提出本文研究目的。

3.2.5 Body

这部分是科技论文的主体,体现出论文的创新性、可行性、所采用的实验材料、仪器设备、学术理论、技术方法和技术路线、研究结果及其分析等内容。有些论文的这一部分还包括讨论。在讨论中,作者根据其研究结果阐述事物的客观规律和内在联系提出自己的见解和观点。正文可以分为几段,每段又可以分为几个小标题。例如 Barbara Scherm 等人的文章正文部分结构如下:

 2 Materials and methods(材料和方法)
  2.1 Fungal strains and media(真菌菌株和培养基)
  2.2 Total RNA extraction and RT-PCR(总 RNA 提取和反转录多聚酶链式反应)
  2.3 Total DNA extraction and amplification(总 DNA 提取和扩增)
  2.4 Aflatoxin extraction and determination by fluorescence detection HPLC(黄曲霉毒素提取和高效液相色谱-荧光检测)
 3 Results(结果)
  3.1 Aflatoxin production determined by fluorescence of *Aspergillus* strains grown on coconut agar(荧光检测椰子琼脂培养基上培养的黄曲霉菌株产生的黄曲霉毒素)
  3.2 Aflatoxin production determined by fluorescence HPLC(高效液相色谱-荧光检测黄曲霉毒素)
  3.3 Analysis of *Aspergillus* strains by reverse transcription-polymerase chain reaction(反转录多聚酶链式反应技术分析黄曲霉菌株)
 4 Discussion(讨论)

3.2.6 Conclusions

在完成了论文的上述几个重要部分以后,要对整篇论文下一个一般不超过三个段落的简短结论。它是作者基于正文资料,经过推理、判断和归纳所得出的新观点。结论对论文有画龙点睛和一锤定音的作用,有助于读者记住作者论文内容。一般读者在阅读一整篇文章之前先看摘要和结论,然后才决定是否看全文。结论主要包括下列几个内容:① 本研究结果说明的问题、得出的规律和解决的问题,② 与前人研究结果或者看法的比较和改进,③ 本研究的不足和将来研究方向。等等。

3.2.7 Acknoledgements

致谢要写得清楚、简练和真实。感谢对本文有贡献的人员和单位:① 支持这项研究的基金委(批准号)和资金赞助单位或个人,② 为本研究提供研究材料、进行实验工作、提供分析方法或实验药品的个人和单位,③ 对论文的修改和编辑提供重要建议、意见和批评的个人,④ 在野外工作以及收集数据的人们。

3.2.8 References

在科技论文的前言、材料和方法、讨论乃至结论中引用大量的参考文献,提供了研究背景和科学问题的现状以及使用的可参考的方法。作者要按照文章将要投稿的杂志稿约要求,在文末,按照一定顺序、一定规律有选择地列出重要的参考文献。

Unit 4 Writing Procedures and Technologies of English Articles for Science and Technology

导语 科技论文写作一般包括写作前准备、选题、研究内容和结果等材料的准备、论文撰写、论文修改、投稿和发表等步骤。其中每一步骤都有其具体写作技巧。

本单元主要介绍科技论文写作的选题、准备和撰写,并且举例说明其写作技巧。

4.1　Selected Topic and Title of EST

科技论文的选题非常重要,一般选择本学科亟待解决的课题或者处于前沿位置的课题,即立题要新。因此,其作者要做到:(1) 结合自身科研工作,选择有科学价值、创新性和现实意义的论题;(2) 从学科边缘或者多学科交叉处选题;(3) 通过参加学术会议、查阅专业期刊、同行交流与研讨了解本学科研究现状、前沿动态和要解决问题等,提炼未经探讨而有意义的课题;(4) 总结学科争论性强的问题,比较其研究方法与结论,从中找出热点作为切入点;(5) 抓住科研生产难题,发现思维闪光点;(6) 思考其可行性。选题确定后,就要定题目了,题目要精准。题目有大有小,有难有易。要从实际出发,量力而行。确定主题和论证的角度,除了量力而行外,还应注意要从自己有基础、有所了解的事情着手。

4.2　Preparation of EST

根据选定的主题,准备写文章。准备包括查阅相关文献,形成论点,收集和分析资料,构思,列出提纲,包括标题、图表和数据以及篇幅等。

4.3　Writing of EST

科技论文的撰写包括撰写初稿、修改和定稿。原则上要简明扼要,指出问题,说明问题,分析问题。初稿形成以后,应再三修改,审查是否符合要求。一篇好的科技论文不仅主题突出,论点鲜明,还应结构严谨,层次分明。要安排好结构,一般应遵循以下五个原则:(1) 围绕主题,选择有代表性的典型材料,根据需要适当安排,使主题思想得到鲜明突出的表现;(2) 疏通思路,正确反映客观事物的规律;(3) 结构要完整而统一,表达要规范,符合客观事物的实际情况;(4) 层次分明,有条不紊;(5) 适合文章体裁。经过反复修改的论文基本上没有太大问题,确定下来,投稿与发表。

4.4　Example Analysis

从 Hladun et al. 2011 年发表在 Environmental and Experimental Botany 期刊上的文章 Selenium accumulation in the floral tissues of two Brassicaceae species and its impact on floral traits and plant performance. 可以看出它属于论证型

(Argument Type)科技论文,具有如下科技英语写作的写作技巧。

4.4.1 Structures of Articles

论文结构层次有三个:整篇论文的结构安排、论文各个部分内部的结构安排和每一个句子的结构。保证一篇论文正确的结构,使各个部分保持相对的匀称,非常重要。该部分仅仅介绍第一个层次——整篇结构,It is seen from this article that its whole structure is composed of the following several parts: ① Title with the names of authors and company (work unit), ② Abstract with Key words (5-8 special terms), ③ Introduction, ④ Materials and methods, ⑤ Results, ⑥ Discussion, ⑦ Conclusions, ⑧ Acknowledgements and ⑨ References。其整篇结构是按以上9个内容的先后顺序依次进行组织。其信息分类和整理(这是形成论文纲要关键性的一步)按两个步骤进行:① 按照论文中信息的重要性进行等级划分,最重要的信息为主要标题,次重要的信息为副标题。② 把等级划分的信息进行排序。这样使论文各部分呈现明确的逻辑关系。文章各个部分内部结构和句子结构将在下面的相关标题下介绍。

4.4.2 Writing Processes and Properties

(1) 选题,决定题目、作者和刊物

植物修复技术是环境科学与技术的热点和前沿领域,hyperaccumulator(超积累)作为植物修复技术的核心和关键而受到广泛关注。本文选题在于验证其中的元素防御假说(the elemental defense hypothesis),确定题目为一种代表元素硒(Selenium)在特定植物(两种十字花科植物的花器官)组织内积累及其对花器官性状和植物表现的作用。该题目以最简短的文字(名词词组)包含了尽可能丰富的内容(结论或发现——accumulation 和 impacts,材料——the floral tissues of two Brassicaceae species,方法—(隐含)硒含量测定和性状 traits),符合选题目的原则:一般题目包含三项内容,即研究的结论或发现,材料和方法)。然后,在精准的题目下面严肃地注明作者姓名及其工作单位。最后,选定杂志(Environmental and experimental botany),按其稿约要求撰写、投稿和发表。

(2) 查阅相关文献,写出本研究要解决的科学问题、研究目的和意义

通过对大量参考文献的阅读、分析和综述,全面了解和掌握本论文所研究的科学问题的研究现状、解决的问题及其程度、尚存问题及其亟待解决的问题以及哪些人曾经用过什么材料、技术和方法等,写出研究的科学问题、目的、意义和引言,并强调本项研究的重要性。本文引言(Introduction)应用了30篇文献,进行分析和综述,在倒数第二段中用两个句子提出科学问题:"These studies did not distinguish which specific parts of the flower (pollen, nectar, or petal) contained Se. Selenium concentrations in specific B. juncea and S. pinnata floral tissues such as pollen and nectar have not been examined to date."[译文:上述这些研究没有区分出花器官的哪些特定部分(花粉、花蜜或者花瓣)含有硒。迄今为止,B. juncea and S. pinnata 的特定花器官如花粉和花蜜内所含硒的浓度还没有人测定。]在最后一段用两个句子写明研究目的:"The first objective of this study was to determine whether plants that accumulate Se in their leaves will also accumulate Se in their pollen, nectar, and other floral tissues. The second objective was to determine the toxic effects of Se uptake in terms of floral traits and plant performance in a hyperaccumulator and accumulator plant species."[译文:本研究的第一个目的是确定叶片中含硒的植物的花粉、花蜜和其他花组织是否也会积累硒。第二个目的是测定超积累和积累硒的植物种所吸收的硒对其花器官性状和植物表现的毒性作用。]其中的两个词(first 和 second)体现了该段落的有机联系(衔接与过渡)。

(3) 列出标题和提纲

既定整篇结构安排以后,又对其各个部分内部结构进行了有逻辑性的安排,特别是对正文的三部分写明了标题和提纲。例如:第二部分 materials and methods 分为六个小部分(2.1~2.6),第三部分 results 分为四个小部分(3.1~3.4),第四部分 Discussion 分为两个小部分(4.1~4.2)。这体现出很好的结构性层次,有简有繁,详略得当。

(4) 写出结果

收集实验数据和图片,使用适当的方法和技术或者软件统计分析实验数据、绘制图表或者处理图片。本文主要用软件 SAS version 9.2 处理分析灌溉箱中 Se 元素和 S 元素的浓度、Se 元素在植物组织内的积累、叶和花组织的重量以及 Se 对良种植物表现的作用数据,制作图表,找出规律或者发现趋势。结果表达的真实、直接、客观,纲举目张,层次分明,思路清晰。本例文使用了两图一表。

(5) 撰写材料和方法

实验结果决定了实验材料和方法的内容,因此在写完实验结果后,再写这一部分比较合理。这一部分包括实验的地点、实验材料及其取样方法、具体实验方法、数据获取的方法和统计方法、图片处理方法等。对于本学科中常用的方法,只需要在其后用括号或者上标列举参考文献;对于新方法,尤其是首次使用的新方法,需要详述,以便读者能够重复使用之。详见本文第二部分 Materials and methods。

(6) 讨论

讨论部分是论文写作的难点和重点,因为它要求作者有丰厚的知识背景,非常熟悉本领域的研究历史和新进展,掌握大量的参考文献,并对其发展前景有一定的预见性。但是,只要作者通过对自己的结果和前人的结果进行全面的比较和分析,有逻辑地回答其文章的新发现及其重要性、重要的观点、科学意义与应用价值、作者的新发现是否能被已有的研究结果支持或者是否一致、其结果和方法有什么不足或受限制的地方、其结果是否需要在哪些方面进一步的研究等问题,就能够把讨论部分写得很好,获得重要的信息和得出本研究的重要意义。因此,其中需要引用大量的参考文献。另外,在讨论中要注意主题句以及各主题下的细节。本文中的讨论部分根据其研究目的,预测:① 硒会最低限度地在两个植物种的花粉和花蜜内积累;② 硒对次级硒积累植物种 B. juncea 的植物表现和花性状的副作用比对超级硒积累植物种 S. pinnata 的强。如:"Se would minimally accumulate in the pollen and nectar of both species and that Se would have a stronger negative effect on plant performance and floral traits in the secondary accumulator B. juncea compared to the Se hyperaccumulator S. pinnata."并且从两个方面 "4.1. Effects of Se treatments on uptake into leaves and floral tissues 和 4.2. Secondary accumulators vs. hyperaccumulators: effects of Se uptake on plant performance" 对自己的结果和前人的结果进行全面的比较和分析,支持作者的正确预测。其间,引用了 16 篇文献,在讨论最后提出(1)在硒积累会增加植物适应性和防御植物繁殖组织的联系方面需要进一步研究(in order to link the adaptive significance of Se accumulation in terms of increased fitness and as a defense of reproductive tissues, additional studies will be required.)和(2)为了确定硒是否在植物内移动在整个实验过程的几个时间点也要采集叶和花器官组织(Also, leaf and floral tissues would have to be collected at several time points throughout the experiment to determine whether Se was being mobilized within the plant.)。另外,我们可以从分属于两个不同段落的两个句子(1)和(2)看出,(2)中的一个词(Also)把前后两个段落的内容有机联系(衔接与过渡)。

(7) 撰写结论

写结论时,一定要写明该论文的关键性发现及其意义、作者想让读者掌握的重要信息和有待解决的科学问题等。本例文结论有三小段内容,写出前人和作者的关键发现和意义以及潜在的危险(for example, the following sentences: ① In our greenhouse study, B. juncea accumulated Se concentrations in the pollen and nectar that could be potentially toxic to pollinators, but Se concentrations of leaves in field studies suggest flower concentrations may be lower. ② Our study provides a snapshot of the Se concentrations during the flowering period that could be available to pollinators visiting flowers on Se-accumulating plants. ③ This study provides crucial information about where some of the highest concentrations of Se are found in two phytoremediators, and may shed light on the potential risks pollinators may face when foraging upon these accumulating plants.)。另外,③的句子结构为长句,复杂句一个主语(This study),两个平行谓语(provides 和 may shed light on),每一个谓语都有一个宾语(information 和 risks)。而且,information 有介词短语 about where-clause 作后置定语,where 引导一个介词宾语从句;risks 有从句 pollinators may face when foraging upon these accumulating plants 做后置定语,从句中非限定性引导词(which)被省略,从句又有一个疑问词 when 引导的时间状语从句(when pollinators forage upon these accumulating plants)因省略了主语而变成的 When + 动名词短语所修饰,该动名词中的介词 upon 的宾语包含了一个代词 these 和一个动名词 accumulating 作为定语。

(8) 摘要

作者写完上述七个部分后,可以从论文的引言到结论找出主要的句子,连贯起来,形成论文摘要,并附几个关键词。摘要必须具体而简洁,能够反映论文的实质性内容,包含论文足够的信息,体现论文的创新性,展现论文的重要梗概。一般包括研究目的、对象、方法、结果、结论和意义等内容。

Abstract: Selenium (Se) is a metalloid that can occur naturally in soils from the Cretaceous shale deposits of a prehistoric inland sea in the western United States(复合句). Agricultural irrigation and runoff solubilizes Se from these shales, causing buildups of toxic levels of selenate (SeO_4^{2-}) in water and soil (对象)(现在时态). Our main objective was to investigate the accumulation of Se in two Brassicaceae species chosen for their potential as phytoremediators of Se contaminated soils(目的). We tested the hypothesis that Se will accumulate in the pollen and nectar of two plant species and negatively affect floral traits and plant reproduction. Certain species of Brassicaceae can accumulate high concentrations of Se in their leaf tissues. In this study Se accumulation in plant tissues was investigated under greenhouse conditions. Se accumulator (Brassica juncea) and Se hyperaccumulator (Stanleya pinnata) plants were irrigated in sand culture with 0 μM selenate (control), 8 μM selenate, and 13 μM selenate(材料和方法). Nectar and pollen in S. pinnata contained up to 150 μg Se mL^{-1} wet weight and 12,900 μg Se g^{-1} dry weight when irrigated with 8μM selenate. Se levels in nectar (110 μg Se mL^{-1} wet weight) and pollen (1,700 μg Se g^{-1} dry weight) were not as high in B. juncea. Floral display width, petal area and seed pod length were significantly reduced in the 13 μM selenate treatment in B. juncea. S. pinnata floral traits and seeds were unaffected by the Se treatments (具体结果)(过去时态).

This study provides crucial information about where some of the highest concentrations of Se are found in two phytoremediators（意义）, and may shed light on the potential risks pollinators may face when foraging upon these accumulating plants. In the field, duration of the plant's exposure, Se soil and water concentrations as well as other environmental factors may also play important roles in determining how much Se is accumulated into the leaf and floral tissues（有待研究内容）. Our greenhouse study shed light on two species'ability to accumulate Se, as well as determined the specific plant tissues where Se concentrations are highest（结论）（现在时态）.

Keywords: *Brassica juncea*, Floral traits, Hyperaccumulator, Pollinators, Selenium, Stanleya pinnata

(9) 写致谢

本例文致谢部分对提供过帮助的人和提供支持的单位表示感谢，如：

The authors thank Woody Smith, David Thomason and Kelly Thrippleton-Hunter for their helpful discussions and assistance. This work was supported by the Department of Entomology at University of California.

(10) 写出重要的参考文献

本例文参考文献在文中用（作者，年）的格式，其中，作者如果为两人，全部写出且两作者间加 and，如果多于三位，只写出第一作者并加 et al.，例如：introduction 中第一篇参考文献（Boyd and Martens, 1992）及其第三段第二篇参考文献（Parker et al., 1992）。在 References 中是按照英语字母表先后顺序依次排列的（从 A 到 W）。

(11) 修改、补充与完善

作者经过上述10步完成了文章写作的初稿以后，应对其进行反复修改、适当的补充和不断完善，直至发表为止。

Keys

Chapter 1

Unit 1

1. (1) 广义地讲,生物学是研究生物的科学,而具体(狭义)地讲,生物学是一门研究生物及其如何与环境相互作用的科学。
   (2) 生物表现出非生物所不表现的几个特征:新陈代谢、生殖、(刺激)反应、调节、独特的结构等。
   (3) 我们(人)的机体对致病微生物(侵染)的(抵御)反应需要(机体)细胞改变(正常的)工作方式,以便(积极)攻击且最终消灭他们。
   (4) 我们(人)在锻炼过程中为了维持(机体的)内环境稳定,有些肌肉收缩更快,加强呼吸,心脏跳动更快,更有力,使(充足的)血液流入肺部。
2. (1) reproduce (2) stimulus (3) genetic (4) homeostasis (5) food production, disease control
3. (1) (A, C), (B, D, E) (2) (B, D), (A, C) (3) (D) (4) (E)
4. Ommitted

Unit 2

1. (1) D (2) C (3) D (4) E (5) A (6) B (7) D (8) D (9) A (10) C (11) D (12) E (13) C (14) E (15) A (16) C (17) E
2. (1) F (2) T (3) F (4) T (5) F (6) T (7) T
3. (1) Because 20 choices for any amino acid, $20 \times 20 \times 20 \times 20 \times \cdots = 20^{129}$ possibilities for a protein 129 amino acid long.
   (2) Proteins can function in structure, contraction, storage, defense, transport, signaling and as enzymes.
4. This is a hydrolysis reaction, which consumes water.

Unit 3

1. (1) Aerobic cellular respiration—Mitochondrion, ATP, Sugar, Water, Oxygen and Carbon dioxide.
   (2) Photosynthesis—Chloroplast, Sunlight, Sugar, Water, Oxygen and Carbon dioxide.
   (3) Cell membrane—Mitochondrion, Chloroplast, Osmosis, Facilitated diffusion, Carrier
2. (1) Cytoplasm. (2) The chemical bonds of molecules.
   (3) Different organelle, opposite reactions and different energy.
3. omitted
4. (1) a (2) b (3) c (4) d (5) e (6) f (7) g (8) h (9) i (10) j
5. (1) C (2) B (3) C (4) B (5) B (6) D (7) B (8) D (9) C (10) C

Unit 4

1. (1) a (2) b 3) a (4) d (5) e (6) f (7) g (8) h (9) I (10) j
2. (1) one-half (2) eukaryotes (3) cell line (4) vaccines (5) embryonic cell, somatic cell (6) nuclear transfer (7) 3 (8) meiosis (9) adult differentiated cell (10) Artificial twinning
3. (1) D (2) A (3) C (4) D
4. Omitted
5. (1) Mouse, pig, bull and cat. (2) Yes. (3) Yes. (4) No.

Unit 5

1. The central dogma is the flow of genetic information from DNA to DNA, from DNA to RNA, from RNA to protein, and from RNA to DNA.
2. It is seen from Fig. 5-2 that the two processes including transcription and translation take place in a eukaryotic cell. a. Transcription happens in nucleus, in which pre-RNAs are synthesized by RNA polymerase which moves along one strand of the double-stranded DNA chain as a template for the synthesis of a single strand of RNA that is complementary to the DNA strand and builds different RNA nucleotides into RNAs in the direction from 5′ to 3′ based on the

base pairing rule. Afterthat, the pre-RNAs are processed into different RNAs such as mRNAs, tRNAs and rRNAs, which go out of the nucleus through its poles to cytoplasm. b. Translation occurs in cytoplasm. rRNAs combine proteins with each other to form ribosomes, tRNAs transfer amino acids into ribosomes by whose amino acid arms link up with amino acids, ribosomes attach to mRNAs carrying codon as templates so that many polypeptide chains are synthesized from it by the pairing of its codons with tRNAs's anticodons.

3. DNA 作为遗传物质,具有四个特点:(1) 能够自我复制(意译);(2) 能够突变或者化学结构(加译)改变,并且把这些改变传递给后代;(3) 能够储藏决定细胞核生物性状的遗传信息(定语从句转换成定语短语,加译);(4) 能够利用其遗传信息指导合成(名词转换成动词)细胞核生物活动(名词转换成动词,意译)所必需的结构蛋白和调节蛋白。

Unit 6

1. 基因是遗传单位,由特异性长度的 DNA(片段)组成,决定生物的表现性状(长句翻译)。特异性基因位于特异性染色体上的特异位点。二倍体生物的每一个性状都有两个基因(控制)(增译),(控制)一个性状的基因的可选择形式叫作等位基因,(控制)一个特定性状的基因可以有很多不同的等位基因,有些等位基因对其他所谓的隐性的基因是显性的。具有两个相同的、控制同一性状的等位基因的生物是纯合的,(而)(增译和意译)具有(两个)不相同的(控制同一性状的)等位基因的生物是杂合的。(但是,基因的表达受环境因素的影响)(增译),环境对基因自我表达作用(名词转化为动词)的结果使生物呈现(过去分词转化为谓语动词)表现型(主语转化为宾语)。

2. (1) chromosomal abnormalities, single gene defects, multifactorial problems and teratogenic problems
   (2) dorminant genetic disorders and recessive genetic disorders
   (3) the carrier identification, prenatal diagnosis, newborn screening, late-onset disorder, and predictive gene testing
   (4) information, genetic disorders
   (5) template
   (6) sense

3. Passage 1
   (1) A pair of homologous chromosomes does not segregate properly during

gametogenesis and both chromosomes of a pair end up in the same gamete.

(2) The correlation between incidence of Down syndrome and age of mother is positive or Down syndrome is much more common among children of older women than that of young women.

(3) The transfer of a piece of one nonhomologous chromosome to another

Passage 2

(1) Recessive inheritance in the recessive condition, codorminance in the heterozygous condition.

(2) Mutation or base sustitution.

(3) In the recessive condition.

4. (1) C (2) A (3) B (4) D

Unit 7

1. (1) d (2) h (3) a (4) e (5) c (6) g (7) b (8) f
2. (1) Monera (2) parasites (3) decomposers
   (4) human immunodeficiency virus (5) nucleic (6) capsule
   (7) retroviruses (8) single-celled or unicellular (9) endospores
3. (1) B (2) A (3) D (4) A (5) B (6) C (7) B (8) C (9) A (10) D

Unit 8

1. (1) b (2) f (3) a (4) c (5) e (6) d (7) h (8) g (9) j (10) i
2. (1) morphology (2) Complex (3) xylem, phloem, cambium
   (4) Guard cells (5) Seed, fruit (6) secondary (7) fibrous
   (8) Taproot (9) Root hairs
   (10) epidermis, vascular tissue system, ground tissue system
3. (1) B (2) E (3) D (4) D (5) C (6) C (7) E (8) A (9) B (10) A
4. (1) Plant tissue culture is the culture and maintenance of plant cells or organs in sterile, nutritionally and environmentally supportive conditions (*in vitro*).

(2) Sterile conditions, nutritive medium and a stable and suitable climate.

(3) Plant tissue culture offers numerous significant benefits over traditional propagation methods.

Unit 9

1. (1) b (2) a (3) d (4) c (5) f (6) e (7) h (8) g (9) j (10) i
2. (1) Organ system (2) Muscle tissues (3) muscles (4) neurons
   (5) endocrine (6) integumentary (7) mammals (8) mechanisms
   (9) excretory systems (10) Immune systems
3. (1) C (2) B (3) B (4) C (5) D (6) B (7) C (8) C (9) E
4. All animals except sponges have organs. An organ consists of several tissues adapted to perform specific functions as a group. The stomach, for example, is mainly composed of three types of tissues such as epithelial tissue, connective tissue and muscle tissue. Higher animals have the following major organs: heart, liver, lung, spleen, stomach, kidney, brain and so on. An organ system is a group of several organs that work together in a coordinated fashion to perform a vital body function. Human beings have ten major organ systems including digestive system, respiratory system, cardiovascular system, lymphatic and immune system, excretory system, endocrine system, reproductive system, nervous system, muscular system and skeletal system.

Unit 10

1. (1) c (2) e (3) g (4) f (5) b (6) a (7) d
2. (1) Biotechnology (2) nucleotide or base (3) DNA (4) Insulin
   (5) Transgenic or genetically engineered (6) vector (7) polymerase
3. (1) C (2) D (3) A (4) C (5) E (6) B (7) C (8) D (9) E (10) D
4. (1) As vectors for introducing normal genes into human tissues lacking them.
   (2) Modifying expression of genes or correcting abnormal genes.
   (3) Technical and ethical questions.

Unit 11

1. (1) c (2) d (3) a (4) e (5) b (6) f (7) j (8) g (9) h (10) i
2. (1) A community ecology (2) A population (3) Ecosystem ecology
   (4) The hierarchy of ecological study (5) temperature, water, sunlight
   (6) photosysthesis (7) physiological response (8) mutation

(9) food and products (10) over-exploitation
3. (1) A (2) D (3) D (4) A (5) D (6) D (7) B (8) A

Unit 12

1. (1) b (2) a (3) d (4) c (5) f (6) e
2. (1) maintain algae growth (2) algae, negative (3) Algaculture (4) pearls
   (5) gourmet food, traditional medicine (6) growout
3. (1) B, D (2) B, D, E (3) A, C, E (4) B, C, D, E
4. (1) B (2) D (3) A (4) B (5) D (6) Fillet size and final trim.

Unit 13

1. (1) j (2) a (3) b (4) c (5) i (6) h (7) d (8) e (9) f (10) g
2. (1) Transcriptomics (2) expression (3) clustering gene expression data
   (4) electrophoresis, protein arrays formats (5) Metabolomics
   (6) mass spectrometry (MS) (7) genomes (8) 0.1%
3.
   Type the following web site into your browser:
   http://www.ncbi.nlm.nih.gov/
   Next to the "Search" box, select Protein, to search the NCBI
   database containing protein sequences.

(1)

The record for hemoglobin S should be returned. Hemoglobin is the protein in our blood cells that Carries oxygen. Click on the link entitled "1HBSB".

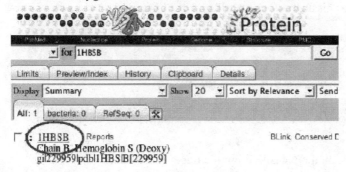

(2)

Next to the word Display in the grey region at the top of the file, change "GenPept" to "FASTA"

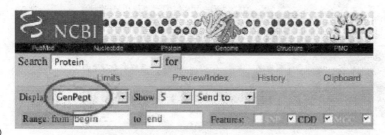

(3)

This will display the amino acid sequence for hemoglobin S in FASTA format.

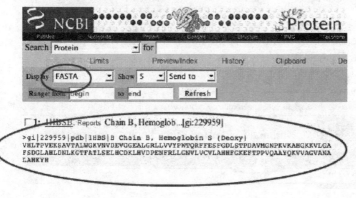

(4)

Hold down the left mouse button while you move the mouse over the sequence. This should highlight the amino acid sequence in blue. Now choose "Edit: Copy" from the browser window, or hit the buttons "Ctrl" and "C" to copy.

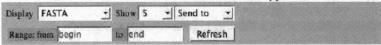

(5)
☐ 1: 1HBSB. Reports Chain B, Hemoglob..[gi:229959]
>gi|229959|pdb|1HBS|B Chain B, Hemoglobin S (Deoxy)
VHLTPVEKSAVTALWGKVNVDEVGGEALGRLLVVYPWTQRFFESFGDLSTPDAVMGNPKVKAHGKKVLGA
FSDGLAHLDNLKGTFATLSELHCDKLHVDPENFRLLGNVLVCVLAHHFGKEFTPPVQAAYQKVVAGVANA
LAHKYH

Now, click on the NCBI logo in the upper left corner of the web page to return to the main page.

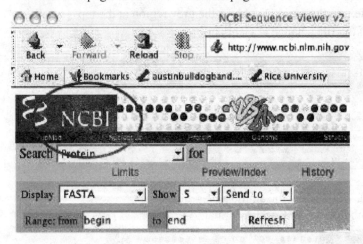

(6)

In the dark blue menu bar at the top of the page, click on the word "BLAST".

(7)

In the box of Protein options, click on the link entitled "Protein-protein BLAST (blastp)".

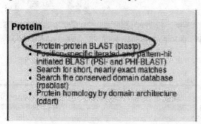

(8)

Click in the Search box and choose " Edit: paste" from the browser menu or hit the "Ctrl" and "P" keys to paste the sequence into the search box.

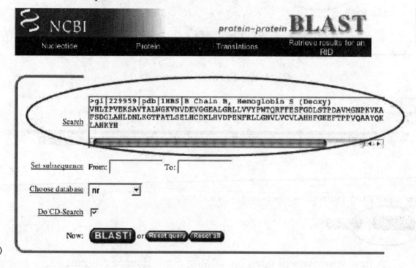

(9)

Change the "nr" database to "swissprot", then click the BLAST! button.

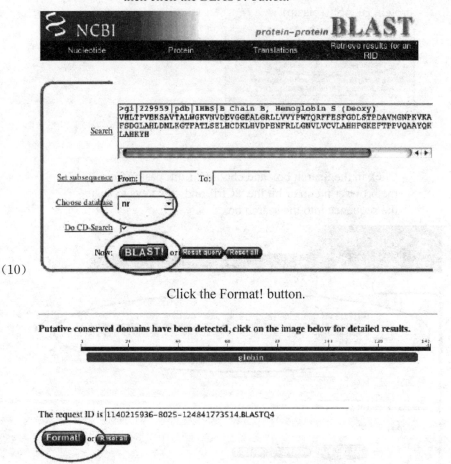

(10)

Click the Format! button.

(11)　　A new window will open containing our sequence alignments.

Under the graph indicating the length of the top alignments, there will be a list of aligning sequences in order of decreasing alignment scores. Click on the score of the first item in the list, which is the highest scoring alignment. This will take you to the section of the file where you can view the alignment.

(12)

```
Sequences producing significant alignments:                           Score    E
                                                                      (Bits)   Value
gi|56749858|sp|P68873|HBB_PANTR  Hemoglobin beta subunit (Hemo...     300     9e-82
gi|232230|sp|P02024|HBB_GORGO    Hemoglobin beta subunit (Hemoglobi   299     2e-81
gi|122528|sp|P18988|HBB2_PANLE   Hemoglobin beta-2 subunit (Hem...    296     1e-80
gi|122616|sp|P02025|HBB_HYLLA    Hemoglobin beta subunit (Hemoglobi   295     4e-80
gi|122668|sp|P02032|HBB_PREEN    Hemoglobin beta subunit (Hemoglobi   292     2e-79
gi|122593|sp|P19885|HBB_COLPO    Hemoglobin beta subunit (Hemoglobi   290     7e-79
gi|122584|sp|P02028|HBB_CERAE    Hemoglobin beta subunit (Hemoglobi   289     2e-78
```

Identify the differences in the sequence
of Query land Subject 2

```
> gi|56749858|sp|P68873|HBB_PANTR  Hemoglobin beta subunit (Hemoglobin beta chain)
  gi|56749857|sp|P68872|HBB_PANPA  Hemoglobin beta subunit (Hemoglobin beta chain) (]
  gi|56749856|sp|P68871|HBB_HUMAN  Hemoglobin beta subunit (Hemoglobin beta chain)
Length=147

Score =  300 bits (768),  Expect = 9e-82
Identities = 145/146 (99%), Positives = 145/146 (99%), Gaps = 0/146 (0%)

Query  1    VHLTPVEKSAVTALWGKVNVDEVGGEALGRLLVVYPWTQRFFESFGDLSTPDAVMGNPKV  60
            V LTP EKS VTALWGKVNVDEVGGEALGRLLVVYPWTQRFFESFGDLSTPDAVMGNPKV
Sbjct  2    VHITPEEKSAVTALWGKVNVDEVGGEALGRLLVVYPWTQRFFESFGDLSTPDAVMGNPKV  61

Query  61   KAHGKKVLGAFSDGLAHLDNLKGTFATLSELHCDKLHVDPENFRLLGNVLVCLAHHFGK  120
            KAHGKKVLGAFSDGLAHLDNLKGTFATLSELHCDKLHVDPENFRLLGNVLVCLAHHFGK
Sbjct  62   KAHGKKVLGAFSDGLAHLDNLKGTFATLSELHCDKLHVDPENFRLLGNVLVCLAHHFGK  121

Query  121  EFTPPVQAAYQKVVAGVANALAHKYH  146
            EFTPPVQAAYQKVVAGVANALAHKYH
Sbjct  122  EFTPPVQAAYQKVVAGVANALAHKYH  147
```

(13) A dissimilar substitution occurs at amino acid number 6.

Chapter 2

Unit 3

1. (1) So much for the principles of ptrotein analyses, go on to determine the structures of several proteins.
   (2) It is understood that biochemistry is one of the fastest developing disciplines in Science, which we have known so far.
2. The translation of some selected English passages in some units of Chapter 1

into Chinese.

(1) 2009 年,日本食品安全委员会得出结论,采用体细胞核移植技术克隆的牛和猪及其后代(生产的)食品,和那些通过传统技术由牛和猪生产的食品一样安全。但是,克隆仍然是一个很有争议的话题。遗传改良使生产者有降低价格的潜能(形容词转换成名词)、提高(意译)肉奶制品的质量和增加抗病性的可能性。不过,很多人(加译)对该技术表现出担忧,对使用(名词转换成动词)克隆动物及其后代生产(加译)肉制品和奶制品(加译)表示愤怒(动词转换成名词),这些消费者和动物福利机构出于(意译)对道德和伦理方面的异议及克隆技术对食品安全和克隆动物及其代孕母畜的潜在伤害。

(2) 微生物是单细胞或者非细胞生物(省略翻译 A 和 an),种类很丰富(意译),包括细菌类、真菌类、古细菌类、原生生物类、绿藻(植物)类、和诸如浮游动物和涡虫等动物类以及病毒等等(复杂长句)。微生物因其大多数成员微小得使(人们)(加译)不用某种放大器不能看见(它们)而得名。(微生物中的)(加译)细菌类、原生生物类和真菌类的成员共有几个区别于动植物的(定语从句转化成定语短语)特征。

(3) "植物"术语表明其与诸如植物是多细胞生物、具有纤维素、能够进行光合作用等特征有某种联系。据估计,2010 年全球有 30～31.5 万种植物,其中大约 26～29 万种植物是种子植物(常用句型和长句)。它们主要分为陆地植物(例如苔类植物、金鱼藻、藓类植物、维管束植物和类似于这些现存植物的化石植物)、绿色植物(包括陆地植物和绿藻)和原始色素体生物(包括绿色植物、红藻、蓝细菌和灰胞藻)几个类群(加译,长句)。绿色植物通过使用叶绿体内的叶绿素(进行的)光合作用把光能转化为化学能,储藏于有机物(意译),获得其绝大多数能量(一个长句翻译成几个短句)。

(4) 如果基因太大,(结构)很复杂,那么就需要使用限制性内切酶把它从染色体(DNA 分子链中)剪切下来。限制性内切酶像分子剪刀一样只在(染色体内的) DNA(分子链)中特定碱基序列内(部)剪切 DNA(分子链)。它们不是以横直方式切割 DNA 分子链,(产生具有平头末端的 DNA 片段或基因),而是以交错方式切割 DNA 分子链,产生(具有)一条链比另一条链略长(结构特点末端)的 DNA 片段或基因。从(这些双链 DNA 片段或基因的末端)伸出的、不(通过互补碱基与其他单链 DNA)配对的、短的、(单链)核苷酸序列因为能够再次与另一条互补的(DNA 分子)链(通过互补碱基)配对而叫作粘性末端。

(5) ① 在当前从高等植物中分离且在现代医学上广泛使用的 120 种活性化合

物中,有80%的化合物在其现代治疗使用(效果)和(用于)提取它们的植物的传统使用(效果)之间具有正相关性。

② 就驯化或者栽培物种而言,(物种)保护就意味着保护它们创造的(适合其生活的)独特环境。通过保护生物多样性,能够保证许多物种的生存和深受人类活动威胁的生境的恢复(意译)。其他保护生物多样性的理由还有(意译)为(我们人类)后代保留有价值的自然资源和保证生态系统健康。

(6) 珍珠生产者把一个"核"(通常就是一片抛光的贻贝壳)放在牡蛎内能够培养珍珠。(含"核"的)牡蛎(培养生长)三至六年后可以产出完美的珍珠。这些珍珠价值不如天然的珍珠,但是看上去(与自然珍珠)完全一样。实际上,自20世纪初几位研究员发现人工培育珍珠的方法以来,人工培养珍珠市场发展得远比天然珍珠市场快。

(7) 搜索一个细菌基因组(的开放阅读框),典型的结果是搜索到几乎肯定是基因的长开放阅读框。它们具有很多部分或者完全包含在一些基因内而位于不同阅读框内的比较短的开放阅读框(组成)。这些短(开放阅读框)序列几乎肯定是核苷酸组合,偶然形成开放阅读框,但不是基因。如果这些短开放阅读框之一完全位于两个基因间,可能被错误地鉴定为一个真正的基因。不过,在绝大多数细菌基因组内,基因之间间隙很小,因此这种问题只会低频出现。

Appendix

1. Amino Acids and their Abbreviations（氨基酸及其缩写）

甘氨酸	Glycine Gly G
丙氨酸	Alanine Ala A
缬氨酸	Valine Val V
亮氨酸	Leucine Leu L
异亮氨酸	Isoleucine Ile I
脯氨酸	Proline Pro P
苯丙氨酸	Phenylalanine Phe F
酪氨酸	Tyrosine Tyr Y
色氨酸	Tryptophan Trp W
丝氨酸	Serine Ser S
苏氨酸	Threonine Thr T
半胱氨酸	Cystine Cys C
蛋氨酸	Methionine Met M
天冬酰胺	Asparagine Asn N
谷氨酰胺	Glutarnine Gln Q
天冬氨酸	Asparticacid Asp D
谷氨酸	Glutamicacid Glu E
赖氨酸	Lysine Lys K
精氨酸	Arginine Arg R
组氨酸	Histidine His H

2. Bases and their Abbreviations（碱基及其缩写）

腺嘌呤	Adenine，A.
鸟嘌呤	Guanine，G.
胞嘧啶	Cytosine，C.
胸腺嘧啶	Thymine，T.
尿嘧啶	Uracil，U.

References

卜玉坤. 2000. 大学专业英语. 农林植物学英语[M]. 北京:外语教学与研究出版社.
高恩光,戴建东. 2003. 英语写作新论[M]. 上海:上海外语教育出版社.
侯宁海. 2001. 英语词语大全[M]. 合肥:中国科学技术大学出版社.
华仲乐. 1999. 新世纪医学英语教程. 生物医学[M]. 上海:上海外语教育出版社.
黄兰宁. 2004. 学校双语课程[M]. 南宁:广西教育出版社.
蒋悟生. 2000. 生物专业英语[M]. 北京:高等教育出版社.
祁寿华. 2000. 高级英语写作指南[M]. 上海:上海外语教育出版社.
任胜利. 2004. 英语科技论文撰写与投稿[M]. 北京:科学出版社.
石坚,帅培天. 2005. 英语论文写作[M]. 成都:四川人民出版社.
司有和. 1984. 科技写作简明教程[M]. 合肥:安徽教育出版社.
王斌华. 2003. 双语教育与双语教学[M]. 上海:上海教育出版社.
王佐良,丁往道. 1987. 英语文体学引论[M]. 北京:外语教学与研究出版社.
吴冰,钟美荪,郭棲庆. 2005. 英语写作手册[M]. 北京:外语教学与研究出版社.
谢江南,何加红. 2005. 使用英文写作[M]. 北京:首都经济贸易大学出版社.
徐东海. 2011. 浅析英语语篇的词汇衔接[J]. 长春大学学报,21(4):106-109.
许建平. 2003. 英汉互译实践与技巧[M]. 2版. 北京:清华大学出版社.
余强. 2002. 双语教育的心理学基础[M]. 南京:江苏教育出版社.
俞天民. 1983. 科技英语写作[M]. 北京:高等教育出版社.
约翰·斯韦尔斯. 1981. 怎样正确运用科技英语[M]. 许才德,方立,译. 北京:地质出版社.
赵萱,郑仰成. 2006. 科技英语翻译[M]. 北京:外语教学与研究出版社.
Scherm B, Palomb M, Serra D, et al. 2005. Detection of transcripts of the aflatoxin genes $aflD$, $aflO$, and $aflP$ by reverse transcription-polymerase chain reaction allows differentiation of aflatoxin-producing and non-producing isolates of *Aspergillus flavus* and *Aspergillus parasiticus*[J]. International Journal of Food Microbiology, 98: 201-210.
Zoller B, Jan S, Jianguang Jia, et al. 2012. Risk of coronary heart disease in patients with cancer: A nationwide follow-up study from Sweden[J]. European

Journal of Cancer, 48: 121-128

Brian D N. 2010. Issues in biosecurity and biosafety[J]. International Journal of Antimicrobial Agents, 365: 566-569.

Brown T A. 2002. Gene Cloning and DNA Analysis: An Introduction[M]. Beijing: Higher Education Press.

Dinakar C, Djilianov D, Bartels D. 2012. Photosynthesis in desiccation tolerant plants: Energy metabolism and antioxidative stress defense[J]. Plant Science, 182: 29-41.

Neumann E G, Neumann G, Leggewie G, et al. 2011. Constitutive overexpression of the sucrose transporter $SoSUT1$ in potato plants increases arbuscular mycorrhiza fungal root colonization under high, but not under low, soil phosphorus availability [J]. Journal of Plant Physiology, 168(9): 911-919.

Karp G. 2006. Cell and Molecular Biology Concepts and Experiments [M]. Beijing: Higher Education Press.

Brum G, McKane L, Karp G. 1994. Biology: Exploring Life[M]. New Jersey: John Wiley & Sons, Inc.

Gu Guangyu, Arthur R B. 2011. Cytogenomic aberrations associated with prostate cancer[J]. Cancer Genetics, 204(2): 57-67

Aoyagi H. 2011. Application of plant protoplasts for the production of useful metabolites[J]. Biochemical Engineering Journal, 56(1/2): 1-8.

Aizaki H, Sawada M, Sato K. 2011. Consumers' attitudes toward consumption of cloned beef. The impact of exposure to technological information about animal cloning[J]. Appetite, 57(2): 459-466.

Junga J, O'Donoghue E M, Dijkwel P P, et al. 2010. Expression of multiple expansin genes is associated with cell expansion in potato organs[J]. Plant Science, 179: 77-85.

Postlethwait J H, Hopon J L, Veres R C. 1991. Biology! Bringing Science to Life [M]. New York: McGraw-Hill, Inc.

Jung J, O'Donoghue E M, Dijkwel P P, et al. 2010. Expression of multiple expansin genes is associated with cell expansion in potato organs[J]. Plant Science, 179: 77-85.

Brooks K R, Lusk J L. 2001. US Consumers attitudes toward farm animal cloning [J]. Appetite, 57(2): 483-492.

Gouveia K, Magalhães A, De Sousa L. 2011. The behaviour of domestic cats in a shelter: Residence time, density and sex ratio[J]. Applied Animal Behaviour Science, 130(1/2): 53-59.

Allison L A. 2008. Fundamental Molecular Biology[M]. Beijing: Higher Education Press.

Lu Ying, Kim S, Park K. 2011. In vitro-in vivo correlation: Perspectives on model development [J]. International Journal of Pharmaceutics, 418 (1): 142-148.

Saleem M, Khan U R, Suleman M, et al. 2011. Experimental study of cake formation on heat treated and membrane coated needle felts in a pilot scale pulse jet bag filter using optical in-situ cake height measurement [J]. Powder Technology, 214(3): 388-399.

Manimaran P, Ramkumar G, Sakthivel K, et al. 2011. Suitability of non-lethal marker and marker-free systems for development of transgenic crop plants: Present status andfuture prospects[J]. Biotechnology Advances, 29: 703-714.

Mandell M, Wisehart G. 1994. Test Bank to Accompany Biology: Exploring Life [M]. New Jersey: John Wiley & Sons, Inc.

Campbell N A, Mitchell L G, Reece J B. 1994. Biology: Concepts & Connections [M]. San Francisco: The Benjamin/Cummings Publishing Company, Inc.

Hoa P, Managaki S, Nakada N, et al. 2011. Antibiotic contamination and occurrence of antibiotic-resistant bacteria in aquatic environments of northern Vietnam [J]. Science of The Total Environment, 409 (15): 2894-2901.

Pickering W R. 2000. Advanced Biology through Diagrams[M]. Oxford: Oxford University Press.

Ribaut J M, De Vicente M C, Delannay X. 2010. Molecular breeding in developing countries: challenges andperspectives[J]. Current Opinion in Plant Biology, 13: 213-218.

Bernstein R, Bernstein S. 1996. Biology [M]. Dubuque: Wm. C. Brown Publishers.

Sindhu S, Chempakam B, Leela N K, et al. 2011. Chemoprevention by essential oil of turmeric leaves (*Curcuma longa* L.) on the growth of *Aspergillus flavus* and aflatoxin production [J]. Food and Chemical Toxicology, 49: 1188-1192.

Theresa M B. 2007. Ecological and Genetic Implications of Aquaculture Activities [M]. Dordrecht: Springer.

Thusith S, Samarakone I, Harold W, et al. 2009. Domestic pigs alter their social strategy in response to social group size[J]. Applied Animal Behaviour Science, 121: 8-15.

Lapitan V C, Redona E D, Toshinori A, et al. 2009. Molecular characterization and agronomic performance of DH lines from the F1 of *indica* and *japonica* cultivars of rice (*Oryza sativa* L.) [J]. Field Crops Research, 112: 222-228.

Klug W S, Cummings M R. 2002. Essentials of Genetics[M]. 4th ed. Beijing: Higher Education Press.

Zhou Y Q, Duan H Y, Zhou C E, et al. 2009. Hairy Root Induction and Plant Regeneration of *Rehmannia glutinosa* Libosch. *f. hueichingensis* Hsiao via *Agrobacterium rhizogenes*-Mediated Transformation[J]. Russian Journal of Plant Physiology, 56(2): 224-231.

Zhou Yanqing, Gu Fengping, Zhou Chune, et al. 2010. Genetic diversity of Rehmannia glutinosa cultivars based on sequence-related amplified polymorphism markers[J]. Scientia Horticulturae, 125: 789-794.

http://www.utsouthwestern.edu.

http://en.wikipedia.org.

http://www.nlm.nih.gov.

http://www.fishfarming.com.

http://www.wri.org.

http://www.ksuaquaculture.org.

http://www.wisegeek.com.

http://www.fish-journal.com.

http://www.kidcyber.com.

http://www.ehow.com.

http://www.thefishsite.com.

http://www.thefreedictionary.com.

http://www.onlineschools.org.

http://www.cnki.com.cn.

http://wenku.baidu.com.

http://www.docin.com.

http://www.religioustolerance.org.

http://zhidao.baidu.com.

http://www.baidu.com.